THE
CASE
FOR
NATIONALISM

THE
CASE
FOR
NATIONALISM

—

HOW IT MADE US POWERFUL, UNITED, AND FREE

—

RICH LOWRY

BROADSIDE BOOKS

HarperCollins books may be purchased for educational, business, or sales promotional use. For information, please email the Special Markets Department at SPsales@harpercollins.com.

Broadside Books™ and the Broadside logo are trademarks of HarperCollins Publishers.

FIRST EDITION

Library of Congress Cataloging-in-Publication Data

Names: Lowry, Rich, author.
Title: The case for nationalism : how it made us powerful, united, and free / Rich Lowry.
Description: First edition. | New York City: Broadside Books, 2019. | Includes index.
Identifiers: LCCN 2019031058 | ISBN 9780062839640 (hardcover) | ISBN 9780062839671 (ebook)
Subjects: LCSH: Nationalism—United States. | National characteristics, American—Political aspects.
Classification: LCC E169.1. L824 2019 | DDC 320.540973—dc23

19 20 21 22 23 LSC 10 9 8 7 6 5 4 3 2 1

TO MIMMY, NINI, AND BAI—I LOVE YOU WITH ALL MY HEART

We mean a principle of sympathy, not of hostility; of union, not of separation. We mean a feeling of common interest among those who live under the same government, and are contained within the same natural or historical boundaries. We mean, that one part of the community shall not consider themselves as foreigners with regard to another part; that they shall cherish the tie which holds them together; shall feel that they are one people, that their lot is cast together, that evil to any of their fellow-countrymen is evil to themselves, and that they cannot selfishly free themselves from their share of any common inconvenience by severing the connexion.

—JOHN STUART MILL

CONTENTS

SECTION IV: THE THREAT TO THE NATION

SECTION I:

IN

DEFENSE

OF THE

NATION

INTRODUCTION: WHAT TRUMP REALIZED

Standing in the shadow of the Arc de Triomphe at a commemoration marking the one hundredth anniversary of the end of World War I, French president Emmanuel Macron had a message for the world, and especially for his American counterpart, Donald Trump.

"Patriotism is the exact opposite of nationalism," Macron said before the assembled world leaders at the 2018 event. "Nationalism is a betrayal of patriotism. By saying 'Our interests first, who cares about the others,' we erase what a nation holds dearest, what gives it life, what makes it great and what is essential: its moral values."

Macron's rebuke of Trump, the self-declared nationalist listening nearby, electrified the international media. Although the Macron speech played to near-universal praise, it garbled the definitions of patriotism and nationalism; slighted France's own great nationalist tradition; and posited a conflict between nationalism and values that doesn't exist (or doesn't have to).

Almost everyone has an opinion about nationalism (usually that it's a very, very bad thing), without really knowing what it is. The esteemed president of France is no different.

Nationalism Is Condemned
Thoughtlessly and Erroneously

When President Trump first openly embraced the term at a 2018 campaign rally, commentators reacted in horror. Patriotism is about love, nationalism about hate, *New York Times* columnist Nicholas Kristof opined. Trump, insisted Jennifer Rubin of the *Washington Post*, is "normalizing a hateful political philosophy that is contrary to our deepest-held beliefs."[1]

The malodor surrounding the idea of nationalism is one reason that Trump picked up on its appeal when more conventional Republicans ignored it or recoiled from it.

Nationalism is traditionally not a partisan affair. Both major political parties have access to it and have made powerful appeals to it over the centuries. The GOP had been most closely associated with nationalism since the 1970s but lost touch with it in the pre-Trump years under the influence of libertarians and a globetrotting business elite and in pursuit of an overly idealistic foreign and immigration policy.

The party was vulnerable to renegade populist politicians with a nationalistic appeal. Pat Buchanan (running from the social-conservative right) took President George H. W. Bush down a notch in the 1992 presidential primaries, and Ross Perot (running from the "radical center") helped finish him off in the general election. But nothing prepared anyone for the unlikely rise of an outlandish political outsider promising to put "America First" and "Make America Great Again."

Although Trump is a nationalist, it's a mistake to attribute everything about him—or even most things about him—to nationalism. There isn't anything inherently nationalistic about wild presidential tweets, extreme boastfulness, excoriating attacks on the media, the browbeating of allies or even protectionism or populism (although in the modern West, nationalism often speaks in a populist voice).

These things define Trump, and his persona, more than nationalism. Nor was there anything nationalistic about his initial reluctance to unambiguously denounce the far-right protests in Charlottesville, one of the low points of his presidency.

The Basic Propositions of Trump's Nationalism Aren't Particularly Radical

Trump's nationalism was encapsulated in his 2016 campaign themes that, stripped down to their essence, were amazingly simple: We need to adopt immigration and trade policies with our own interests foremost in mind. We should protect ourselves with the utmost vigilance from foreign threats, whether via the so-called Muslim ban or Trump's promise to "bomb the shit" out of ISIS. Without borders we don't have a country, and the one to our south needs to be protected by a big, beautiful wall. Most important, our country, not any other nation or international body or alliance, should always come first.

These constituted the basic axioms of Trump's nationalism. Immigration was such a focus because it involves foundational questions: Do the American people have the sovereign authority to decide who gets to come here or not? How should we weigh the relative importance of the interests of American vis-à-vis foreign workers? And finally, what emphasis are we going to put, if any, on assimilation?

When abstracted from his combative rhetorical style and more idiosyncratic policy enthusiasms (e.g., taking Iraq's oil), the rudiments of Trump's nationalism should be hard to oppose—or would be in a more rational time than the one we live in.

In his widely panned inaugural address, Trump said that "a nation exists to serve its citizens" and that "we are one nation," sharing "one heart, one home, and one glorious destiny." What is supposed to be the alternative to this vision? Serving the citizens of other countries? The nation as a collection of tribal and other interest groups that don't share a common destiny?

On foreign policy, Trump was considerably more grounded than his predecessors. In his 2005 inaugural address, George W. Bush, a champion of universal freedom, quite seriously promised to spread freedom everywhere around the world. In 2009, Barack Obama, in his more soaring moments a self-styled "citizen of the world," predicted that "as the world grows smaller, our common humanity shall reveal itself" and averred that "America must play its role in ushering in a new era of peace."

Trump simply left it at: "We will seek friendship and goodwill with the nations of the world—but we do so with the understanding that it is the right of all nations to put their own interests first."

This, too, should be uncontroversial. Where, historically, many nationalists around the world have failed is in not recognizing the right of other people to self-government. Trump has repeatedly made it clear that his nationalism is broadly applicable.

In his 2018 address to the UN General Assembly, he declared, "We believe that when nations respect the rights of their neighbors, and defend the interests of their people, they can better work together to secure the blessings of safety, prosperity, and peace." He made a nod to the remarkable variety that makes up the international tapestry: "Each of us here today is the emissary of a distinct culture, a rich history, and a people bound together by ties of memory, tradition, and the values that make our homelands like nowhere else on Earth."

As a consequence, he continued, "America will always choose independence and cooperation over global governance, control, and domination." It will "honor the right of every nation in this room to pursue its own customs, beliefs, and traditions." All we ask, he stipulated, is "that you honor our sovereignty in return."

After years of worry over purported American imperialism, these sentiments should have been a relief to the international media and assembled foreign potentates, yet, of course, there were few plaudits.

Trump most eloquently expressed his nationalism in a fine 2017 speech at Krasiński Square in Warsaw, in front of a monument to the Warsaw Uprising. He spoke of a Polish nation that is "more than one thousand years old" and that persisted during long periods of occupation and despite a long Communist political and cultural offensive against its very identity. "While Poland could be invaded and occupied," he said, "and its borders even erased from the map, it could never be erased from history or from your hearts."

Trump put an emphasis on culture and called Poland a "nation devoted to God." He invoked Pope John Paul II preaching his famous 1979 sermon in Warsaw and an adoring throng chanting in response, "We want God." The foundation of Poland's resilience, Trump noted, was knowing its identity and staying true to it: "The story of Poland is the story of a people who have never lost hope, who have never been broken, and who have never, ever forgotten who they are."

Finally, he warned of a crisis of civilizational confidence: A stalwart defense of the West "begins with our minds, our wills, and our souls," and depends on "bonds of history, culture, and memory."

All of this occasioned eye rolling, if not active hostility, among left-wing pundits and intellectuals. They scoffed at the notion of a crisis of Western confidence. Never mind the last decade of European misgovernance, including periodic crises threatening the European Union's common currency, a disorderly mass influx of migrants across Europe's borders, and homegrown terror attacks in the cities of France and Great Britain. Peter Beinart of *The Atlantic* objected that "the West" is supposedly "a racial and religious term," proving, once again, that commonplace expressions can be deemed offensive at a moment's notice.

Trump obviously represents a broader turn in the Western world (sorry, there's that phrase again) toward a reassertion of national identity and sovereignty. The forerunner of his election victory was the United Kingdom's stunning vote to leave the

European Union. Great Britain, which has given us such land-marks of accountable government as the Magna Carta, which has produced foundational thinkers on the road to democratic rule including John Locke, Algernon Sidney, and John Milton, and which has resisted continental threats to its sovereignty emanating from Spain (King Philip II), France (Napoleon), and Germany (Adolf Hitler) over the centuries, decided for self-government. And rightly so.

Elsewhere in Europe, prodded by the European Union's arrogance, nationalist figures and parties have been on the rise. They are a motley bunch, some not deserving the hysteria they occasion in elite circles (Hungarian prime minister Viktor Orbán is a democrat, although with rough edges), others doomed never to outrun the sorry pasts of their parties (Marine Le Pen, the leader of France's rebranded National Front, founded by her anti-Semitic father). But all stand for the proposition that nations should decide their own fates and control their own borders.

The Charge That Nationalists Are Racist Is a Smear

The accusation against all nationalists is that they are racists, almost by definition. Even Brexit, a simple vote for a great nation to have control over its own affairs, including immigration policy, has been tarred as an act of rank bigotry.

In a 2017 essay in *The Atlantic* titled "The Nationalist's Delusion," Adam Serwer made the case at length that Trump's nationalism constitutes racism. The piece made no effort to define nationalism or to set out what is distinctive about Trump's version but argued that Trump's election was driven by racial animus and simply took it as a given that racism and nationalism are the same thing.

This is embarrassingly reductive about nationalism and not convincing about Trump's 2016 election, either. To support the proposition that Trump's win wasn't class based but instead a victory for so-called white hegemony, Serwer writes, "Trump defeated Clinton among white voters in every income category." This is untrue. As Zach Goldberg notes on the website Quillette, the very reliable American National Election Studies (ANES) survey showed Hillary Clinton handily beating Trump among white voters making $175,000 or more—suggesting that Trump's strength was indeed with working-class and middle-class voters.

Racism doesn't make much sense as an explanation of Trump's win given that voters who switched from Obama in 2012 to Trump in 2016 were a crucial increment of his support. These voters—who often lived in congressional districts that hadn't fully felt the effect of the economic recovery—tended to think that the country was on the wrong track, needed a strong leader, had become less secure, and should have more protection from imports.

None of this sounds hateful or especially unreasonable. Adam Serwer's bizarre answer is that these voters, too, are racists and were bigoted even when they were voting for the nation's first black president.

Much of the critique of Trump and his supporters comes down to an unwillingness to concede the legitimacy of their views, especially on immigration. These critics hold a dim view of the nation and of borders, believe that putting Americans first is somehow small-minded and selfish, and dismiss the notion that we are a people whose nature can be changed depending on who we welcome here or not.

In short, much of the debate at bottom is over how we should regard nationalism and nationalistic attitudes.

It is to this question that this book addresses itself. This is not a book about Donald Trump, although it was occasioned by him. His rise put the debate over nationalism at the top of the national agenda, and I got interested in the topic after his 2017 inaugural address. But this book doesn't adjudicate every controversy related to Trump's nationalism, except to acknowledge the legitimacy and power of it.

Nor is this a partisan book. Nationalism is flexible enough that either party can appeal to it. I think it was a mistake for many

Republicans to lose touch with nationalism. It has been even more of a mistake for Democrats to throw in almost entirely with identity politics and a cosmopolitanism that is hostile to the prerogatives of the nation-state and emotionally detached from routine expressions of patriotism.

Finally, this book doesn't directly engage with the intra-conservative doctrinal debate over classical liberalism, although readers will gather that I don't agree with the contention that liberalism in this sense is a mistake and incompatible with nationalism.

A word on organization: The first section of this book sets out its fundamental argument about the centrality of nationalism to the American experience and knocks down common misconceptions about nationalism in general.

The next section delves into the roots of the American nation by following the lamp of enlightened nationhood from ancient Israel to England and then to the United States, especially via the settlement of New England.

The following three chapters excavate and defend the American nationalist tradition running through the Revolution and its aftermath in the 1790s; the expansion across the continent and the Civil War; and the rise of America to a world power in the twentieth century and its role as vindicator of the prerogatives of other democratic nation-states.

The final section makes the case for American nationalism against its contemporary challengers and argues, in particular, for an emphasis on cultural nationalism.

I don't get into policy disputes except very roughly at the end, when I outline what I believe is a sensible, broad nationalist agenda.

If nothing else, I intend to prove that Emmanuel Macron and his ilk don't know what they're talking about. They traffic in clichés and misunderstandings about nationalism that obscure the true nature of a force that has shaped the modern world—and, yes, made America great.

CHAPTER 1

AMERICA THE NATION

Prior to the Civil War, a sea captain from Massachusetts named William Driver moved to Nashville, Tennessee, where he proudly flew the Stars and Stripes from his house every holiday.[1]

His mother, with the help of a group of young women, sewed the flag for him in 1824, when he took command of his own ship as a twenty-one-year-old. The legend has it that Driver declared when first raising the seventeen-by-ten-foot banner up his mast, "My ship, my country, and my flag, Old Glory."

This is probably too pat to be true. But somewhere along the line of his extensive travels and adventures, including in the Far East (he knew a little Fijian), the flag earned its famous nickname. "It has ever been my staunch companion and protection," Driver wrote. "Savages and heathens, lowly and oppressed, hailed and welcomed it at the far end of the wide world. Then, why should it not be called Old Glory?"

We know of the affectionate nickname only because of what happened during the Civil War. Driver's enthusiastic display of the flag drew unwelcome attention after Tennessee seceded from the Union. Local Confederates wanted to seize it, but Driver confronted the group who came knocking. "Gentlemen," he said, "if you are looking for stolen property in my house, produce your search-warrant." He rebuffed a subsequent armed party. He then thought it prudent to hide the flag away, and it was sewn into a coverlet.

In February 1862, Union forces took Nashville. Driver sought out the local commander, General William "Bull" Nelson, at the capitol. An adjunct of Nelson, Horace Fisher, recalled later: "Capt. Driver—an honest-looking, blunt-speaking man, was evidently a character; he carried on his arm a calico-covered bedquilt; and, when satisfied that General Nelson was the officer in command, he pulled out his jack-knife and began to rip open the bedquilt without another word. We were puzzled to think what his conduct meant." Driver produced the banner, according to Fisher's account, "which he handed to Gen. Nelson, saying, 'This is the flag I hope to see hoisted on that flagstaff in place of the [damned] Confederate flag set there by that [damned] rebel governor, Isham G. Harris. I have had hard work to save it; my house has been searched for it more than once.' He spoke triumphantly, with tears in his eyes."[2]

It was run up the flagpole, Fisher writes, "when all heads were uncovered and the troops presented arms."[3] Another report says the raising of the flag occasioned "frantic cheering and uproarious demonstrations by soldiers."[4] The 6th Ohio Infantry, which had led the Union troops into Nashville, began to refer to itself as "Old Glory," and as the legend of Driver's flag spread, so did its nickname. A monument at his gravesite is inscribed, "HIS SHIP, HIS COUNTRY, AND HIS FLAG, OLD GLORY."

Why does our flag elicit such strong feelings, whether at epic events such as its raising on Iwo Jima or atop the pile of the World Trade Center after September 11, 2001, or more mundane incidents, say, Chicago Cubs outfielder Rick Monday snatching the flag from protestors about to burn it in the outfield in 1976 or Weather Channel meteorologist Paul Goodloe picking up a battered flag from amid the debris of Hurricane Harvey and respectfully folding it away?

America Is a Nation, Not an Idea

The sentiment around the flag speaks to a loyalty to nation that is deep, abiding, and emotional. Critics might describe this feeling as "atavistic." The better word is *human*. Americans aren't immune to the same natural devotion to their home and country that has animated people since time immemorial, nor should anyone expect them to be.

If anything, we feel this commitment more intensely. Consider the flag. We have long been one of the most flag-soaked societies in the world: we fly our flag more than any other country; our national anthem is about the flag; and we, of course, pledge allegiance "to the flag of the United States of America and to the Republic for which it stands." Flag Day has been celebrated since 1877 and became an official holiday in 1916.[5] We have a flag code with quasi-religious overtones. We adopted these forms of veneration before any other country.[6]

Nonetheless, America is a nation that has trouble accepting that fact. It is often said that America is "an idea," or, as the historian Richard Hofstadter wrote, "It has been our fate as a nation not to have ideologies but to be one."[7]

This is one of our most honored national clichés. The great twentieth-century journalist Theodore H. White wrote, "Americans are not a people like the French, Germans, or Japanese, whose genes have been mixing with kindred genes for thousands of years. Americans are held together only by ideas."[8] The political commentator Cokie Roberts maintains, "We have nothing binding us together as a nation—no common ethnicity, history, religion, or even language—except the Constitution and the institutions it created."[9] South Carolina senator Lindsey Graham insisted during a heated debate over immigration, "America is an idea," and Joe Biden launched his 2020 presidential campaign by averring the same. The columnist Mike Barnicle goes so far as to say that America is "not a democracy, it's not a republic before it is an idea."

Almost all of this is simply wrong as a factual and historical matter. America is a nation, whose sovereignty and borders are dear to it, whose history and culture are an indispensable glue, whose interests guide her actions (or should). What makes us different from other nations isn't the fact that we have national ideals—so do France, England, and Russia, China, Japan, and India. Nor that we consider ourselves distinctive or chosen and honor our Founders. These, too, are fairly common national characteristics.

What makes us different is that our ideas are true. That our claim to chosenness has been better demonstrated, by our essential goodness and power, than that of any other country. That our Founders aren't mythical figures—we don't have to strain to venerate chieftains who a couple of millennia ago fought the Romans (Hermann the Cheruscan for the Germans, Vercingetorix for the French) because we have real giants whose heroism and wisdom are extensively on the historical record.[10] But of course I'd say all these things: I'm an American nationalist.

Nationalism Shouldn't Be a Dirty Word

Of course, the term is widely considered a dirty word. Nationalism has fierce critics on both the Right and the Left, making it a true trans-ideological bogeyman.

Conservatives such as Jonah Goldberg see nationalism as dangerous and at odds with both American exceptionalism and a patriotism that reflects the ideals of the American founding. Goldberg writes that nationalism is a form of tribalism that undermines important attributes of a free society, "from the rule of law to the right to dissent to the sovereignty of the individual."[11]

Progressives such as Jamelle Bouie of the *New York Times* and the aforementioned Adam Serwer of *The Atlantic* write as if nationalism is indistinguishable from "white nationalism" and as such is hideously racist and exclusionary.

Libertarians such as Ilya Somin, a George Mason University law professor, consider nationalism a horror show. "I believe," he writes, "that nationalism is second only to communism as the greatest evil of modern politics." He alleges that "it is a leading cause of mass murder," and even short of that, "many non–mass murdering nationalist regimes still use nationalism as a justification for protectionism, discrimination against minority groups, suppression of dissent, and the like."[12]

The democratic socialist Elizabeth Bruenig of the *Washington Post* denies our nationhood itself. "America simply isn't a nation-state," she asserts. "Nations are made up of people who claim to share certain unchosen characteristics: language, ethnicity, historic religion, mystical destiny. In America, not only is it the factual case that we do not share such things, but it's rather the point of our existence as a country—or was, once. Liberal democracies prize freedom and self-determination, so it follows that Americans are made by beliefs and choices, not by blood and tongue. American nationalism can shatter lives and breed violence, but it won't ever amount to the creation of an American nation. Such a thing does not exist."[13]

Or as Max Fisher, a co-author of an explainer column at the *New York Times*, puts it more broadly, "If you think about it, nationality is weird. The idea that you identify with millions of strangers just based on borders. That's because *national identity is made up*."[14] It is, per Fisher, "the myth that built the modern world, but it also primes us for dictatorship, racism, genocide."

This is all misbegotten. Nationalism should rightly be infused with a country's ideals and its sense of mission; it should be a unifying force hostile to racism and all invidious distinctions that play into sub-national loyalties and identity politics; it should be respectful of the prerogatives of other nations, even as it is jealous of its own. And the fact is that nationalism is an age-old phenomenon that is natural and incredibly widespread.

Nationalism Is Often Wrongly Defined and Understood

First, some terminology. What is a nation? Any definition is open to quibbles, but that of John Stuart Mill is as good as any: "a portion of mankind may be said to constitute a Nationality if they are united amongst themselves by common sympathies, which do not exist between them and any others—which make them co-operate with each other more willingly than with other people, desire to be under the same government, and desire that it should be government by themselves or a portion of themselves exclusively."[15]

As for national identity, it is what used to be known as national character. It is the culture that marks off one country from another, that makes France so French and England so English. Or, to state it more precisely, quoting the great scholar of nationalism Anthony Smith, "it is the continuous reproduction and reinterpretation by the members of a national community of the pattern of symbols, values, myths, memories and traditions that compose the distinctive heritage of nations."[16]

Why use the term *nationalism* instead of *patriotism*? Patriotism is often taken to denote all that is good in national feeling and nationalism all that is noxious. This is simply an attempt to deem nationalism a swear word and end all discussion on that basis. There isn't that much of a practical distinction between the two terms, and in common usage, they should be largely interchangeable. But since anti-nationalists try to put so much weight on the difference, let's pause to examine it more closely.

The root of the word *patriotism* goes back to the Romans and the word *patria*, or "fatherland," the same root as in *patriarchy*. It is love of homeland, of the land of your fathers, of your own.

G. K. Chesterton has a lovely passage on the importance of patriotic appreciation for what's peculiar to your country. "Wherever there is a strangely-shaped mountain upon some lonely island," he wrote, "wherever there is a nameless kind of fruit growing in some obscure forest, patriotism insures that this shall not go into darkness without being remembered in a song."[17]

Whereas patriotism is loyalty to what is your own, particularly your own people and government, nationalism is more specific, namely, as the scholar Azar Gat writes, "the doctrine and ideology that a people is bound together in solidarity, fate, and common political aspirations."[18] Anthony Smith describes the national ideal as "a belief that all those who shared a common history and culture should be autonomous, united and distinct in their recognized homelands."[19]

A key contention of nationalism is that a nation has its rights and claims. This is the thread that runs through the Declaration of Independence, the Gettysburg Address, and the Atlantic Charter. A nation has the right to break off from larger sovereignties in the cause of self-determination (see, for instance, 1776), and to remake its regime or foundational governing rules (see, for instance, 1789).

So if a nation's rights and interests are being trampled, loyalty to the nation, i.e., nationalism, may require treason against the government, the object of patriotic loyalty. As Michael Lind explains, "The nationalist is willing to sacrifice patriotic duty to national loyalty, if necessary—as in 1776, when the American Patriots decided that the needs of the American nation had to prevail over their patriotic allegiance to the British Empire. Governments should serve nations, not nations governments."[20]

Civic Nationalism Is an Illusion

Another distinction that anti-nationalists sometimes make is between civic nationalism, which they consider roughly another term for patriotism, and ethnic nationalism. The liberal writer Michael Ignatieff calls the civic nation "a community of equal, rights-bearing citizens, united in patriotic attachment to a shared set of political practices and values." Ethnic nationalism, in contrast, entails "that an individual's deepest attachments are inherited, not chosen," and "it is the national community that defines the individual, not the individuals who define the national community."[21]

It is certainly true that different forms of nationalism can be more or less inclusive and democratic. But no nation has ever been entirely civic in this sense.

Not France, which is often cited as a leading example of civic nationalism.[22] It undertook an intensive, far-reaching campaign to wipe out distinctive regional cultures and dialects to forge the common national culture that is the basis of its civic nationalism. In 1863, about a quarter of the population spoke no French.[23] As one French observer put it, "France is a deliberate political construction for whose creation the central power has never ceased to fight."[24]

And certainly not the United States. Our cultural nation was extremely important at the outset, and remains so today. At the time of the Revolution, the colonists were 80 percent British and almost entirely Protestant. As John Jay wrote in the Federalist 2, "Providence has been pleased to give this one connected country to one united people—a people descended from the same ancestors, speaking the same language, professing the same religion, attached to the same principles of government, very similar in their manners and customs."

The fact is that culture is seeded with ideas. Would America be the same if its people spoke Russian, the language of a country that has never effectively supported property rights, the rule of law, or limited government, rather than English? Would our political culture as we know it have emerged if practically every home in America a couple hundred years ago had had a Koran on the bedstand rather than a King James Bible? Of course not.

At the beginning, this was a country not necessarily for Englishmen but by Englishmen, including their notions of liberty, which defined the American experience from the outset. Tocqueville famously wrote that the American was the Englishman left alone. If the eastern seaboard had been settled by Spaniards, you could have "left them alone" for a very long time and marinated them in all the Enlightenment philosophers, and they still never would have come up with the American founding.

Even today, when America largely fulfills the standard of a civic nation, it still has a cultural basis. The English language remains a pillar of our national identity (language is often considered a foundation of exclusive ethnic nationalist states). Our rituals and holidays reflect the dominant culture. Christmas is a national holiday; Yom Kippur is not. And they reflect our national identity. Independence Day is a holiday; Cinco de Mayo is not.

Our national heroes, our ancestors, are afforded a prized place of honor in our collective life. The ascension of George Washington to a quasi-sacred status in our country began almost immediately. Today, he's still visible in a fresco inside the US Capitol dome, dressed in purple, and surrounded by the gods of mythology. (Upon the centennial of Washington's birth in 1832, the statesman Edward Everett was part of a movement to disinter the former president from Mount Vernon and bury him at the center of the Capitol: "The sacred remains are . . . a treasure beyond all price, but it is a treasure of which every part of this blood-cemented Union has a right to claim its share.")[25]

We bear the stamp of our national character wherever we go. "The Americanism of American culture," Azar Gat writes, "is deeply felt around the world, regarded either with approval or disapproval, and Americans become very conscious of it when- ever they encounter the outside world. This common American culture far transcends the political-civic culture that many theo- rists have posited, naively, as the exclusive binding element of the American nation."[26]

The devotees of the idea of civic nationalism, at the extreme, make it sound as if a country is a voluntary association of indi- viduals who have decided to live together under a certain set of political institutions and ideas. This is a fantasy. Nations are thicker than that. They are homelands that are felt as such by the people who live there and are connected by a web of associ- ations and memories.

If political institutions were all that mattered, Americans would be just as comfortable living in any major English-speaking country. Canada or Australia don't have our Constitution, but they are liberal societies with ample protections for the freedom of the individual. Yet after every election, when famous people on both sides of the political divide threaten to move to Canada if the result goes the wrong way, no one actually moves.

The French intellectual Ernest Renan gave expression to the voluntarist idea of the nation in his oft-quoted 1882 lecture: "A nation's existence is, if you will pardon the metaphor, a daily plebiscite, just as an individual's existence is a perpetual affirmation of life." But Renan also cited the importance of "a rich legacy of memories" and thought that "the nation, like the individual, is the culmination of a long past of endeavours, sacrifice, and devotion."[27] Just so.

Nationalism Is Not Illiberalism

Underlying most critiques of nationalism is the mistaken assumption that the rumble of Prussian jackboots can be heard underneath it, leading inexorably to fascism and Nazi Germany. As I'll explain in the next two chapters, this is wrong as history and analysis.

Liberalism and a vision of cooperation among nations animated, for the most part, the nationalist movements of the nineteenth century.[28] Their leaders tended to believe deeply in individual rights and popular sovereignty.[29] Prominent nationalists included Giuseppe Mazzini, the Italian revolutionary who sought "one, free, independent, republican nation," and Tomáš Masaryk, the philosopher and humanist who agitated for Czech independence from the Austro-Hungarian Empire.[30]

When Europe went off the rails in the early twentieth century, nationalism as such didn't cause its crash so much as social Darwinism, militarism, and the cult of charismatic leadership. The aftermath of World War I added its own poison.

Nazism exploited nationalist tropes but was also something completely different—a totalitarian ideology based on biological racism.[31] Nazi intellectuals believed in what one historian has called "a SS German-led Europeanism," fired by a lunatic vision of an Aryan Europe cleansed of allegedly inferior peoples.[32] This was not nationalism but supranational racism.

If anything, the conclusion from the horrors of World War II shouldn't be, "Don't be a nationalist" but rather "Don't be a German (or for that matter Austrian, Japanese, Italian, or Spanish)." At least not a German in the era when the illiberal predicates established by the Iron Chancellor, Otto von Bismarck, spun out of control.[33] Nationalism has been a current in the world for centuries, touching every corner of the globe, and somehow only the Germans produced Nazism.

True nationalism, represented by the likes of Charles de Gaulle in World War II and Lech Wałęsa during the Cold War, proved the antidote to the twin totalitarianisms of the twentieth century, what Anthony Smith calls "rival collectivities." Challenged by fascism and communism, nationalism "has met and outlived the crisis posed by these two opposed 'world salvation' movements."[34]

Even if you don't accept this line of argument, deriving a sweeping aversion to nationalism based on the experience of twentieth-century Europe makes no sense. Would anti-nationalists have sided with Napoleon rather than his nationalist opponents from Spain to Egypt?[35] Would they have rooted for the British Empire against Mahatma Gandhi? For the Soviet Union against Hungary and Poland? For Czechoslovakia over the Czech Republic?

American Nationalism Is Different

Regardless, American nationalism in particular is not to be feared. It is, as with so many other things about this country, more benign than the versions to be found in Europe and other places around the world.

This is true for a number of reasons. First, we are the inheritors of an Anglo-American tradition—including the Scottish Enlightenment—that has profound respect for the individual and the rule of law and is woven into the fabric of our country and a fundamental part of our national identity.[36]

The sheet anchor of American sovereignty, the US Constitution, makes it clear where authority ultimately resides: "We the people of the United States . . . do ordain and establish this Constitution for the United States of America." It also happens to be the most inspired and durable mechanism of self-government ever devised by man and is itself an object of patriotic loyalty and national pride.

The United States was never infected with the dream of universal empire that Europe inherited from Rome and that has lingered on in differing forms from Charlemagne to the European Union.

We weren't beyond our national insecurities, especially as we developed our own literature and high culture and emerged from the shadow of Great Britain. "Nothing can betray a more despicable disposition in Americans, than to be the apes of Europeans," pronounced the great nineteenth-century lexicographer Noah Webster.[37] Yet these anxieties never curdled into something fetid. In the sweep of the last few centuries, England and the United States didn't have cause to resent the leaders of the West—a distorting factor in the nationalism of Germany and Russia, among others—because we *were* the leaders of the West.

Finally, we never encountered territorial depredation by our neighbors (even if we have subjected Mexico to it). We have never had to work ourselves into a fever pitch of irredentism over, say, the equivalent of Alsace-Lorraine, the French territory annexed by Germany in the Franco-Prussian War.

American nationalism is not opposed to American exceptionalism, the way anti-nationalists allege. We can acknowledge that we are a nation and give nationalism the place it deserves while honoring all those things that set us apart from other countries: our founding documents, our skepticism about overweening government, our strong commitment to negative rights ("Congress shall make no law . . ."), our middle-class orientation, our celebration of commerce, our broadly democratic politics, our gun culture, our brassy self-confidence and optimism.

An Exclusively Idealistic Account of America Is a Mistake

It is actually an exclusively political and idealistic account of America that puts its exceptionalism in doubt. At the inception of the American nation-state in 1776, we were truly revolutionary in our thoroughgoing commitment to democratic ideas. This is no longer the case. Even Japan, the country of the shogunate and of the emperor, of the military regime that launched the attack on Pearl Harbor, is now a liberal polity that seeks to buttress democracy and the rule of law around the world. If our political system is what supposedly makes us different, we are just another country in the OECD.

For much of the world, our nationalism is, indeed, a prominent feature of our exceptionalism. In a book mostly critical of the phenomenon, Anatol Lieven writes of how the strength of nationalism in this country makes us "very much the 'outlier' in the developed world" and sets us apart "from what Europeans have come to think of (in their own Eurocentric way) as central patterns of post-1945 modernity." He refers to "the nationalist cult of American 'exceptionalism.'"[38]

The boasts of American idealists who believe they are forswearing all connection to nationalism can't be terribly convincing to foreign observers. Consider how the contention that we are a "universal nation" must strike their ears, i.e., as the most bumptiously nationalistic sentiment that they have ever heard. If we are the universal nation, what does that say about every other grubby, small-minded, non-universal nation?

The anti-nationalists are resistant to a more grounded, realistic and truthful understanding of American history because it gets in the way of a definition of America as an ethereal abstraction. In an anti-nationalist speech in 2017, George W. Bush said, "Our identity as a nation, unlike other nations, is not determined by geography or ethnicity, by soil or blood." It is certainly true that "blood and soil," the rallying cry of ethno-nationalists and the Charlottesville Nazis, is deeply inimical to the America project. Yet denying the contribution of geography and land to our identity is willful ignorance.

The criterion for citizenship in the United States is not attachment to a set of ideas but birth within our borders. This standard is enlightened by some standards but also speaks to a deep belief in the specialness of the land such that it confers extraordinary privileges to those born here.[39] Birthright citizenship also implies that the nation doesn't choose us and we don't choose it; we are born into a community of mutual rights and obligations.

From the beginning, we have celebrated the beauty and bounty of our land in the most exalted terms, appreciated the importance of being separated from Europe by an ocean, thought that the frontier had a formative influence on our national character, and pushed to occupy more and more western land. We didn't acquire a continental nation, in the famous quip about the British and their empire, in a fit of absentmindedness.

"America is a poem in our eyes," wrote Ralph Waldo Emerson, "its ample geography dazzles the imagination, and it will not wait long for metres."[40] We believed that geography pointed to our national destiny. "This country and this people seem to have been made for each other," John Jay wrote in the Federalist 2. The Dutch Reformed preacher John B. Johnson argued in a 1794 oration that "PROVIDENCE designed us to be a great and a *united* Nation[.] Our lines are marked by the very hand of nature." A congressman coveting Texas in the early nineteenth century explained that "the great Engineer of the Universe has fixed the natural limits of our country, and men cannot change them."[41]

The process of expansion involved brutality and duplicity in our dealings with the Indians and Mexicans in particular, along with much else that we shouldn't be proud of. But does anyone want to give back any of the land we gained? Does anyone believe that Texas and California would be better governed, freer, or more prosperous under the suzerainty of Mexico? If, by the way, anti-nationalists are so certain that this country doesn't care about soil, they should propose giving an acre of land in the middle of nowhere back to Mexico as symbolic compensation for the Mexican-American War and see how that goes over.

As for blood, it obviously matters that our land is where patriots who came before us bled and died and that most of us have buried our fathers here. These are essential notes in Lincoln's "mystic chords of memory."

The point was eloquently put by the future president of Harvard John Thornton Kirkland in a 1798 speech: "We have learned to love our country, because it is our country; because we are near it, and in it, and have an opportunity of being useful to it; because we breathe its air and share its bounties; because the sweat of our fathers' brows has subdued its soil; their blood watered its fields, and their revered dust sleeps in its bosom; because it embraces our fathers and mothers, our wives and children, our brothers and sisters; because here are our altars, and here our firesides; because patriotism is the combined energy of the social affections, and he who can tear it from his heart, commits sacrilege upon his nature."[42]

James Madison made a similar appeal in the Federalist 14: "Hearken not to the unnatural voice which tells you that the people of America, knit together as they are by so many cords of affection, can no longer live together as members of the same family." No, he argued, "the kindred blood which flows in the veins of American citizens, the mingled blood which they have shed in defense of their sacred rights, consecrate their Union, and excite horror at the idea of their becoming aliens, rivals, enemies."

Ambitious, Nationalist Projects Defined America

Throughout our history, we have pursued half a dozen significant, broadly nationalist projects: to achieve independence from Great

Britain; to forge—and maintain—a government capable of holding the nation together; to take over the continent from the Atlantic to the Pacific; to muster enough national strength to ward off foreign threats; to assimilate immigrants to this country; to establish an international system of nation-states, ideally democratic, but certainly independent and sovereign, free of the control of hostile neighbors and totalitarian empires.

This was the work of Washington and Hamilton, of Jackson and Polk, of Lincoln and TR, of FDR and Reagan. It has been absolutely central to our fate as a nation and essential to our greatness.

America could have been just another nation housed within the British Empire, like Canada or New Zealand; it decided for national independence. It could have been a collection of squabbling statelets with no central government to speak of; it decided for a national government. It could have been split asunder between the North and a new quasi nation in the South; it decided for national unity. It could have been content to huddle against the eastern seaboard as we did at the beginning; it decided for continental expansion.

Anti-nationalists may want to focus on only our ideals, but these ideals were directly implicated in these nationalist projects. If we had agitated about the importance of rights only from within the British Empire, without making the bold statement of republican self-government that was the Revolution, no one would have paid attention. If we had brought disgrace on ourselves by collapsing into chaotic ungovernability in the immediate aftermath of our independence, it wouldn't have mattered what we wrote in the Declaration. And if the North hadn't maintained the union through force of arms, the rump of the United States of America might have been stirringly idealistic—yet embroiled in costly, distracting, and enervating contention with an ideologically and territorially ambitious competitor nation-state in the South.

Anti-nationalists especially want to ignore or excoriate our conquest of the continent. But if we had remained the coastal country we were in the eighteenth century, we would have been a significant, but not a world-historical, nation. Size matters. The Swiss have ideals. Does anyone give a damn?

The Founders themselves were too realistic and practical-minded to doubt that they had established a nation. Alexander Hamilton understood the cultural roots of national loyalty and the central importance of such loyalty to the American project. He wrote in a pseudonymous newspaper essay in 1802, warning of unchecked immigration, "The safety of a republic depends essentially on the energy of a common national sentiment; on a uniformity of principles and habits; on the exemption of the citizens from foreign bias, and prejudice; and on that love of country which will almost invariably be found to be closely connected with birth, education, and family."[43]

Thomas Jefferson opposed the nationalist program of Hamilton and is often portrayed as a kind of universalist, but even he wasn't a citizen of the world in the modern sense. "The first object of my heart is my own country," he maintained. "In that is embarked my family, my fortune, and my own existence. I have not one farthing of interest, not one fibre of attachment out of it."[44]

He wrote from Paris to James Monroe in 1785 and said he wished Monroe could travel to France: "it will make you adore your own country, it's soil, it's climate, it's equality, liberty, laws, people & manners. my God! how little do my countrymen know what precious blessings they are in possession of, and which no other people on earth enjoy. I confess I had no idea of it myself."[45]

America Is Old, Not New

Another cliché that obscures more than illuminates is the notion that the United States is a young country, unburdened by a defining national history and culture.

Most countries reach back into the mists of time for their forebears: America does the opposite and foreshortens its history, forgetting what came before its formal founding, besides a few high points right at the beginning of our settlement. The belief in our newness and youthfulness is itself a national characteristic. When a Frenchman in the nineteenth century wondered of the United States, "If such is the youth of the republic, what will be its old age," Senator Lewis Cass of Michigan replied, "Sir, it will have no old age."[46] This attitude has a considerable upside, but it is based on a myth.

Mark Twain noted, acutely, in his classic *Life on the Mississippi*, "The world and the books are so accustomed to use, and over use, the word 'new' in connection with our country, that we early get and permanently retain the impression that there is nothing old about it." He brought this up in the context of Hernando de Soto first encountering the Mississippi River in 1542, "still two years before Luther's death; eleven years before the burning of Servetus; thirty years before the St. Bartholomew murder; Rabelais was not yet published; 'Don Quixote' was not yet written; Shakespeare was not yet born."[47]

The United States might not be an old nation—certainly not compared to, say, Japan, whose beginnings stretch back too far to be known—but it is a very old nation-state. The historian Henry Steele Commager noted that the United States is "the oldest republic, the oldest democracy, the oldest federal system; it has the oldest written constitution and boasts the oldest of genuine political parties."[48]

Michael Lind invites us to consider the history of the English language, the fantastically successful legacy of the Angles, who invaded England from Denmark in the sixth century.[49] "Modern English stabilized around the year 1500," he writes. "The first permanent British settlement in North America was in 1607. For four-fifths of the time that there have been modern English speakers—almost half a millennium—there have been Anglo-Americans."[50]

Of course, America has made itself anew across its history, especially regarding race. A country that, at its beginning, granted suffrage only to white males and tolerated chattel slavery gradually opened up, abolishing slavery and recognizing the rights of African Americans. The national government was the (obviously much-belated) vehicle of this progress, crushing a bigoted regionalism both during the Civil War and in the civil rights era.

In sketching out the predicates and history of American nationalism in what follows, I will give the appropriate due to both material considerations—land, above all—and inescapable human emotions such as national honor and pride. I will emphasize how far back our history goes and how important culture—religion, geography, inherited folkways and tropes, and so on—have been to our formation, as a corrective to the pervasive, yet wholly erroneous notion that our nation somehow emerged exclusively from the pen of Thomas Jefferson in 1776, like Athena from the head of Zeus.

Before delving into the American experience, though, I'll clear out some of the underbrush about the phenomenon of nationalism in general in the next two chapters.

All of this is offered in support of the proposition that we need to recover the sense of America as a nation, that although we may look different and have different tenures in America, we are bound by a defined geography, a common history and set of customs, and an inheritance from a particular place that attracted others from outside that tradition.

It is only in tending to this understanding of ourselves as a people and a culture that we can preserve this country's distinctiveness, including its belief in universal ideas.

It has long been assumed by those who consider themselves the great and good that the nation-state is inevitably going to fade away. To the contrary, it is critical to any American future worthy of the name. We will lose something essential and irrecoverable if William Driver's Old Glory ever fails to elicit our passion and our devotion.

CHAPTER 2

LOVE, NOT HATE

In 1425, a thirteen-year-old French peasant girl experienced a vision of Saint Michael the Archangel in her father's garden. It began a journey that would make her a world-famous martyr and transcendent national hero whom Mark Twain deemed "the most noble life that was ever born into this world save only One."

Joan of Arc's visions told her to free France from the English, and that was what she set out to do, in one of the least likely stories of martial valor the world has ever known. A slender teenage girl defied every norm of class and gender to convince the authorities that she was born to liberate her country and should be allowed to lead troops into battle. When she did, she won a stunning victory against the English besieging the city of Orléans.

In the mid-fourteenth century, the English sought to conquer French lands that they claimed as their own, beginning the Hundred Years' War that would reduce the French population, ravaged by famine and plague, by about half.[1] The English king Henry V had won his famous victory at Agincourt in northern France in 1415. With his French allies (the Burgundians sided with him, the Armagnacs against), he held Paris and a swath of northern France and had forced the French to recognize his heirs as the rightful rulers of France.[2]

Born a few years before Agincourt, her country riven by civil war and under foreign occupation for seventy-five years, Joan of Arc followed the voices that told her to fight to restore to the throne the French heir who had been pushed aside by the English, Charles of Valois.

She sent a note to the English prior to the battle at Orléans that they should get out of France. If they refused, she assured them with wonderful temerity, "I am a captain of war, and wherever I find your men in France, I will force them to leave, whether they wish to or not. If they refuse to obey, I will have them all killed. I am sent by God, the King of Heaven, to chase you one and all from France."[3]

The English weren't overly impressed by their young female interlocutor. She sent another warning in a message shot over to the English camp tied to an arrow: "I am writing this to you for the third and final time; I will not write anything further."[4] The English troops yelled back, "News from the whore of the French Armagnacs."[5] Joan cried the tears of an insulted teenage girl—and soon enough got her revenge.

The Maid of Orléans led the French troops to victory riding a white horse and carrying a twelve-foot banner with an image of Christ sitting in judgment. Soon enough, in keeping with her outlandish prediction before she took up arms, Charles VII was crowned in the cathedral of Rheims.

Joan's run of success eventually gave out. The Burgundians captured her and handed her over to the English, who threw the book at her in preparation for a show trial: she had dressed as a man (a charge that consumed an inordinate amount of attention and energy), deceived the people, and was a heretic and a witch.

Joan deftly handled her inquisitors, who had no interest in anything other than trapping her in a damning admission and killing her.[6] But she gave no ground. Asked whether God hated the English, "she said she knows nothing about the love or hate that God has for the English, nor what he will do with their souls; but she knows for certain they will be driven from France, except for those who stay and die, and that God will grant the French victory over the English."[7] The verdict was foreordained.

The English burned her alive—she proclaimed the name of Jesus during the ordeal—and scattered her ashes in the Seine River. She was nineteen years old.[8]

Critics of nationalism contend that it is a relatively recent phenomenon, a contrivance of modern rulers to control and manipulate their populations and therefore inherently illegitimate. The Maid of Orléans tells us otherwise.

Joan both expressed the national identity of France—a chosen people ruled by "the most Christian" king and inhabiting their own distinct land—and came to represent it. Charles VII annulled her trial when he finally expelled the English, and in 1920 she became a saint. The Free French during World War II adopted Joan's symbol, the Cross of Lorraine, as their own, flying it on their ships and painting it on their planes.[9] The home village of Charles de Gaulle, himself a formidable symbol of the French nation, erected a 145-foot-tall Cross of Lorraine in his honor.

Nationalism Is Powerful

The allergy to nationalism and the belief that it should be dismissed and resisted are built on widespread misperceptions.

Nationalism, or at least national feeling, isn't new or manufactured but quite old and entirely natural. It isn't based on hatred, instead on love: our affection for home and our own people. It is caught up in culture, in the language, manners, and rituals that set off any given country from another. It is an elemental force that can't be effaced without government coercion, and even then has proved impossible to wipe out. Empires and totalitarian ideologies have failed to eradicate it.

Modern nationalism developed in the nineteenth century as largely a liberal movement, intimately associated with the rise of popular sovereignty. The nation-state is what gives us accountable government and the possibility of a self-governing polity at all. Places such as the Middle East and Africa where nation-states have never properly developed aren't more enlightened or peaceful but the opposite—they're blighted by ruinous tribal and ethnic conflict.

All of this means that it would be impossible to suppress nationalism and foolish to try. The critics would be better advised to hone nationalism to their own ends rather than to pretend that it will go away, here in the United States or anywhere else.

Just ask the English who grappled with a fearlessly patriotic French girl so many centuries ago. They captured her, humiliated and attempted to discredit her, and finally executed her to bury her memory forever, yet the example and spirit of Joan of Arc inspire her countrymen and people around the world to this day.

Nationalism Is Natural

Attachment to the nation is deeply rooted. We get the term *natio* from ancient Rome; it means "birth" or "descent."[10] It is closely related to the word *gens*, meaning "clan" or, more broadly, "people." The Roman historian Tacitus referred to the Germans as a *gens* who had constituent *nationes*. The medievalist Susan Reynolds explains that the terms were used fairly widely in the Middle Ages and denoted "a community of custom, descent, and government—a people."[11]

As the political scientist Benedict Anderson observes, in a variety of languages, the nation is commonly described "either in the vocabulary of kinship (motherland, *Vaterland*, *patria*) or that of home (*heimat* or *tanah air* [earth and water, the phrase for the Indonesians' native archipelago])."[12] This is no accident. Almost every nation rests on an ethnic core and consequently a deep sense of natural, unchosen ties, like those of family.

The great Italian nationalist Giuseppe Mazzini, the nineteenth-century writer and activist who agitated for the unification of Italy under a republican government, expressed this feeling: "Our country is our home, the home which God has given us, placing therein a numerous family which we love and are loved by, and with which we have a more intimate and quicker communion of feeling and thought than with others."[13]

His sentiment underlines how loyalty to nation is ultimately built on a foundation of love—for its landscape, arts, traditions, and people; for, in short, what is *ours*. Nationalist songs and poems typically aren't bloodthirsty or hateful but simply express a devotion to country.[14] G. K. Chesterton put it well. "Cosmopolitanism gives us one country, and it is good," he wrote. "Nationalism gives us a hundred countries, and every one of them is the best."[15]

All of this is why the nation can make a call on our sacrifice—to kill and be killed—that very few causes can outside of family and faith. The World War I–era tombs of unknown soldiers symbolize this intense, almost mystical identification of citizen-warriors and the nation. The tomb in Arlington Cemetery is inscribed simply but powerfully, HERE RESTS IN HONORED GLORY AN AMERICAN SOLDIER KNOWN BUT TO GOD; it has been watched over by a sentinel every minute of every day since 1937. In France, every evening a Committee of the Flame relights a torch at the Tomb of the Unknown at the base of the Arc de Triomphe. In Great Britain, the unknown soldier rests in Westminster Abbey, the church of kings, underneath the inscription BENEATH THIS STONE RESTS THE BODY OF A BRITISH WARRIOR UNKNOWN BY NAME OR RANK BROUGHT FROM FRANCE TO LIE AMONG THE MOST ILLUSTRIOUS OF THE LAND.

Any attempt to disrupt these commemorations would be taken as a grave offense against the nation, which depends on—and must honor—the sacrifices of its citizens.

Nationalism Is Old

Counter to the evidence of the depth of national feeling, the students of nationalism known as the modernists contend that nationalism really only arose in the nineteenth century.[16] There is no doubt that beginning with the Industrial Revolution, innovations such as railroads and newspapers brought a new national integration. They conquered space, promoted mass political mobilization, and standardized vernacular languages.[17] (Prior to 1500, roughly three-quarters of books in western Europe were printed in Latin, a dominance that rapidly gave way.)[18] But this didn't create nations as such, just modern nations.

Modernism works, in effect, as a just-so story for critics of nationalism, who want to believe that national feeling is a contrivance of cynical leaders. "Nationalism is a doctrine invented in Europe at the beginning of the 19th century," insists the acclaimed British historian Elie Kedourie.[19] "Nationalism," according to the influential modernist Ernest Gellner, "does not have any very deep roots in the human psyche."[20] This is nonsense, and much of human history provides a record of why.

States with a national basis have existed for a very long time. Ancient Egypt constituted a unified state, ruling an ethnically homogeneous people with a distinct culture, for thousands of years. The same was true of China, Korea, and Japan.[21]

Consciousness of nations existed in the Middle Ages. The Benedictine churchman Regino of Prüm noted in the tenth century that "the various nations and peoples are distinguished from each other by descent, customs, language and laws." The basic map of Europe had taken shape by the twelfth century. "France, England, and Scotland, the three Scandinavian kingdoms, Aragon, Castile, Portugal, Sicily, Hungary, and Poland had all of them taken their places as units of Latin Christendom by 1150," the historian Johan Huizinga wrote.[22]

Even multinational empires had a strong ethno-national element. As Azar Gat points out, the medieval Holy Roman Empire might not have been holy, Roman, or an empire, in Voltaire's famous quip, but it sure as hell was German.[23] In 1512, it changed its title to the Holy Roman Empire of the German Nation, although as late as 1782 the emperor still insisted, "the capital and true center of the empire is Rome."[24]

Long before the modern era, people felt an attachment to their countries. The French believed in their special status centuries prior to Joan of Arc. An eighth-century prologue to the medieval Salic Law described "the illustrious nation of the Franks, chosen by God, valorous in arms, constant in peace, profound in wisdom, noble in body, spotless in purity, handsome without equal, intrepid, quick and fierce, newly converted to the Catholic faith, and free of heresy."[25]

In the early twelfth century, the abbot and historian Suger wrote (as he's been paraphrased) that "France is 'our land' . . . the mother of us all, of the king and of the commoner. The land gives us life and everything associated with it. We are all born French of France, all 'from the same womb,' part of one and the same flesh, protected by this earth and sky. We all owe it therefore our love and support."[26]

Nations already defended their interests. In the fourteenth century, the Catholic Church held ecumenical councils that voted separately by nation and featured intense national contention. The French wanted England either subsumed in the German nation (as it had been in a former ecclesiastical division) or split up. The English vigorously defended the integrity of their nationhood and the principle at stake: "Nations in a general council should be considered equals and each should have the same rights."[27]

National stereotypes had taken hold. A French diplomat and historian reported on a 1467 meeting in Brussels between the Duke of Burgundy and a German counterpart, Frederick the Victorious of the Palatinate. "The Duke's people said the Germans were dirty, that they took off their boots and flung them on the freshly made beds and had no such manners as we have." *Those uncouth Germans.* "The Germans, on the other hand, as though consumed with envy, disapproved of all the luxury." *Those high-living Frenchmen.*[28]

And foreign threats were considered intolerable. Nations often achieved their identities, in part, in the elemental act of resisting foreign enemies.[29] The English and the Dutch sharpened their sense of national self in resisting the Spanish, the Irish in resisting the English, and the Polish in resisting the Prussians and Russians (among others).[30]

Even if native rulers mistreated the masses, they were preferable to an alien yoke. Appeals to national feeling constituted a natural and powerful calling card even for otherwise high-handed or tyrannical leaders. Fighting off invading Swedes in the early eighteenth century, Peter the Great of Russia exhorted his troops, "You should think that you are fighting not for Peter, but for the state, entrusted to Peter, for your kin, for fatherland."[31]

He knew, as so many after him have realized as well, that his subjects had a deeper attachment to their country and home than to his rule.

The Nation Rests on Language

The prospect of being ruled by a people speaking a foreign tongue is especially offensive. Our sense of community depends heavily on a common language. Where one is present, it creates a cultural glue; where it isn't, there are deep-seated divisions.

Nice, pleasant Canada has been nearly torn apart in recent decades by the presence of a French-speaking province, Quebec, in an English-speaking country.[32] Equally nice, pleasant Belgium is perennially riven between its French-speaking and Dutch-speaking regions. Spain has been buffeted by an independence movement in Catalonia, where, despite the best efforts of the Spanish central government over the centuries, Catalan is still spoken by much of the population.

On the other hand, the cleavage of Charlemagne's empire in the 843 Treaty of Verdun between German- and Romance-speaking parts, corresponding roughly to Germany (in all its various forms over the centuries) and France, has endured for more than a millennium.[33]

People have long cared about the status of their language. As early as the fifteenth century, proto-Protestant Hussite rebels agitated in the Holy Roman Empire for more Czech officeholders and greater recognition of their own tongue. The revolt was both religious and national, against an emperor deemed "a great and brutal enemy of the Czech kingdom and language." Years after the Hussite rebellion had ended, dissidents still accused the pope of seeking "to destroy, wipe out, and utterly suppress the Czech language."[34]

Language runs very deep. Benedict Anderson writes of how each language "looms up imperceptibly out of a horizonless past." This is why languages "appear rooted beyond almost anything else in contemporary societies. At the same time, nothing connects us affectively to the dead more than language." The weight of the words "Earth to earth, ashes to ashes, dust to dust," for instance, "derives only in part from their solemn meaning; it comes also from an as-it-were ancestral 'Englishness.'"[35]

The spark for nationalist movements has often been historians, writers, lexicographers, and folklorists who celebrated and promoted vernacular languages and excavated a glorious literary past. The German dictionary of the Brothers Grimm, who famously collected folk- and fairy tales, nodded to the primacy of language with its logo "In the beginning was the word." Poets came to exemplify the national traditions and aspirations of their countries: the Irish had W. B. Yeats, the Poles had Adam Mickiewicz, the Zionists had Haim Bialik, and so on.[36]

This was true as well of composers (Franz Liszt for the Hungarians, Frédéric Chopin for the Poles, Antonín Dvořák for the Czechs), painters (Jacques-Louis David for the French, Henry Fuseli for the Swiss, Viktor Vasnetsov for the Russians), and novelists of great historical epics such as Walter Scott and Leo Tolstoy.[37] The spectacle of opera provided a particularly powerful tableau for national themes. A performance of Daniel Auber's *La muette de Portici*, the first French-language grand opera, in Brussels in 1830 helped spark a national rebellion, with the southern provinces splitting from the Netherlands and becoming Belgium.[38]

Tolstoy's *War and Peace* is a classic of the national genre. Set during Napoleon's invasion in 1812, it limns and extols an irreducible Russian national character. Tolstoy describes how Natasha Rostov, a young noblewoman who grew up in an aristocratic setting soaked in French culture, instinctively takes to a folk dance out in the countryside: "Where, how and when could this young countess, who had a French émigrée for governess, have imbibed from the Russian air the spirit of that dance?"[39] But she did. As Roger Scruton writes, "The art and literature of the nation is an art and literature of settlement, a celebration of all that attaches the place to the people and the people to the place."[40]

Once this attachment exists and is expressed and exemplified in art and literature, it makes for an almost indissoluble bond.

Nationalism Protects Self-Government

The eighteenth-century Scottish philosopher David Hume observed how accretions of culture add up over time to a national identity: "Where a number of men are united into one political body, the occasions of their intercourse must be so frequent, for defense, commerce, and government, that, together with the same speech or language, they must acquire a resemblance in their manners, and have a common or national character, as well as a personal one, peculiar to each individual."[41]

His Genevan counterpart Jean-Jacques Rousseau considered this a formidable bulwark of national independence. He wrote of Poland, "The virtue of its citizens, their patriotic zeal, the particular form that national institutions can give to their spirit, that is the only rampart always ready to defend it, and which no army could breach. If you arrange things such that a Pole could never become a Russian, then I can assure you that Russia will never subjugate Poland."[42]

This proved, of course, not literally true (at the time Rousseau wrote, Poland had already been partitioned by the Russians). Yet no one has been able to extinguish Poland for exactly the reasons Rousseau set out.

His insight applies more broadly. Consider Scandinavia. The Russians annexed the Finns in the early nineteenth century, wrenching them from their centuries-long union with Sweden. The Finns realized that they could survive only by resisting Russification and protecting and strengthening their own national culture. Their informal motto became "We are no longer Swedes, we cannot become Russians, therefore let us become Finns."[43] The nationalists made promotion of the Finnish language a major project and the country declared its independence in 1917.[44]

In the tumult of the Napoleonic Wars in the early nineteenth century, Norway broke away from its union with Denmark, only to get yoked to Sweden. The country's nationalists, too, focused on language. They distinguished Norwegian from what had been a common language in Denmark-Norway and reached back to Old Norwegian manuscripts, an act of recovery in support of something new, namely their nation's independence, achieved in 1905.[45]

Rousseau presumably wouldn't have been surprised.

Empires Never Last

When a political authority runs against the grain of a nation's culture and identity, its legitimacy inevitably comes into question. The eighteenth-century German philosopher of nationalism Johann Gottfried Herder wrote of how "the most natural state is . . . *one* nation, an extended family with one national character." He warned against empires that mixed various "nationalities under one sceptre. A human sceptre is far too weak and slender for such incongruous parts to be engrafted upon it. Such states are but patched-up contraptions, fragile machines, appropriately called state-machines, for they are wholly devoid of inner life, and their component parts are connected through mechanical contrivances instead of bonds of sentiment."[46]

The old multinational empires of Europe, built on conquest or dynastic unions, constituted precisely such fragile machines. In 1830, the Austrian dramatist Franz Grillparzer compared the nationalities collected within the Habsburg Empire to "horses absurdly harnessed together." He predicted that they "will scatter in all directions as soon as the advancing spirit of the times will weaken and break the bonds."[47] So it proved.

The Habsburg, Ottoman, and Russian empires all dissolved as their repressive apparatuses gave way and the drive toward national self-determination gained ground.[48] Empires can't rely on the fellow feeling and social trust that are at the foundation of democracy. John Stuart Mill wrote that such states are beset by "mutual antipathies" and that "none feel that they can rely on others for fidelity in a joint resistance." He concluded that it is "a necessary condition of free institutions that the boundaries of government should coincide in the main with those of nationalities."[49]

This has been borne out. Azar Gat writes that "while there have been many national states without free government, free government has scarcely existed in the absence of a national community."[50] Despite massive effort via the education system and other instruments of indoctrination and persuasion, the old empires couldn't forge themselves into single, all-encompassing nations. As soon as the infrastructure of imperial power began to break down, the constituent nations went their own ways and, as Gat remarks, have endured since, even when they didn't have a tradition of independence.[51]

The Habsburg Empire succeeded the Holy Roman Empire. It encompassed a vast collection of territories in central and east-central Europe broadly grouped as Austria, Bohemia, and Hungary, which included much of modern Romania, Croatia, and Slovakia. Loyalty centered on the dynasty, which took its name from its ancestral fortress in what is now Switzerland, the Castle of the Hawk, or Habichtsburg. The House of Habsburg ruled for six hundred years, with the next-to-last emperor, Franz Joseph, alone reigning for sixty-eight years.[52]

An undeniable majesty attached to the project. The Habsburgs mastered ritual and patronized culture, such that Vienna became a watchword for musical genius. But there's a reason that the empire was known as the "prison of nations."[53] Hungarian revolts periodically broke out on national grounds. As the leader of a rebellion in the early seventeenth century put it, "It should be demanded that every man who loves his country and fatherland stand up for his nation and hasten against our common enemy."[54] The Revolution of 1848 rocked the empire as the nations rose up in the cause of democracy and self-rule but were defeated.

In the aftermath, the imperial authorities concluded that Hungary couldn't be completely subsumed into the empire and agreed to divided rule between Austria and Hungary in 1867. Despite centrifugal pressures, the Habsburgs held it together up until the catastrophe of World War I, which smashed it into oblivion. Near the end, Franz Joseph conceded, "I have been aware for a long time of how much an anomaly we are in the modern world."[55]

The same could have been said of the "sick man of Europe," the Ottoman Empire, with its exotic court featuring routine fratricide and the harem of the sultan's wives and concubines, guarded by black eunuchs.[56] It grew in extent in the fourteenth and fifteenth centuries, conquering Constantinople from Byzantium and gobbling up the Balkans. A century later, it acquired Arab lands, including Mecca and Medina. This gave the empire a more Muslim cast that only grew more pronounced as it shed its Christian nations in Europe after repeated reversals in the nineteenth century.[57]

The Greeks won their independence in 1830 after a national revolt derived, in the words of one historian, "from their common language, from the traditions of their church . . . and from a consciousness of being under alien rule." Serbia constantly rebelled, beginning in the sixteenth century, before finally making its exit in 1878. Other Balkan states departed as well, and soon enough the empire lost everything in Europe. The Ottoman Empire, too, reached the end of its tether in World War I, supplanted by the nation-state of Turkey.[58]

The Russian Empire, for its part, long existed in tandem with the Russian nation. Already in the fifteenth century, a crude state ruled an enormous swath of territory. In the formulation of the Russian expert Michael Karpovich, "the body of Russia grew too fast for its soul."[59] Russia became one of the largest empires ever in terms of sheer landmass. Imbued with a messianic sense of mission as the Orthodox "Third Rome" after the fall of Rome and Constantinople, it relied on force and, depending on the circumstances, Russification as key instruments of control. It stamped out Polish rebellions, incorporating the Kingdom of Poland as the "Vistula province" and attacking the Catholic Church. It tried to suppress the Ukrainian and Belarusian languages.[60]

All the non-Russian nations sought their freedom after Russia's defeat in World War I. Poland, Finland, and the Baltics got out, while the Bolsheviks crushed the other independence movements, taking almost a decade to bring Kazakhstan to heel. During World War II, the Soviets retook the Baltics, Belarus, and western Ukraine, then extended the old empire even further, with Joseph Stalin's ravenous eye looking as far afield as Xinjiang and northern Iran. Moscow controlled the Eastern Bloc countries, even if they weren't directly incorporated into the USSR.[61]

Like the empire it had supplanted, the Soviet Union occupied a sixth of the world's territory. Like the old empire, it imagined a world-historical mission for itself, although an ideological, not a religious one. Like the tsarist project, it resorted to Russification, mandating instruction in the Russian language and the teaching of Russian history and culture.[62] And it rolled the tanks as necessary to keep the captive nations in the fold. It operated as a fearsome example of the state as, in the phrase of Herder, a "cold monster."[63] As soon as the empire's resolve waned at the end of the 1980s, the non-Russian nations became triumphantly independent.[64]

And they have never looked back.

Colonialism Inevitably Failed

When the great French and British colonial empires liberalized and no longer resorted to crushing force to maintain their control over subject countries, they lost their grip just as the old European empires had. They fought to hang on, but not with the ferocity of prior centuries or the brute, at times genocidal force of imperial Germany in Africa in the early twentieth century. And so they, too, gave way to the tide of national self-determination.[65]

The French imperial project, which endured and transformed across the centuries, always supremely culturally self-confident and infused with a sense of civilizing mission, staggered under the reverses of World War II.[66] The humiliating defeat at the hands of the Nazis undermined French prestige, while Japanese military success in Indochina sent an encouraging message to anti-colonialists bristling under the European yoke. De Gaulle promised a more open empire, but not nearly open enough for the subject peoples. France suffered successive disasters in wars in Indochina, fought from 1946 to 1954, and Algeria, from 1954 to 1962. After that, it became clear that there was no keeping the empire, and the French liquidated the rest of it in short order.[67]

The British Empire, a globe-spanning enterprise that at its height included almost a quarter of the world's population, slowly came undone during the same period. In the immediate aftermath of World War II, India, Burma, and Ceylon became independent and the British left Palestine.[68] They fought to hold Malaya, Kenya, and Cyprus in the 1950s, but the fiasco of the Suez Crisis—the British went to war with Egypt to hold the canal and were abandoned by the Americans—began the unraveling in earnest. The British unloaded possession after possession and made the famous announcement of withdrawal of their forces from east of Suez as of 1971. The phrase originated with Rudyard Kipling: "Ship me somewheres east of Suez, where the best is like the worst,/Where there aren't no Ten Commandments an' a man can raise a thirst."[69] Thirsts would heretofore have to be raised closer to home.

The reality underlying decolonization was that other peoples besides the European nations had their pride, their ideals, their sense of mission. In 1928, Gandhi called colonial rule "this living death of a whole people." He spelled out his own version of national chosenness: "My ambition is much higher than independence. Through the deliverance of India, I seek to deliver the so-called weaker races of the earth from the crushing heels of Western exploitation in which England is the greatest partner." Indeed, he believed that "India's coming into her own will mean every nation doing likewise." He envisioned the creation of a world commonwealth, with a leading role for—what else?—his own country: "India has the right, if she only knew, of becoming the predominant partner by reasons of her numbers, geographical position and culture inherited for ages."[70]

Given the choice, no nation or people picks "living death."

Without Nationalism, Democracy Is Impossible

The circumstances of India's independence, as it proved, didn't justify the high-flying rhetoric. The ensuing partition between Hindu and Muslim territory, creating Pakistan and ultimately Bangladesh, resulted in a humanitarian catastrophe. In swaths of the former colonial empires, especially in the Middle East and Africa, decolonization brought its own misery. If the experience of empires proved that ultimately, foreign peoples couldn't be denied self-government without resorting to force, the experience of many of the new countries demonstrated that states without a strong unifying sense of nationality can't establish peace and order within their own borders.

They confronted the same issue raised by the nineteenth-century statesman Massimo d'Azeglio at the inaugural meeting of the parliament of a united Italy: "Italy is made, but who will now make the Italians?"[71]

New African states that emerged in the mid-twentieth century corresponding to arbitrary colonial borders generally lacked an ethnic core and a strong national identity. They accepted the old lines in the interest of stability, although the borders weren't conducive to it. Ethnic rebellions, wars of secession, and wars between states over border-straddling ethnic populations have been the norm, killing and displacing millions of people. In many countries, democracy hasn't smoothed over the deep-seated sources of hatred and division. It's not lack of democracy but lack of a true nationalism that is the source of the chaos and discontent.[72]

Consider the British colonial legacy alone. The British cobbled together Nigeria out of 250 ethnic groups; Igbos lost a quarter of their population trying to gain independence in the Biafran war in the late 1960s, and the country has had a long history of ethnic-based coups and conflict between Christians and Muslims. The British performed a shotgun marriage between the mutually hostile Nilotic and Bantu people in Uganda, leading to perpetual conflict, including the horrors of the 1970s dictator Idi Amin. The British made Sudan out of sundry African tribes and Arab peoples; after endemic warfare, the country split in two between the Arab Muslim north and the African Christian south in the 2000s, while the government has prosecuted a genocidal campaign against Africans in the western region of Darfur.[73]

All of this tragic history is negative evidence for the proposition that having a functioning democracy requires a demos, or a people who feel attached to one another. We are well beyond the era of the city-state, when all free citizens could gather on the Pnyx, the Athenian hillside within sight of the Acropolis, and listen to the likes of Pericles and Alcibiades before voting on important matters of state. Now the nation-state is the best way to delineate a people sharing bonds of language, history, culture, and institutions. It is telling that the era of the modern nation-state has overlapped with the rise of democracy.

"It is no accident," the scholar Craig Calhoun writes, "that projects of linguistic reform have been nearly universal features of nationalist (and democratic) projects. Aristocracies used language partly to parcel out differential standing, forever distinguishing refined from vulgar usage. Democracies claimed rights to public participation for all people—the nation. Equally, advocates of national self-strengthening sought the education of those same people, and often their inclusion in the political process."[74]

National loyalty gives everyone in society a common interest that is deeper than any specific power struggle. It transcends tribe and sect. It establishes the parameters within which a discrete people and its government can arrive at something approximating the social contract imagined by philosophers such as John Locke. It renders a society, as Roger Scruton puts it, in the first-person plural "we."[75] Only on this basis is it possible to create citizens with equal rights and reciprocal obligations, living together under the rule of law. This arrangement, in turn, makes possible the social trust that lubricates everyday life and the market economy.

In short, nationalism isn't just old, natural, deep seated, and extremely difficult to suppress, it is the foundation of a democratic political order. This is another reason why it is foolish to dismiss and diminish it based on the common misunderstanding that it is synonymous with racism, warfare, and the most hideous totalitarianism that the world has ever known.

CHAPTER 3

THE SMEAR AGAINST NATIONALISM

Tolui, the youngest son of Genghis Khan, must have been in a generous mood. He spared a contingent of skilled craftsmen from the conquered city of Merv in 1221—and killed perhaps 700,000 others.[1]

Controlling modern Iran and swaths of central Asia, the Empire of Khwarezmia was bound to clash with the adjacent Mongols, already on their way to forging the most territorially extensive empire of all time. When a Khwarezmian governor killed a caravan of Mongol traders and then a subsequent Mongol ambassador was beheaded, war became inevitable and militarily overmatched Khwarezmia all but doomed. Genghis Khan and his ferocious force of cavalrymen ran over city after city. "They came, they sapped, they burnt, they slew, they plundered and they departed," reported one survivor.

In charge of a division of his father's army, Tolui surrounded Merv, in present-day Turkmenistan. The city's commander decided to surrender. After the Mongols took whoever was desirable or useful to them, they slaughtered everyone else and utterly destroyed the city. As if this enormity weren't enough, a rear guard later showed up to kill whoever had somehow escaped the first massacre.[2]

The Mongols didn't kill out of religious or ethnic animus. As a matter of fact, they were quite tolerant. They massacred as a means of coercion—submit or die—and to secure vengeance for acts they believed humiliated or dishonored them. By some estimates, the Mongols killed 30 million people across two centuries of empire building and reduced the population of Hungary and China by half.[3]

The Case against Nationalism Is Ill Informed and Ahistorical

Anti-nationalists claim that modern nationalism is the inevitable progenitor of war and precursor of fascism, that it is shot through with racism and anti-Semitism. This is an ill-informed and ahistorical smear. It is certainly true that nationalism has more and less desirable forms, and some deserve all the obloquy heaped on them, but it is not inherently militaristic, undemocratic, or racist.

Military conflict existed long before the modern nation-state—indeed, long before the existence of the state at all. Researchers have established that prehistory was less a blissful period of noble savages living at peace as a series of raids and massacres that occasionally wiped out entire populations.[4]

Peace has been the exception rather than the norm throughout much of human history. The gates of the Temple of Janus, which were closed to signal that the Roman Empire was at peace, were shut only extremely rarely. The Romans fought against cities, tribes, and other empires; they fought to extend their empire and repel invaders; they fought against one another in civil wars over imperial succession—and nowhere to be found in this bloody tableau of constant conflict is the modern nation-state.

Of course, nation-states can be bumptious and aggressive, but a constant source of war throughout history isn't nationalism but its opposite: the quest for dominion, the drive not to govern ourselves but govern others. It's ultimately why Genghis Khan, and many of the world's other great conquerors, fought.[5]

As for fascism, it makes an appeal to nationalistic sentiment yet is a distinct phenomenon that in important respects runs against the grain of nationalism.

Finally, racism, like warfare, is endemic to the human condition. In the broadest gauge, the golden era of the modern nation-state over the last hundred years or so has been a time of declining racism around the globe, although bigotry is still with us and, realistically, always will be.

In general, what are taken to be the sins of modern nations or nationalism—aggression, fascism, racism—are really human failings across all epochs and all forms of human organization, as is abundantly clear from the historical record.

Nationalism Has Done More to Promote Peace than War

During the Peloponnesian War in the fifth century BC, Athens wiped out the Spartan island colony of Melos—almost on principle. According to Thucydides, they "put to death all the grown men whom they took, and sold the women and children for slaves, and subsequently sent out five hundred colonists and inhabited the place themselves."[6]

This in the course of a devastating twenty-seven-year-long war of one Greek city-state against another Greek city-state.

In 146 BC, the Romans gained the upper hand on the Carthaginians in their long struggle and demanded that the city of Carthage be destroyed. When the Carthaginians resisted, the Romans leveled the place and tried to efface all memory of it.[7]

This in the third installment of bitter warfare between two great cities cum rival Mediterranean empires.

Pope Urban II kicked off the First Crusade in 1095. Soldiers drawn from around Europe marched on the East and captured the city of Antioch. "With the battle and the booty won," the chronicler Raymond d'Aguilers wrote, "we carried the heads of the slain to camp and stuck them on posts."[8] The Crusaders plundered their way to the gates of Jerusalem, finally broke through in July

1099, slaughtered the inhabitants (particularly the Muslims), and stacked the bodies to be burned outside the city.

This from a transnational military force fired by a religious mission sanctioned by the universal church.

In 1618, three officials representing the Habsburg Empire were tossed from a window in Prague by Bohemian Protestants opposed to the Catholic drift of imperial policy. The famous Defenestration of Prague precipitated a sectarian war that became a Europe-wide conflagration known as the Thirty Years' War. It killed as many as 8 million people.

This in a war that began as a conflict over religion between an empire and its motley collection of subnational entities including principalities, bishoprics, duchies, and free cities.[9]

It's not just that the nation-state isn't necessarily a cause of war; the absence of effective state authority itself constitutes a great peril. In his book on declining violence, the psychologist Steven Pinker writes, "Tribal battles, slave raids, pillagings by raiders and horse tribes, pirate attacks, and private wars by noblemen and warlords, all of them nonstate, were scourges of humanity for millennia. During China's 'warlord era' from 1916 to 1928, more than 900,000 people were killed by competing military chieftains in just a dozen years."[10]

Tribalism tends to be red in tooth and claw. Pinker cites evidence that warfare accounts for 30 percent of the deaths of the Jivaro in Amazonian Ecuador. He also quotes the anthropologist Rafael Karsten for the proposition that wars between different tribes "are in principle wars of extermination. In these there is no question of weighing life against life; the aim is to completely annihilate the enemy tribe."[11]

It's been the world of greater respect for borders and sovereignty created by democratic nationalists in the twentieth century that has led to an extraordinary period of peace in the developed world. When people are allowed national self-determination, it removes an endemic cause of tension and resentment; nationalism no longer has to be fought over or resisted but can simply be accepted as the natural right of people to self-government.[12]

As Pinker points out, the great powers haven't fought since 1945, nor have the countries of western Europe, nor have developed countries (putting aside Moscow's incursions on the Russian periphery in the Soviet era and more recently). Territorial conquest has become a thing of the past for advanced nations besides the illiberal, neo-imperialist regimes in Russia and China. What was once a fairly common occurrence, of states being occupied or subsumed by stronger neighbors, basically doesn't happen anymore.[13]

None of this is to deny the role of nationalism and the nation-state in the modern era's conflagrations. An extreme or authoritarian nationalism (usually the same thing), as well as a nationalism of unquenchable grievance (also often associated with authoritarianism), is dangerous. This is especially so given that it tends to feed into imperialism and colonialism. The age-old drive for universal dominion, or at least Europe-wide dominance, is almost by definition an illiberal project that depends on war and tramples on the prerogatives of other peoples and nation-states, denying them their legitimate nationalism.

The French Revolution Gave Way to Imperialism

Consider the French Revolution and the subsequent Napoleonic Wars, which killed up to 4 million people.[14] They were initially fired by revolutionary fervor and then the imperial ambitions of a protomodern dictator who anticipated much worse to come in the twentieth century.

The French Revolution shifted the locus of the French nation from the monarchy to popular sovereignty, a pillar of modern nationalism. The Declaration of the Rights of Man in 1789 stated it plainly: "The nation constitutes the principal source of all sovereignty. No assembly or individual may exercise a power that does not derive expressly from the nation."[15] Many of the symbols of French nationhood go back to this period, from Bastille Day to the signature French tricolor flag to the national anthem, "La Marseillaise."[16] But the project was tainted from the beginning with a radicalism that spiraled out of control.

At first, the revolutionary regime forswore wars of conquest. Then, under military pressure from hostile foreign governments, it took up the mission of spreading its universal values: cosmopolitanism via the French nation in arms. When France realized that occupied lands weren't as interested in being "liberated" by its troops as it had hoped, the idealism curdled into contempt for the recalcitrant foreigners.

At home, the Revolution moved through its bloody phases from regicide and civil war to political terror to order imposed by a man on a horse.

Under Napoleon, France shifted from the initial nationalism of the Revolution to something closer to a traditional imperialism. Napoleon drew on Roman, Byzantine, and Carolingian influences for the emblems of his regime and relied on a pan-European elite to carry out a civilizing mission to bring the Enlightenment to dark corners of the empire. His army that invaded Russia, mostly never to return, was only one-third French. Napoleon had no use for the nationalism that inspired resistance to his conquests in other countries.[17]

German Imperial Ambition Drove World War I

The next all-consuming cataclysm, World War I, killed more than 8 million people in combat and roughly 15 million altogether.[18] Shelves of books have been devoted to the causes of the war, a topic beyond the scope of this work, although the fevered prewar intellectual environment and the role of Serbia and Germany as arsonists of the European order stand out.

The nationalisms of early-twentieth-century Europe tended to be tainted with malign influences. National honor and prestige got caught up in a competition for overseas colonies and over the size of naval fleets. Nations became obsessed with threats both external and internal. The rise of Social Darwinism buttressed a grim view of the world, fixated on power, struggle, and war. The German historian Heinrich von Treitschke wrote that the individual should be willing to sacrifice himself "for a higher collective, of which he is a member; he counts for something only in so far as he is part of his nation." The French thinker Georges Sorel mused about "a great foreign war that might invigorate us once again."[19]

The immediate cause of the war was Serb nationalism, putrid with grievance, violence, and conspiracy. The Serbs could never forget or forgive how they had supposedly lost their kingdom to the Ottoman Turks at the Battle of Kosovo in 1389.[20] Serbia became the termagant of the ethnically and religiously fraught Balkans. It expanded its territory in two Balkan wars early in the twentieth century and hated the Austro-Hungarian Empire for checking its designs on Bosnia, to which it had no legitimate claim. In 1903, Serb army officers shot a king and queen they considered too warm toward the empire and tossed their naked bodies out a window. The assassins founded the terror group Black Hand, which in turn gave the world the assassin who killed the Archduke Franz Ferdinand, heir to the Austro-Hungarian Empire.[21]

The crisis ignited a European-wide war rather than yet another Balkan war, largely because of the designs of imperial Germany. The kaiser's Germany exemplified how an aggressive (and authoritarian) nationalism slides into overweening imperial ambition. It couldn't tolerate the power and influence of other nations and treated weaker foreign countries as disposable pieces in its grand design.

The Germans hated the idea of an international order defined by the British. In his 1917 book, *Mitteleuropa*, the German politician Friedrich Naumann captured the attitude. He rejected the prospect of becoming "the junior partner in the English world-firm." No, he maintained, "a great nation only does a thing like this when nothing else remains to it." Instead, "a greater aim tempts us in virtue of our strength and experience: to become a central point ourselves!"[22]

Hence, to simplify, the Great War. Imperial Germany's quest for European dominance drove the conflict. As set out in its September program right after the beginning of the war, Germany wanted to seize French territory, make Belgium a vassal state, create German-dominated buffer states from western parts of the Russian Empire, and expand its colonial holdings in Africa. The kaiser put it succinctly in 1915: "The triumph of Great Germany, destined one day to dominate all of Europe, is the sole object of the struggle in which we are engaged."[23]

Fascism Isn't Nationalism

The horror of World War I, in turn, set into motion the forces that led to World War II and the rise of fascist movements that took power in Italy and Germany.

The name derives from the Italian word *fascio*, meaning "bundle" or "sheaf," used by nineteenth-century Italian revolutionaries to denote their fervent unity. Benito Mussolini, a former schoolteacher who started out a socialist and opponent of colonial expansion, picked up the term for his movement of demobilized World War I veterans and radical socialist syndicalists.[24]

Fascism had different iterations wherever it arose. The Italian version, at least before the 1930s, wasn't particularly race obsessed, and fascism in western Europe tended not to be as virulent as that in the east. Of course, Nazism was the most extreme form.

The Fascists had nationalistic appeal. Mussolini wrote in the party's manifesto in 1921 that the nation "is the supreme synthesis of all the material and immaterial values of the race," and "we desire the greatness of the nation, both material and spiritual." As for the Nazis, they sought a racially pure national community, captured in the phrase "blood and soil" popularized by the ideologist Richard Walther Darré. Upon becoming chancellor in 1933, Adolf Hitler addressed his countrymen as "national-comrade."[25]

But fascism is not the same thing as nationalism, which, as

Anthony Smith writes in a brilliant discussion of this topic in his book *Nationalism in the Twentieth Century*, has as its common priorities citizen autonomy, territorial unity, and historical identity. Fascism opposes or distorts all of these in service of its distinct, and distinctly noxious, program.

As a general matter, fascists hated parliamentary democracy and sought to substitute loyalty to the party and its leader to the squabbling of democratic politics. They believed in an all-consuming state and had no use for citizenship, instead hoping to create an elite vanguard. They had contempt for bourgeois life and promoted a cult of warrior youth. Fundamentally, fascism celebrated violence and the triumph of the will, in a nihilistic rejection of rationality and elevation of strength and struggle.[26]

Mussolini saw a new elite in the "trenchocracy," which, he wrote in 1917, "is the aristocracy of tomorrow! It is the aristocracy in action. It comes from the depths. Its 'quarterings of nobility' are a splendid blood red. On its coat of arms one may depict a Friesian horse, a trench pit and a hand grenade." They would become his Blackshirts, or *squadristi*, the party's street-fighting paramilitary whose uniforms were drawn from those of elite World War I troops. The Nazis, likewise, initially appealed to former soldiers and to the spirit of the World War I front, which the author Ernst Jünger called "blood socialism."[27]

The fascists emphasized action and strife. The early Italian Fascist slogan was simply "I don't give a damn."[28] Shortly before he took power, Mussolini asked, "The democrats of *Il Mondo* want to know our program? It is to break the bones of the democrats of *Il Mondo*. And the sooner the better."[29]

Anthony Smith runs through other contrasts: nationalism has its founding fathers, but nothing like the charismatic fascist leaders who demanded total loyalty and submission—it's the difference between Mazzini and Gandhi, on the one hand, and Mussolini and Hitler, on the other.

Smith points out how the characteristic paintings of French nationalism in the eighteenth and nineteenth centuries, Jacques-

Louis David's *Oath of the Horatii* and Eugène Delacroix's *Liberty Leading the People*—still beloved cultural artifacts in French, indeed Western, culture—valorized resistance to tyranny but not fascism's violence for its own sake.[30]

For the fascist, as Smith writes, the nation is not the main point, it is a tool, "a 'power house,' a repository and weapon for the exercise of will and force." Similarly, the homeland isn't enough for the fascist; the object is foreign conquest.

Nationalism is a flexible sentiment and doctrine and historically has infused any number of different political movements, whether on the left or on the right. Fascism, on the other hand, was all-encompassing and exclusive.[31]

Nationalism acted within the Western heritage; fascism wanted to destroy it. Smith argues that twentieth-century nationalism attempted "to give concrete political form to the aspirations of both rationalism and romanticism, however uneasy their conjunction: fascism set out to destroy both, and replace the whole Western cultural heritage by men and regimes built on brute instinct and primitive appetite."[32]

Modern nationalism predated the rise of fascism by 150 years, an extraordinary interval of time if there is supposed to be an organic connection between the two.[33]

The Great War Created the Opening for Fascism

The rise of fascism would have been impossible without the crisis-ridden aftermath of World War I, even if there were fetid stirrings before then.

France had protofascist currents, in the writers and factions who supported the bogus turn-of-the-century treason case against the Jewish army officer Alfred Dreyfus, a notorious instance of anti-Semitic paranoia.[34] The term *national socialism* was apparently first used by the right-wing French author Maurice Barrès, who championed "Nationalism, Protectionism and Socialism."[35]

He called the Marquis de Morès "the first national socialist," a distinction the wild-eyed adventurer and duelist earned by wedding his socialism to anti-Semitic agitation that included leading a band of slaughterhouse ruffians who intimidated Jews.[36] (Bizarrely, they wore cowboy hats, reflecting the time Morès had spent in the 1880s in the Badlands of the American West, where he had nearly challenged Teddy Roosevelt to a duel.)[37]

In Germany, romantic nationalism in the early nineteenth century was cultural, not racial. After Bismarck's military victories united Germany, though, there was a wider acceptance of overawing statism and a growing glorification of militarism.[38] Some of the worst trends were crystallized in Vienna mayor Karl Lueger, who combined socialist measures with anti-Semitism, all sold in populist terms.[39] Living in the city as an aspiring artist, Hitler took note.[40]

But it was the Great War that blew a hole in Western political culture, making it possible for fascists to gain traction. The war created aggrieved parties. Germany was a flat-out loser, while Italy was a resentful winner, denied what it considered its rightful spoils. Cultural optimism lost ground, and democracy, and liberal values in general, lost prestige. Bolshevism loomed, an enormous threat to the liberal order from the left. In this context, extremists took the initiative, exploiting the new possibilities of mass politics.[41]

Functioning liberal democracies had antibodies against the fascist threat. The movement fizzled in Great Britain, Scandinavia, and the Low Countries and didn't have electoral success in France.

In fact, we shouldn't exaggerate the electoral appeal of any of the fascist parties in Europe. Neither Hitler nor Mussolini won power at the ballot box but by invitation from the political establishment. In the one free parliamentary election they ran in, the Italian Fascists won less than 10 percent of seats. Before Hitler took power, the Nazi high mark in a parliamentary election was 37.2 percent of the vote in 1932.[42]

Nazism Had a Race-Obsessed Imperial Vision

The Nazis were the most politically potent fascist party and obviously the most lunatic. Hitler believed in an existential struggle between the species ("one creature drinks the blood of another"), a conflict that the German race must win in a vicious war of annihilation against inferior peoples. The state was supreme, and the Nazi Party's Aryan vanguard, wielding all power, would protect its racial purity. The "Jewish virus" was a dire threat and had loosed liberalism, capitalism, and Marxism on the world. Individuals had no standing outside of their race and owed it their loyalty.[43]

Hitler joined nationalist themes to a vile imperial vision. The "First Reich," after all, had been the Holy Roman Empire.[44] He had only disdain for the nationalism of the peoples subjugated by the Soviets, even when it would have been to his practical advantage to foster it.[45] When Germany, thankfully, proved unequal to the task allotted to it by Hitler, he ordered the destruction of his own country in his infamous "Nero Decree."

The idea that this cracked worldview has anything important in common with that of run-of-the-mill nationalism, with the intellectual tradition running through Mill, Rousseau, and Herder, let alone with American nationalism, is frankly absurd. Gone is any respect for the citizenry as such, for the various peoples of the world and the different character of their nations, for borders, even for the German nation, which is also subjugated to racial categories and ultimately expendable.

Communism, Not Nationalism, Was the Great Killer

Overall, the twentieth century was horrifically bloody. About 80 million people were killed by their governments and an additional 40 million in government-created famines.[46]

The greatest killer by far was transnational ideology. More than 80 percent of the government-caused deaths were the responsibility of totalitarian regimes, the lion's share Communist. Mao's China alone killed 20 million to 30 million people in the Great Leap Forward and another 7 million in the Cultural Revolution.[47]

Nonetheless, Marxism still retains a better reputation than nationalism in many elite and academic circles.

The Neo-Imperial European Union Threatens Self-Government

The champions of the European Union take credit for the postwar peace on the Continent. Its architects believed the only way to avoid another world war was to subsume the European countries in a supranational entity. Former European Commission president Jean-Claude Juncker cites François Mitterrand for the proposition "Le nationalisme, c'est la guerre." Juncker says, "This is still true, so we have to fight against nationalism."

It's no accident that Juncker, like other key EU potentates over the years, is from Luxembourg, a premodern, prenational anachronism in contemporary Europe.[48] The EU project represents another version of the ambition for a unified Europe dating back to Charlemagne. Its premises are deeply wrong, and as a practical matter, it can't possibly work over the long term.

Peace in Europe has been guaranteed not by the European Union but by the nature of postwar states in the West that are liberal, democratic, and committed to European norms. This would be true whether they were tethered to the European Union or not. In addition, this postwar order has been buttressed by NATO and ultimately American military power. If Jean-Claude Juncker wants to dole out credit for preserving peace in Europe, a much larger share should go to the US armored cavalry regiments that patrolled the Fulda Gap during the Cold War than to Brussels.

Regardless, the European Union is perhaps the greatest threat to self-government in the West. The organization of nearly thirty different countries doesn't have the bonds of loyalty of a nation. It is too big and too sprawling for true accountability. No one in Poland cares how Finland is governed, and vice versa. Forging a Europe-wide government has always been an elite project that necessarily operates outside democratic channels, accruing more authority, mostly out of sight (with an occasional national referendum on treaties, usually revoted if it goes against Brussels).

Brexit was an appropriate reaction to this high-handedness, and the European Union faces more turbulence as its pretensions to being a single country are buffeted by the irreducible fact that it emphatically is not.

Racism Is Not a Product of Nationalism

The final large-scale charge made against nationalism is that it is inexorably intertwined with racism. Yet racial animus existed long before the nation-state. As the political scientist Samuel Huntington put it in a bracing formulation, "It is human to hate."

The historian Benjamin Isaac argues that forms of proto-racism "were common in the Greco-Roman world."[49] There's a debate over how to categorize older forms of prejudice and whether "racism" is the best term prior to the modern era, but the contempt for others is clear enough.

The Greeks scorned outsiders and gave us the term *barbarians*, which they used to denote people who spoke languages—sounding to their ears, evidently, like bar-bar-bar—that they didn't understand.[50] For his part, the Roman poet Juvenal disapproved of the Greeks and their ways, while the Roman historian Tacitus trafficked in the image of the East as corrupt and lascivious, as did the poet Horace.

The traditional explanation for group differences was culture, as well as geography and climate. Aristotle believed that the environment of the Greeks uniquely suited them for excellence.[51] And it was long believed that proximity to the sun blackened the skin. Even this unsophisticated prejudice had its bite.

But a more "scientific" racism arose with the Enlightenment and its focus on classification, including a new emphasis on inherent characteristics and racial hierarchy.[52] David Hume opined in his 1748 essay "Of National Characters," "I am apt to expect the negroes, and in general all the other species of men (for there are four or five different kinds) to be naturally inferior to the whites. There never was a civilized nation of any other complexion than white."[53] (This way of thinking was not exclusively Western—it may have been Muslims who first came up with the poisonous idea that sub-Saharan Africans were burdened with the "curse of Ham" and deserved bondage.)[54]

Hume was relatively mild. The French writer Joseph Arthur de Gobineau, a counterrevolutionary who yearned for a return to aristocratic supremacy and the medieval order, wrote of the struggle of the different races as the defining force in societies. In his volume published in the 1850s *The Inequality of the Human Races*, he explained commoners as belonging "to a lower race which came about in the south through miscegenation with the negroes and in the north with the Finns." He played a key role in developing the noxious theory of the supremacy of the Aryans.[55]

At least those holding the old prejudice didn't believe that everything was reducible to race and that it had an immutable biological source. Emerging in the nineteenth century, the racial Darwinists saw the individual only as a member of his biological group, and at the extreme, they were obsessed with breeding pure racial groups through eugenics.[56]

Anti-Semitism took roughly the same course. The "longest hatred" was hideous enough in its traditional forms. The Jews were massacred during the First Crusade and expelled from Spain in 1492, and they were the subject of paranoid lies, from the "blood libel" that Jews made Passover matzos from Christian blood to the belief that they poisoned wells during the Black Death.[57]

In the late nineteenth century, anti-Semitism began to take

on a biological cast in places such as Austria, Romania, Poland, France, and obviously Germany.[58] The term itself was coined by Wilhelm Marr, a German agitator who posited an ineluctable racial conflict between Germans and Jews and founded the Anti-Semitic League.[59]

What does any of this have to do with nationalism? Racism and nationalism tend to be confused, Anthony Smith believes, because they both loosely have their roots in love of one's own and because of coincidental timing: modern nationalism arose in the late eighteenth century, scientific racism in the nineteenth.[60]

Racism infected the nationalism of nineteenth-century and interwar Europe, of 1930s Japan, and of South Africa. Smith notes, though, the different dynamics of the two phenomena. In the case of nationalism, the belief in the superiority of one's own people was largely cultural and religious, and over time, it came to be minimized and the prerogatives of other peoples recognized. On the other hand, racism pulled the other way. As we have seen, it deemphasized the cultural element in favor of physical qualities, of blood and hierarchy, and elevated the racial caste above all.[61]

All of this is to say that nationalism, like anything else in this fallen world, is susceptible to corruption and abuse, but it is not intrinsically destructive or hateful. It is not the same thing as militarism, Social Darwinism, authoritarianism, racism, or imperialism. It doesn't deserve its bad name.

Indeed, a well-considered nationalism has defined the American project, and its roots go back to one of the world's oldest and most inspiring nations.

SECTION II

THE

ROOTS

OF THE

AMERICAN NATION

CHAPTER 4

THE EXEMPLAR OF ANCIENT ISRAEL

On a visit to Judea in AD 130, the Roman emperor Hadrian had a vision: he'd extinguish Jerusalem and construct his own city on top of it.[1]

An inveterate builder, Hadrian planned a new street grid along Roman lines. To honor his family, known as *gens Aelia*, and the king of the gods, Jupiter Capitolinus, he intended to rename the city Aelia Capitolina. He wanted to build a temple to Jupiter on the site of the old Jewish Temple.[2]

For the Jews, Hadrian's plans represented a dire provocation. The prospect of rebuilding their temple—destroyed first by Nebuchadnezzar of Babylonia in 587 BC and then by the Roman emperor Titus in AD 70 after the First Jewish Revolt—faded into oblivion.[3] The Mishnah, or the Oral Torah, reports that a Roman plow drove over the temple's grounds, a ceremonial first step toward the construction of the new pagan shrine. The Roman historian Cassius Dio noted how "the Jews deemed it intolerable that foreign races should be settled in their city and foreign religious rites planted there."[4] The Jews launched a desperate rebellion, known as the Bar Kokhba revolt. The doomed insurgency testified to the depth of Jewish longing for national independence and became a symbol of national resilience when a Jewish nation-state was—once again against fierce resistance—reestablished almost two thousand years later.

Shimon ben Koseva led the rebellion. A warrior who imagined himself the national leader and vindicator of the Jews, he called himself the "Prince over Israel." Rabbi Akiva, a towering religious leader, declared him the messianic "son of a star," Bar Kokhba. (The rabbi would eventually be captured, flayed, and executed by the Romans, perhaps in retaliation.) Bar Kokhba knew scripture and drew extensively on Akiva's rabbinical students for recruits.[5]

He sought to break the Roman occupation and retake Jerusalem. He'd seize Judea using classic hit-and-run guerrilla tactics, exploiting an extensive system of caves for concealment. Then, having liberated the district, he would endeavor to govern and hold it and force the Romans to recognize the Jewish nation.[6]

The wonder isn't that this audacious project failed but that it enjoyed a period of stunning success. Local Jewish workshops manufactured light arms. Bar Kokhba mustered an army of tens of thousands. "I shall deal with the Romans," he vowed, and at least for a time, he made good on his boast.[7]

The Jews, Cassius Dio wrote, "did not dare try conclusions with the Romans in the open field," an obvious formula for defeat. Instead, "they occupied the advantageous positions in the country and strengthened them with mines and walls." They stunned the occupiers and may have destroyed a legion. The rebels managed to establish a relatively stable government in the area they controlled.

The Jews overstruck Roman silver and bronze coins with their own iconography. They wiped out the pagan symbols, replacing them with depictions of the Temple and evocative agricultural images. The coins declared, "Year One of the Redemption of Jerusalem," "Year 2 of the Freedom of Israel," and "For the Freedom of Jerusalem" (despite Bar Kokhba's hopes, he never did manage to liberate Jerusalem).[8]

The revolutionary dating—Year One—speaks of the presumed world-historical importance of the reestablishment of Israel. The vaulting ambition of the insurgency, and its dependence upon an indelible national and historical memory, is a marvel of human history.[9]

Hadrian eventually got a handle on the rebellion—as the Romans almost always did. At the height of the Bar Kokhba War, the emperor may have hurled a dozen legions at the Jews. Bar Kokhba holed up in the Judean Hills, in a town called Betar. In AD 135, two legions cut off the supply of water and kept anyone from entering or leaving. According to the historian Eusebius, the siege drove the rebels "to final destruction by famine and thirst." The Romans killed Bar Kokhba and, according to one legend, presented his head to the emperor.

The Jews fled to caves, taking all they could carry, to no avail. The Romans ground them underfoot. "Fifty of their most important outposts and nine hundred and eighty-five of their most famous villages were razed to the ground," Cassius Dio reported. He exaggerated the numbers, if not the outlines of the debacle: "Five hundred and eighty thousand men were slain in the various raids and battles, and the number of those that perished by famine, disease and fire was past finding out."[10]

Captured Jews flooded the slave market in Hebron, crashing prices.[11] The Romans banned the Jews from Jerusalem. Judea no longer existed. Hadrian merged it with Syria and deemed it Syria-Palaestina, after the ancient rival of the Jews, the Philistines.[12]

After the calamity, one rabbinic tradition condemned Bar Kokhba as "Son of a Liar." Over time, though, his image changed. Zionists held him out as a figure of strength and sacrifice. A 1905 bronze statue of the rebel by the sculptor Henrik Glitzenstein is heavily muscled in the heroic style, standing and leaning forward toward his destiny. The Jewish holiday of Lag Ba'Omer, originally devoted to the memory of a second-century spiritual leader, came to focus in part on Bar Kokhba and his warrior spirit.[13]

The modern state of Israel buried bones of survivors of the revolt, discovered by archaeologists in a cave near the Dead Sea, with full military honors in 1982. Prime Minister Menachem Begin delivered a eulogy, declaring that "we have redeemed Jerusalem." He spoke directly to those long-ago rebels: "Our glorious fathers, we have a message for you: We have returned to the place from whence we came. The people of Israel lives, and will live in its homeland in Eretz Israel for generations upon generations. Glorious fathers, we are back and we will not budge from here."[14]

That is the true voice of nationalism.

Ancient Israel Gave Us the Template of a Nation

In the story of the ancient Israelites, we see the creation not just of a great religion but of a nation, one that would, through the Torah, spread its example throughout the world and that would never be abandoned by its people despite nearly two millennia of exile and catastrophe.

Ancient Israel bears all the hallmarks of a nation. The Israelites were a people with a homeland, centered on the holy city of Jerusalem. Their genealogy, history, traditions, law, and language set them out as different. They acted on a deeply felt imperative to govern themselves, escaping from Egypt, the "house of slavery," and resisting foreign conquerors. They were a Chosen People, and their particularism (they belonged to one place and to the one true God) existed side by side with a sweeping universal vision (theirs was the God of all people).[15]

Of course, the template of an ancient society isn't directly comparable to contemporary societies, but even that defining feature of modern nationalism, popular rule, can be seen in embryo thousands of years ago. Ancient Israel was ruled first by judges, then by kings. Yet the land didn't belong to the kings but rather to the people, with God exercising the highest authority, expressed through the Covenant. The historian Aviel Roshwald argues that through its egalitarianism—i.e., it applied to everyone—"the Covenant conferred the functional equivalent of popular sovereignty on the Israelites."[16]

The national creed of ancient Israel is, of course, a religion, something that can't be said of the core beliefs and founding myths of most other nations—although they aren't necessarily that distinct. "Nationalisms may be secular, or better secularizing," writes Anthony Smith, "but they retain many 'religious' features—sacred texts, prophets, priests, liturgies, rites, and ceremonies—as well as specific ethnoreligious motifs."[17]

The Old Testament Tells the Story of a People and Its Land

A defining aspect of nationality is the belief that "a people has its land and a land has its people," as Steven Grosby puts it.[18] The Torah is, in part, a long elaboration of this theme, and therefore a kind of how-to guide for nationalism.

It sets out a world inhabited by different and often clashing peoples, "the families of the earth." The book of Genesis traces their genealogy through the sons of Noah, "after their families, after their tongues, in their lands, after their nations." The tale of the Tower of Babel describes the source of the world's various, mutually uncomprehending peoples: "The Lord did there confound the language of all the earth: and from thence did the Lord scatter them abroad upon the face of all the earth."[19]

The Jews considered themselves an 'am and a gôy, roughly a people and a nation. Key pillars of their nationhood—their creed, law, and territory—depended on their Covenant with God.[20]

Its first expression is with Noah, who, upon the characteristically meticulous orders of the Lord, saves mankind from the Flood. Then God commands Abram, whose name will change to Abraham, to go to Canaan: "And I will make of thee a great nation, and I will bless thee, and make thy name great; and thou shalt be a blessing."[21]

Abraham is a pivotal figure in Jewish, nay, in human, history and a man in full. The Bible depicts him dealing with the mundane details of life: conflict between his herdsmen and those of his nephew Lot, disputes over water rights, powerful men desiring his attractive wife, jealousy between his wife and his concubine.

He is just, diligent, magnanimous, and, above all, faithful and obedient to God—but not without expressing doubts and even challenging the Lord. When God says that his wife, Sarah, will bear his son and become "a mother of nations," he "laughed, and said in his heart, Shall a child be born unto him that is an hundred years old? and shall Sarah, that is ninety years old, bear?" Sarah, too, laughs sardonically when she overhears this promise. (The historian Paul Johnson believes that this is the first recorded human laughter.)

Yet when God tells him, "Get thee out of thy country, and from thy kindred, and from thy father's house, unto a land that I will shew thee," he goes. When God makes circumcision a condition of the Covenant, he is circumcised at age ninety-nine, along with "all the men of his house." When God demands that he sacrifice his son, Isaac, in a terrifying episode, one that theologians and philosophers have grappled with over the centuries, Abraham complies—until the Angel of the Lord stays his hand.

Abraham's obedience leads to a reaffirmation of the Covenant, including an unmistakable universalist promise: "I will multiply thy seed as the stars of the heaven, and as the sand which is upon the sea shore; and thy seed shall possess the gate of his enemies; And in thy seed shall all the nations of the earth be blessed; because thou hast obeyed my voice." Abraham set out the predicates of Judaism and the Israelite nation—a chosen people, elected by God, living in or yearning for their homeland. [22]

The Law Was Centrally Important to Israel's Nationhood

The other towering figure of the Old Testament, Moses, enacted the chief drama of Jewish history, the return from exile. He delivered his people to the cusp of the Promised Land and gave them another central pillar of their identity, the law. In the famous sculpture by Michelangelo, he is clutching the Commandments in one arm and looks as formidably bearded, wrathful, and muscled as Neptune.

The outlines of his story are irresistible and well known. His Levite mother, fearful for his life after the Pharaoh has ordered the newborn sons of the Jews killed, hides him in the reeds of the Nile in a floating basket. He is discovered by Pharaoh's daughter and raised as an Egyptian prince. As a young man, he intervenes and kills an Egyptian overseer abusing a Jewish slave. Moses flees Egypt and marries, and while he is tending his father-in-law's flock, God comes to him in a burning bush and commands him to free the Jews from their captivity.[23]

Moses is more complex than the depictions of him as a stereotypical prophet in statuary and film suggest: the modest shepherd ("Moses was very humble, above all the men which were upon the face of the earth"), so inarticulate that God allowed his brother to be his spokesman; the fierce warrior and religious enforcer; the intimate of God, who is the only figure in the Hebrew Bible to speak to Him "face to face, as a man speaketh unto his friend";[24] the lawgiver, judge, and statesman whose sweeping vision and gargantuan will shaped a people and a nation.[25]

When he took his people out of captivity, Moses turned his back on Egypt and its oppression, its static culture, its multitude of gods—and its lack of impartial law. The Jewish God gave his people a detailed and exhaustive code encompassing, in one tradition dating to the third century, 613 total commandments. The Bible depicts Moses himself attempting to adjudicate all legal questions arising among his people, until his father-in-law advises that he set up a trained judiciary to relieve the overwhelming burden.[26]

The code is a bedrock of Israeli nationality, a foundational expression of sovereignty, and, as the Scottish scholar William Barclay put it, "the law without which nationhood is impossible."[27] It binds the people of the nation to one another and the nation to God. In this light, Moses is not just a great lawgiver, as he is often depicted, including on two friezes at the US Supreme Court, but a great nation builder.

The foundation of the law is the Covenant. God tells Moses on Mount Sinai, "Now therefore, if ye will obey my voice indeed, and keep my covenant, then ye shall be a peculiar treasure unto me above all people: for all the earth is mine: And ye shall be unto me a kingdom of priests, and a holy nation."

God Gave Israel Borders

The Israelites became a fully formed people. By the book of Joshua, relating the story of the successor to Moses who conquers Canaan, there are routine references to "all Israel," a collectivity above and beyond divisions of tribe and clan.[28] "Before they went to Egypt," Paul Johnson writes, "the Israelites were a small folk almost like any other, though they had a cherished promise of greatness. After they returned, they were a people with a purpose, a program and a message to the world."[29]

And with a land, as promised by the Lord, "from Dan to Beersheba," referring to the northernmost and southernmost cities of Israel. Borders are a key part of a nation, and God couldn't have set them out more specifically to Moses absent a map and a surveyor: "And your border shall turn from the south to the ascent of Akrabbim, and pass on to Zin: and the going forth thereof shall be from the south to Kadeshbarnea, and shall go on to Hazaraddar, and pass on to Azmon," and so on.[30]

This is "a land of brooks of water, of fountains and depths that spring out of valleys and hills; a land of wheat, and barley, and vines, and fig trees, and pomegranates; a land of olive oil, and honey." It is a holy land for a holy people—"Defile not therefore the land which ye shall inhabit, wherein I dwell: for I the Lord dwell among the children of Israel." The land and the people become so intimately related that the two become synonymous.[31]

David, the shepherd boy plucked from obscurity by the Lord, contributed much to this relationship of people and territory. A leader of genius and an inspired warrior, he established the united monarchy that brought together the kingdoms of Judah and Israel and, through his remarkable success in the field, created a territorially extensive kingdom circa 1000 BC. In his most important conquest, he took Jerusalem, an elusive goal of the Israelites for centuries.[32]

He thus gave his people a religious and national capital, the City of David, that endures to this day. He housed his "mighty men" in the city and repaired the walls. He built a palace and brought to the city the Ark of the Covenant, the magnificent receptacle for the tablets of the Ten Commandments that the Israelites had carried with them on their wanderings. But building the temple fell to his son, Solomon.

A grandiose king celebrated for his unsurpassed wealth and wisdom, Solomon constructed the temple over seven years with an army of workers. Thirty thousand conscripted laborers went to Lebanon in shifts of ten thousand for timber. Eighty thousand stonecutters and seventy thousand carriers went to the hills.[33] "And they brought great stones, costly stones, and hewed stones," the Bible relates, "to lay the foundation of the house."

By the end, the Israelites had a shimmering locus for their nation and faith, a symbol that would never dim, even when Solomon's temple and its successor were eventually leveled, even during their exile from the Promised Land. Psalm 137 laments the separation from Jerusalem during an ensuing disaster centuries later, the sieges of Nebuchadnezzar that led to the Babylonian Captivity, mass deportations from the Kingdom of Judah:

> By the rivers of Babylon, there we sat down,
> yea, we wept, when we remembered Zion.
> We hanged our harps upon the willows in the midst thereof.
> For there they that carried us away captive required of us a song;
> and they that wasted us required of us mirth, saying,
> Sing us one of the songs of Zion.
> How shall we sing the Lord's song in a strange land?

This lament would be repeated down through the centuries after invasions, failed rebellions, and expulsion, yet the nation always survived.

The Jews Never Turned Their Back on Their Nation

The Jewish nation persisted because its traditions and beliefs never died out. Israel powerfully demonstrates the importance of historical memory and ritual, of texts, language, and reading, to nationalism. With them, a nation can endure despite unfathomable adversity; without them, it is nothing.

The institutions of the Torah and the synagogue meant that Jewish identity endured wherever Jews lived in the diaspora, from eastern Europe to North Africa. The Torah set out the religious creed and constituted the great national epic. Memorized and recited, it stimulated an extraordinary literacy.[34] Even if vernacular languages differed across the diaspora, the language of scripture, Hebrew, provided a basis for cohesion (and it was revived as a spoken language in the modern era).[35]

Jewish culture is steeped in a deep sense of history, ever mindful of common origins and a common purpose and destiny.

Feasts and remembrances and rituals ensured as much; that was the point. The Lord tells Moses of Passover, "And this day shall be unto you for a memorial; and ye shall keep it a feast to the Lord throughout your generations; ye shall keep it a feast by an ordinance for ever." Moses speaks of the educative function of the observance: "And it shall come to pass, when your children shall say unto you, What mean ye by this service? That ye shall say, It is the sacrifice of the Lord's passover, who passed over the houses of the children of Israel in Egypt, when he smote the Egyptians, and delivered our houses."[36]

The suffering of the people is woven into these remembrances. The Yom Kippur prayers include the story of the Ten Martyrs, rabbis killed by the Roman oppressors in the period after the destruction of the second temple, including in the Bar Kokhba revolt. None of this is a cause of despair. It is a sign of the stalwartness of the Jewish people, who will abide until the restoration of the Jewish state.[37]

The trauma and dispossession of the Jews showed that God

continued to hold them to the Covenant, and still promised a return to Davidic glory—"I will be with thee, and build thee a sure house, as I built for David, and will give Israel unto thee."[38] Yearning for this "sure house" remained key to Jewish identity. A central prayer of the daily liturgy, the Amidah, ends, "May it be your will that the Temple be rebuilt soon in our days." And the Passover dinner always concludes, "Next year in Jerusalem." Amazingly enough, by the nineteenth century, thousands of years after the united kingdom had been destroyed, this was no longer just a far-off hope.[39]

Zionism Was a Great Nationalist Movement

It's no accident that this faithfulness and historical memory spawned one of the great nationalist movements of the modern era.

Zionism arose in a nineteenth century that brought emancipation, a revolution in Jewish standing in Europe: equality before the law, a shift from the rural fringe to the great urban centers, prominence in academia, the arts, and finance. For hundreds of years, as the Israeli political scientist Shlomo Avineri observes, Jews were (loosely speaking and with horrific exceptions) tolerated but relegated to second-class status as religious outsiders in Christian societies.[40] Yet the most prescient Jewish leaders and intellectuals realized that Jewish security and self-respect depended on the restoration of the nation.

Consider Moses Hess, a nineteenth-century socialist intellectual, an exile from Germany living in France, close for a time with Karl Marx and Friedrich Engels. Marx called him "my communist rabbi," although Hess eventually split with him over doctrinal differences and, most notably, gave up his assimilationist universalism for a Jewish nationalism.[41]

In his 1862 book *Rome and Jerusalem: The Last Nationality Question*, Hess declared his change of heart. "After an estrangement of twenty years," he wrote. "I am back with my people. I have come to be one of them again, to participate in the celebration of the holy days, to share the memories and hopes of the nation, to take part in the spiritual and intellectual warfare going on within the House of Israel, on the one hand, and between our people and the surrounding civilized nations, on the other."

The book sold 160 copies in its first year; Hess suffered the author's nightmare of the publisher asking him to buy up the remainder at a discount. But he made arguments and observations that stood up.

He warned of the abiding danger of anti-Semitism, at a time when many assumed it was fading away, particularly in Germany: "Even an act of conversion can not relieve the Jew of the enormous pressure of German antisemitism. The Germans hate the religion of the Jews less than they hate their race—they hate the peculiar faith of the Jews less than their peculiar noses." Given this awful truth, Jews should embrace their distinctiveness and return to their land: "The Jew in exile who denies his nationality will never earn the respect of the nations among whom he dwells."[42]

Seventy-five years after his death, the exile found his true home: in 1961, the Israeli government transferred his remains from Germany to the shores of Lake Tiberias.[43]

Theodor Herzl Understood the Power of Nationhood

Three decades after Hess's book, Theodor Herzl wrote *The Jewish State: An Attempt at a Modern Solution of the Jewish Question*. A journalist and playwright living in Vienna, Herzl animated the Zionist movement and put it unalterably on the world agenda.[44]

Like Hess, he feared the worst from European anti-Semitism and was shocked, in particular, by the drummed-up treason case against French army officer Alfred Dreyfus, an illustration of what could befall even an assimilated Jew in an advanced western European country.[45] Like Hess, he believed that the only way out was a Jewish homeland, a very ancient idea, not a new one: "I have discovered neither the Jewish situation as it has crystallized in history, nor the means to remedy it."

Herzl threw everything into his activism in the eight years he lived after publication. He spoke of himself as the leader of the Jews and got world leaders and the Jewish public to take him seriously as such. He was a living commentary on the advantages of audacity. "It is the simple and fantastic," as he once said, "which leads men."

He lobbied, cajoled, and propagandized for the cause. He wanted the sultan of the Ottoman Empire to give the Jews a homeland in Ottoman-controlled Palestine (Argentina and Uganda were other, fanciful options). He failed. Herzl complained to the British colonial secretary of the endless delay of Ottoman negotiations, which his people could ill afford: "You know what Turkish negotiations are. If you want to buy a carpet, first you must drink half a dozen cups of coffee and smoke a hundred cigarettes; then you discuss family stories, and from time to time you speak again a few words about the carpet."

He soldiered on, despite reality not always according with his grand visions. He described Jerusalem upon his first visit as having "the musty deposits of two thousand years of inhumanity, intolerance, and uncleanliness lying in the foul-smelling little streets." Undergirding his tireless advocacy was a profound understanding of the power of the national idea. He rejected the notion that a flag was just a rag on a stick: "With a flag people are led—perhaps even to the Promised Land. For a flag men live and die." So it proved. He died in 1904, his ultimate dream not close to realization. But the goal he set out at the first Zionist Congress had been considerably advanced: "To lay the foundation stone of the house which is to shelter the Jewish nation."[46]

The road to the Jewish state involved decades of convoluted international diplomacy; a cataclysm for European Jewry beyond the imagining of even the most despairing Zionist pioneers ("Give us the right to fight and die as Jews," begged the future Israeli prime minister David Ben-Gurion in 1942); and, at the state's inception in 1948, warfare for its survival against Arab adversaries on every side.[47] Yet it prevailed and endured, its Declaration of Independence calling Herzl "the spiritual father of the Jewish state."

His belief in the potency and utility of nationalism had proved out.

The National Idea Spread via the Old Testament

If the restoration of the Jewish homeland took millennia, the example of ancient Israel fortified nations and national movements long before 1948. The Old Testament acted as a conveyor belt carrying biblical notions of nationality directly into the mind of Europe. "The Bible provided, for the Christian world at least, the original model of the nation," the historian Adrian Hastings writes. "Without it and its Christian interpretation and implementation, it is arguable that nations and nationalism as we know them, could never have existed."[48]

The word *nation* suffuses the King James Bible, the translation of unsurpassed importance in the English-speaking world. The Latin Vulgate version used the word *natio*, which became *nacioun* in English. Hastings points out how consistent the use of the word remained across time. A verse in the book of Revelation was translated differently in the mid-fourteenth century ("kyndes & tunges & folkes & nacions") than in the Wycliffe Bible later in the century ("each lynage and tunge and people and nacioun") than in the King James Version in the seventeenth century ("every kindred, and tongue, and people, and nation") than in the Jerusalem Bible in the mid–twentieth century ("of every race, language, people, and nation"). The rendering of every other word in the line changed over six hundred years, yet *nation* always stayed the same.[49]

The rise of the vernacular Bible in Europe spread the national idea throughout Europe, especially in Protestant countries such as England and Holland, Denmark and Sweden.[50] It depicted a united people, governing themselves in their own land, with their own laws, special relationship with God, and mission in the world.

Practically any self-respecting nation conceived of itself as the new Israel, a chosen people with its own Promised Land. This became central to England's self-understanding, and to the self-image of its adversary, France. The Dutch thought of themselves as contemporary Israelites; "O Lord," the poet and composer Adrianus Valerius wrote in 1626, "when all was ill with us You brought us up into a land wherein we were enriched through trade and commerce and have dealt kindly with us, even as you have led the Children of Israel from their Babylonian prison." So did the Armenians, and the Afrikaners, and the Ethiopians, who believed a son of Solomon had brought the Ark of the Covenant from Jerusalem to Ethiopia.[51]

But it was the English as the new chosen people that had the greatest influence on world history.

CHAPTER 5

OUR ENGLISH FORERUNNER

"**B**RITAIN, an island in the ocean, formerly called Albion, is situated between the north and west, facing, though at a considerable distance, the coasts of Germany, France, and Spain, which form the greatest part of Europe.""[1]

Thus the Venerable Bede began his *Ecclesiastical History of the English People*, completed in about 730.[2] The English monk, who entered the twin monastery of Wearmouth-Jarrow in the Kingdom of Northumbria at age seven, was a great literary genius of his age.

Benedict Biscop, a well-traveled, learned man, founded the monastery at Wearmouth about the time of Bede's birth and only about fifty years after the kings of Northumbria converted to Christianity. The monastery at Jarrow was built several miles away less than ten years later, together with one of the largest churches in northern Britain.[3]

Despite its remoteness, Wearmoth-Jarrow stood as a cultural jewel of the British Isles.[4] Benedict accumulated books and manuscripts during his travels and built an extensive library that made Wearmouth-Jarrow a significant center of learning. The monasteries had collections of art and featured stained glass, extremely rare at that time and place (it is said that Jarrow today has the oldest stained glass in the world that is actually part of a window).

Through its reputation, Wearmouth-Jarrow attracted visitors who made it a kind of cosmopolitan hub.

For all these reasons, Wearmouth-Jarrow became an inviting target in subsequent decades for rampaging Vikings, who burnt and sacked the monasteries. But during Bede's time, they were an ideal home for his astonishing scholarly output.

The only record Bede left of his own life is a spare, modest autobiographical note at the end of his *History* that relates, "I have spent all of my life in this monastery, applying myself entirely to the study of the Scriptures; and, amid the observance of the discipline of the Rule and the daily task of singing in the church, it has always been my delight to learn or to teach or to write."[5]

He delved into poetics and grammar (*On the Art of Metrics*), science (*On the Nature of Things*), and chronology (*On the Reckoning of Times*), among other topics. He popularized the system of dividing time before and after the birth of Christ, i.e., BC and AD. He wrote poetry and hymns, some of which are still performed. He worked to the very end, translating the Gospel of John on his deathbed. With justification, a Swiss monk reached for the greatest superlative in his praise of Bede: "God, the orderer of natures, who raised the Sun from the East on the fourth day of Creation, in the sixth day of the world, has made Bede rise from the West as a new Sun to illuminate the world."[6]

For our purposes, Bede's most enduring achievement is his conception of a unified English people. According to the famous formulation of Benedict Anderson, a nation is an "imagined community" ("imagined because the members of even the smallest nation will never know most of their fellow-members, meet them, or even hear of them, yet in the minds of each lives the image of their communion").[7] If so, the English nation first took hold in the imagination of the Venerable Bede.

At a time when England remained divided among various kingdoms, Bede wrote of a unified geographic entity with a unified history that stretched from the campaigns of Julius Caesar to the present. He assumed an ecclesiastical unity, centered on Canterbury, over and above the island's political divisions. Yes, England had been settled by different Germanic peoples who had established their own kingdoms, but, as Adrian Hastings writes, Bede "takes it for granted that this whole medley of peoples and kingdoms has become a single nation, 'gens Anglorum,' the people of the English, and he regularly uses the name 'English' to include not only Northumbrians and other Angles, but Saxons and Jutes."[8]

At the end of Bede's preface, Hastings notes, "he reaffirms that he has written the 'historia nostrae nationis,' the history of our own nation."[9]

The English Nation Gave Birth to Ours

The English nation was the most important in Europe. It created a successful model of the nation-state that would be emulated, and envied, around the world. Over time and imperfectly, it developed a conception of the nation as a society of equals with truly revolutionary implications. And it spawned another nation, ours, that would take these premises and push them to their logical conclusion in a great experiment in liberty.

Every polity has its flaws. English history is blighted by its share of brutality (Henry VIII's sacking of the monasteries) and disgraces (Oliver Cromwell's massacres in Ireland). Yet England set the pace in the development of parliamentary government, individual rights, and the rule of law. Its chief competitors for centuries, the centralizing monarchies of Spain and France, were less free and less tolerant.[10] Nationalism wasn't a diversion or obstacle to these developments in England but central to them.

The English experience demonstrates the falsity of the contention that nationalism is a modern innovation. It exposes as a smear the charge that nationalism inevitably leads to fascism or other forms of authoritarianism. It shows how, to the contrary, nationalism at bottom expresses the impulse of people to rule themselves and not be merely the pawns of kings. Finally, it establishes that the United States is the product of a tradition that stretches back centuries before this country's formal founding and that left a deep imprint on our own nationality.

Before there was American exceptionalism, there was English exceptionalism.

The English Nation-State Has Millennium-Old Roots

One reason for the English nation-state's relative effectiveness and stability is the fact that it has existed so long. Historian James Campbell writes that in no other state in Europe "has there been such continuity in the exercise of effective authority over so wide an area for so long," and "in the institutions of government."[11] The boundaries of the shires, i.e., counties, remained essentially the same from the eleventh century to the twentieth.[12]

The signs of a budding nation-state abound in the Anglo-Saxon period even before the Norman Conquest in 1066. The coinage, pennies struck by the millions at mints throughout the country, spoke of an impressive administrative apparatus (a great volume of these pennies would be sent as Danegeld to buy off the Vikings). The kings were able to levy taxes. The country had a large, thriving commercial center, London, with its own distinct culture transcending the various regions. A vernacular literature of remarkable range already existed.[13]

The Norman Conquest in the eleventh century brought a strong monarchy and a more centralized, administratively rigorous state.[14] It also delivered a blow to English nationality. William the Conqueror came from France and, once he had subdued England, ruled it from France. In the end, though, the English assimilated the Normans rather than the other way around.[15]

The English kings nonetheless long retained a fixation with ruling France, until the Hundred Years' War, fought over the succession to the French throne, disabused them of this interest. The English won stirring victories—most famously at Agincourt—but lost their continental possessions and ambitions.

This was a blessing, one of a number of salutary nationalizing trends. An important national institution that brought people together from across the country, Parliament gained in strength.[16] The success of the English armies on the strength of the longbow, wielded by yeoman archers, symbolized the contribution of the common man to the national cause.[17] More and more of the country's energy was poured into commerce, loosening the hold of the medieval world and fostering the beginnings of a middle class.

The English Reformation Was a Step toward the Primacy of the Nation

The rise of the House of Tudor eventually brought a new stability after a period of civil wars.[18] The monarchy was, as of yet, at the center of English nationality.[19] Henry VIII believed his own power and prestige inseparable from the nation's and took the same title as the Holy Roman Emperor, "Majesty."[20] The signal event of his reign, the Reformation, was a testament to his power. Yet, most important for our story, it unleashed forces that, over time, undermined the monarchy and advanced a liberalizing nationalism.

Henry made Parliament central to the Reformation, occasioned, of course, by his marital misadventures.[21] He referred to his "wise, sage, politic commons," and the key measures were enacted by statute.[22] The crucial 1533 Act of Appeals, forbidding appeals of judicial decisions to Rome, made England's independence clear: "Where by dyvers sundrie old authentike histories and cronicles it is manifestly declared and expressed that this realme of Englond is an Impire, and so hath ben accepted in the worlde, governed by oon supreme heede and King."[23]

The Church, associated with the hostile powers of France and Spain and based in Rome, imposed unpopular taxes and owned about a third of the land in England. The Reformation asserted the primacy of the English Crown and showered it with resources diverted—and confiscated—from the Church. Henry plowed them into patronage and state building.[24]

Henry's revolution shattered medieval universalism. At bottom, the offense of Henry's former chancellor Sir Thomas More, charged with treason and executed, was his failure to accept the new status of the nation, instead hewing to the old unity of the medieval Christian world. "I am not then bounden," More maintained, writing from the Tower of London, "to change my conscience and confirm it to the council of one realm, against the general council of Christendom." He represented a worldview that considered nationality an accidental division and an incidental loyalty, a perspective that would steadily lose ground.[25]

The English-Language Bible Became a Bedrock of Anglo-America

The English Reformation gave us one of the most consequential events in English, and by extension American and therefore world, history: the widespread printing of the Bible in English. Catholic religious and secular authorities had fiercely resisted vernacular translations of the Bible. Prior to the Reformation, attempting to translate it into English involved considerable risk to life and limb. Only the incredibly brave, and thoroughly committed, would attempt it.

Someone, in short, like William Tyndale. He left England for the Continent to work essentially as an outlaw, hoping his translations would be smuggled back into England as samizdat. The literary quality of his work was exemplary—he gave us such phrases as "powers that be," "apple of his eye," and "cast the first stone." Back in England, the authorities weren't favorably impressed. Bishop Cuthbert Tunstall burned Tyndale's translation of the New Testament—"Pestiferous and most pernicious poison"—at

St. Paul's Church in London. Tracked down by the authorities in
Antwerp, Tyndale was gruesomely executed for his offenses.[26]

Tyndale's dying prayer was that God would open the king
of England's eyes. Henry VIII had once deemed possession of
English-language Bibles a crime. After the Reformation, he sanctioned the publication of the Great Bible—so called because of its
physical heft—and enjoined parish priests to display a copy "in
some convenient place within the said church that ye have cure
of, whereas your parishioners may commodiously resort to the
same and read it."[27]

The English became a Bible-soaked people. The churchman
William Chillingworth declared, "The BIBLE, I say, THE BIBLE
only is the Religion of the Protestants." It was much more com-
plicated than that. Protestants couldn't agree among themselves
what the Bible meant for church and secular government.[28] But
the availability of the Bible and the emphasis on it for direct access to the word of God put a premium on literacy, and England
became a highly literate society by the standards of the day. The
act of reading the Bible impressed on people their own dignity,
a revolutionary spark that wouldn't be extinguished. They were
also exposed to the Old Testament notions of chosenness and nationality, which came to have such a central role in English and
American history.[29]

Bloody Mary Failed to Restore the Old View of the Nation

Mary Tudor, the only surviving adult child from the marriage of
Henry VIII and his first wife, Catherine of Aragon (a Catholic from
Spain), sought to return England to the Catholic fold.[30] The failure
of her ambition is attested by the fact that she became known to
history as "Bloody Mary." She banned the English-language Bible,
repealed her father's religious measures, and reinstituted harsh
heresy acts.[31]

Relentless and unbending, she executed nearly three hundred

Protestants in the years 1555 to 1558, and many others fled.[32] In the catalogue of atrocities in world history, this barely rates. But her persecutions backfired spectacularly and took on an outsized significance in establishing England's (and with time, America's) national identity. The martyrdoms were recorded in the second most influential book in the English language, John Foxe's *Book of Martyrs*. Himself an exile from Mary's reign, Foxe left England when threatened with arrest by the authorities. While abroad, he wrote a precursor of his famous volume and then, in 1554, its initial edition in Latin. Back in England, he published the first English edition, a formidable 1,800-page tome in folio, illustrated with harrowing woodcuts of the executions.[33]

The book became a de facto supplement to the Bible. Running through six editions during Foxe's lifetime, the Convocation of Canterbury ordered it placed alongside the Bible in cathedral churches.[34]

Foxe believed that the Church is "universal and sparsedly through all countries dilated." Yet his point of view is unmistakably national. England's royal history, not the tenure of the popes, provided the framework for his work, which is divided by the reigns of kings and queens.[35]

Foxe connected English national identity to Protestantism and created the predicate for the belief in its chosenness. Adrian Hastings calls the *Book of Martyrs* "a sort of English Book of Maccabees," which relates the Jewish revolt against foreign rule by the Seleucids.[36] Foxe described and celebrated a community of believers, whose ability to read and understand the Bible on their own gave them a status that didn't depend on the monarchy or the church hierarchy. The implications were radical and far-reaching.

Mary Tudor's failure constituted a disastrous blow to her conception of the English polity. "For Mary," Liah Greenfeld writes, "England was not a nation; it was indeed a patrimony which she wished to rule in the interests of the Roman Catholic Church." The exiles rejected this idea and instead insisted that people owed the nation, separate and distinct from the monarchy, their truest allegiance.

The exile John Poynet insisted that "men ought to have more respect to their country than to their prince, to the commonwealth than to any one person. For the country and the commonwealth is a degree above the king."[37]

Elizabethan England Became a Chosen Nation

After Mary, her half sister Elizabeth, prudent and moderate, forged a compromise Protestant settlement that felt like a deliverance. Elizabeth wanted to avoid the excesses of the religious repression of Mary; she forswore any desire to "make windows in men's souls." Given the hostility of Rome to her reign, though, she considered Catholics a potential threat to her rule. She justified her expulsion of the Jesuits from England in 1585 on grounds that they intended "to stir up and move sedition," and when she executed priests it was for treason, not doctrinal differences per se.[38]

Elizabeth personified the joining of Protestantism and the nation, and signal events of her long, stable reign increased the sense that she was an instrument of English distinctiveness and righteousness.[39] She persisted even after Pope Pius V excommunicated her in a bull that functioned as an open invitation for her Catholic subjects to assassinate her (the pope deemed her "the pretended Queen of England and the servant of crime").[40] And she prevailed over the Spanish Armada. "I know I have the body but of a weak and feeble woman," she said in a stirring speech to the troops at Tilbury as the Spanish navy loomed, "but I have the heart and stomach of a king, and of a King of England too."

Her devotees regaled her with an exalted iconography. They held her up as Gloriana, the character representing her in Edmund Spenser's poem The Faerie Queene, or as the British Constantine, the first Christian emperor of Rome.[41] John Jewel, bishop of Salisbury, wrote, "When it pleased God to send a blessing upon us, He gave us His servant Elizabeth to be our queen, and to be an instrument of His glory in the sight of the world."[42]

All of this provided the backdrop for the patriotic effusions of Elizabethan literature, most importantly and memorably in Shakespeare's history plays written in the aftermath of the defeat of the Spanish Armada.

John of Gaunt, Duke of Lancaster, famously celebrated England in his dying speech in *Richard II*:

> This royal throne of kings, this scepter'd isle,
> This earth of majesty, this seat of Mars,
> This blessed plot, this earth, this realm, this England,
> This nurse, this teeming womb of royal kings, . . .
> This land of such dear souls, this dear dear land

Henry V, in the play centered on the battle of Agincourt, urges his troops as they besiege the French city of Harfleur:

> On, on, you noblest English.
> Whose blood is fet from fathers of war-proof,
> Fathers that, like so many Alexanders,
> Have in these parts from morn till even fought . . .
> And you, good yeoman,
> Whose limbs were made in England, show us here
> The mettle of your pasture; let us swear
> That you are worth your breeding; which I doubt not;
> For there is none of you so mean and base,
> That hath not noble lustre in your eyes.

Shakespeare exalted a country whose common people are united by a sense of their own worth, which lends them the advantage over their more hierarchical foreign adversaries.[43] In Henry's words, "upon one pair of English legs/Did march three Frenchmen."

The exiles who had left under Mary's rule returned to take up top positions in Elizabeth's government. They asserted England's chosenness. John Aylmer, who assisted John Foxe while in exile and eventually became bishop of London, insisted in 1559 that "God is English."[44] The poet and playwright John Lyly wrote of the divine favor that the nation enjoyed: "So tender a care hath he alwaies had of that England, as of a new Israel, his chosen and peculier people." Adrian Hastings notes that the word *peculiar* is often used in expressing such sentiments, an echo of 1 Peter 2:9: "But ye *are* a chosen generation, a royal priesthood, an holy nation, a peculiar people; that ye should shew forth the praises of him who hath called you out of darkness into his marvellous light."[45]

The apotheosis of Elizabeth effectively fused the monarchy and English national identity. The democratizing tendency of the budding English nationalism remained submerged, although not for long. All that it took for it to rise to the fore was the right combination of religious contention and royal presumption. The successor to the childless Elizabeth, the ill-fated House of Stuart, provided both.[46] The provocations and high-handedness of the Stuarts—James I believed the authority of kings was comparable "to the Divine power" and "to the fathers of families"—led to Parliament literally waging war against the king.[47]

Parliament Stood Up for the Nation

Popular sentiment was extremely vigilant about any Catholic threat, foreign or domestic, and the Stuarts, especially the son of James, Charles I, got on the wrong side of this feeling. Charles had a Catholic wife from France. He played diplomatic footsie with Spain even as it warred against Protestants in the Netherlands. He tilted toward greater toleration of Catholics and even thought about a rapprochement with the pope.[48]

Charles himself inclined toward a "high church Arminianism" which was too formal and ritualistic, i.e., too close to Catholicism, for Presbyterians and Independents in Parliament. He made the rigid William Laud, who implemented changes in this direction, his Archbishop of Canterbury. Popular opposition to a perceived drift toward Catholicism—Archbishop Laud built altar rails; drunken troops tore them down—became inextricably linked to opposition to the king's overweening assertions of royal power.[49]

In an epic change, the locus of the nation shifted from the Crown to Parliament as the protector of the nation's faith and its liberties. Charles, of course, begged to differ, and the issue was contested between the royalist "Cavaliers" and parliamentary "Roundheads" on the battlefields of Marston Moor, Naseby, and Worcester. By some estimates, the country suffered its highest military casualties as a proportion of population until World War I.[50]

Charles lost the war—and his head. The parliamentary act establishing a court to try him for treason made it clear that the king existed separately and apart from the nation. It declared that "no Chief Officer or Magistrate whatsoever may hereafter presume traiterously and maliciously to imagine or contrive the Enslaving or Destroying of the English Nation."

The Puritans, originally a derogatory term, drove the parliamentary side in the Civil War, although the anti-Stuart coalition was broader than that and included politically moderate aristocrats and the likes of the great jurist Sir Edward Coke. For their part, the Puritans wanted, first of all, to reform the Church. They had no use for bishops and wanted to institute Presbyterian Church governance. They wanted people to be able to read and understand the Bible, unmediated, on their own. This hostility to established authority and emphasis on individual conscience inevitably had radical political implications. In King James I's pithy formulation, "No Bishop, no King." Or, as Thomas Hobbes put it, the fundamental issue in the revolution was "that liberty which the lower sort of citizens under the pretence of religion, do challenge to themselves."[51]

Indeed, the parliamentary cause attracted artisans and yeomen, "the middling sort" (at first "roundhead" was an insult directed at London mechanics with short haircuts). As the parliamentary leader, Oliver Cromwell, put it, "I had rather have a plain, russet-coated Captain, that knows what he fights for, and loves what he knows, than that which you call a Gentle-man and is nothing else." Parliament found its geographical base in East Anglia and London in the southeast of the country, heavily commercial areas with a disproportionate number of Puritans, as well as Protestant refugees from continental Europe.[52]

"The religious enthusiasm of the Puritan Revolution blazed the trail for a new liberty," the historian Hans Kohn writes. "The feeling of a great task to be achieved was not restricted to the upper classes; it lifted the people to a new dignity. They were no longer the common people, the object of history, but the nation, the subject of history, chosen to do great things in which every one, equally and individually, was called to participate."[53]

John Milton Forecast the Anglo-American Future

The great poet John Milton gave Puritanism its most exalted expression. At a time when political choices were a matter of life and death, Milton staked all on the parliamentary cause. He wrote fiercely in favor of it, including the decision to execute Charles I, and served in the republican government established after the king's death. When the Crown again gained the upper hand, he was briefly jailed during the Restoration and, after his release, wrote the greatest epic poem in the English language, *Paradise Lost*.

His polemics understandably aren't as well remembered, but they are exceptionally eloquent and forward looking. Marinated in the Old Testament and fervent in his faith, Milton represented something that might strike our more secular age as unusual, which is the joining of religious zeal to the cause of liberty, reason, and temporal progress. He wrote in a nationalist key that emphasized the special English role in the world.

He referred to England as "this nation chosen before any other." He wrote, in a passage that could appear in a patriotic speech in Shakespeare, "Consider what Nation it is whereof ye are, and whereof ye are the governours: a Nation not slow and dull, but of a quick, ingenious, and piercing spirit, acute to invent, suttle and sinewy to discours, not beneath the reach of any point the highest that human capacity can soar to."[54]

In his early work, Milton emphasized England as a leader in the Reformation; in his later work, he emphasized it as a leader in liberty.[55] He believed that God would incline people "to the voice of our Supreme Magistracy, calling us to liberty and the flourishing deeds of a reformed Commonwealth." Once known as "the hotbed of tyranny," Britain "will hereafter deserve to be celebrated for endless ages as a soil most congenial to the growth of liberty."[56]

In Milton, we hear, before John Locke and well before the American Founders, a description of the philosophical foundations of self-government: "No man who knows aught, can be so stupid to deny that all men naturally were born free, being the image and resemblance of God himself. . . . It being thus manifest that the power of Kings and Magistrates is nothing else, but what is only derivative, transferred and committed to them in trust from the People, to the Common good of them all, in whom the power yet remains fundamentally, and cannot be taken from them, without a violation of their birthright."[57]

If Milton was the exemplary writer of the English revolution, Cromwell was the exemplary figure, for better or worse. He rose from parliamentary backbencher to become a celebrated cavalry officer in the New Model Army of Parliament and, finally, the head of government as Lord Protector of the Commonwealth established after the execution of Charles I.[58] Cromwell marched to the cadences of the Old Testament, as did his army. The Old Testament provided the lion's share of material for a 1643 pocket Bible for the troops to illustrate "the qualifications of His inner man, that is a fit Souldier to fight the Lord's battles." Cromwell thought the English were "a people that have had a stamp upon them from God."[59] With their chosenness came responsibility. "We are apt to boast that we are Englishmen," he noted, "and truly it is no shame to us that we are so; but it is a motive to us to do like Englishmen, and seek the real good of this nation, and the interest of it."[60]

What was that? In the extraordinary Putney Debates, the army argued about what would be the basis of a new regime. The radical faction, the Levellers, made the case for popular sovereignty and widespread suffrage. The famous statement of the Leveller Colonel Thomas Rainsborough proved ahead of its time by a couple of centuries, but put down a marker. "Really," he said, "I think that the poorest he that is in England has a life to live as the greatest he." He believed "that every man that is to live under a government ought first by his own consent to put himself under that government." If not, then "the poorest man in England is not at all bound in a strict sense to that government that he has not had a voice to put himself under."[61]

Cromwell himself was no Leveller. He had no sense of the secular realm in the modern sense, and for his critics, his government descended into military dictatorship. He contributed to Britain's early forays into overseas empire. His reign was a wrong turn that wouldn't last and would give way to the Restoration after his death. But England would never be the same.

England Changed Forever and Seeded America

Royal absolutism of the sort that would long dominate on the Continent had been dealt a blow from which it never truly recovered. In time, England would get its Bill of Rights and its Toleration Act (although full Catholic emancipation had to wait all the way to 1829).[62] Censorship of the press would end.[63] Parliament, especially the House of Commons, would come to dominate the country's affairs. The nation would overawe the monarchy rather than the other way around. All this had to wait for the Glorious Revolution, when James II, a Catholic, was ousted in favor of his Protestant daughter Mary and her Dutch husband, William, who arrived at the invitation of prominent figures in England. The (initially) bloodless revolution led to a durable constitutional settlement.

But that's a story for another day. In the meantime, during the Civil War and Restoration, something like 80,000 Protestant dissenters and other discontents left England. A third of them crossed the Atlantic and undertook an errand in the wilderness in North America.[64] And therein lies a tale.

CHAPTER 6

A NATION OF SETTLERS

In 1634, the Massachusetts Bay Company prepared for war—against the king of England.

Some 140 years before the American Revolution, the fire of rebellion smoldered in a remote, hard-pressed outpost of North America established a mere four years earlier. Long before Boston revolted against George III, it prepared to revolt against Charles I.

If there isn't a direct line from John Winthrop, the governor of the Massachusetts Bay Colony, to the Founding Fathers, there is a clear connection. The historical resonance of recalcitrant New Englanders insisting on their rights and defying the English Crown is obvious. Nearly four hundred years ago, when not enough Englishmen occupied New England to fill a hockey arena, a key component of what would be the American national identity had already made itself plain.

The Massachusetts Bay Company received a surprisingly generous charter from Charles I, even though it was a Puritan project inimical to the king's own interests and beliefs.[1] The charter didn't require religious conformity, nor did it call for the establishment of the Church of England.[2] It didn't demand that company officials swear an oath of allegiance to the Crown in front of a royal official. It didn't limit what laws the company could pass, so long as they didn't contradict those of England.[3] Finally, it didn't stipulate that the charter itself should physically remain in England.

The leaders of the company took advantage of the loophole and made off with the charter.[4] The New World thus became the venture's seat of government, far from meddling royal officials. In the words of a company official back in England, the transfer to North America meant the government belonged "to those that shall inhabit there, and not to continue the same in subordination to the Company here."[5] Three thousand miles from the mother country, the Massachusetts Bay Company gladly created facts on the ground, whether to the liking of the English authorities or not.

The company had established an advance outpost in 1629 at a location that they called Salem, after the Hebrew word *shalom*.[6] The main body of settlers, numbering in the hundreds, arrived a year later in seventeen ships under the leadership of John Winthrop.[7] They ended up at Boston, named after a town in Lincolnshire, England. Across the decade, roughly twenty thousand emigrants arrived in what is known as the Great Migration, one of the most consequential movements of people in the history of the world.[8]

With a background as a fairly conventional country gentleman and lawyer from Suffolk in East Anglia, Winthrop didn't stand out except for a conversion experience in his youth that made him a Puritan.[9] Close to people imprisoned for resisting Charles I's back-door taxes and opposed to the king's anti-Puritan religious policy, he began to consider emigrating.[10]

His friends discouraged him. "To adventure your whole family upon so many manifest uncertainties standeth not with your wisdom and long experience," counseled one. Not to mention that the rigors ahead were daunting for a man in his forties— "Plantations are for young men, that can endure all pains and hunger."[11]

Yet Winthrop feared England's drift. "I am verily persuaded," he wrote a friend, "God will bring some heavy affliction upon this land, and that speedily; but be of good comfort. . . . If the Lord seeth it will be good for us, He will provide a hiding place for us and others." Why, he asked his wife, should we "suffer a whole continent, as fruitful and convenient for the use of man, to lie waste without any improvement?"[12]

The continent at first didn't seem particularly fruitful. Starvation and illness killed as many as half of the settlers the first winter, and a bounty had to be established to kill and stave off the wolves.[13] A dozen members of Winthrop's own household died between June and November 1630.[14] Yet the settlement hung on, committed to a vision of a truly reformed commonwealth impossible to achieve in Charles I's England.[15] Tellingly, the first item on a list of supplies compiled before the voyage—running from wheat to rabbits to pewter bottles—was "ministers."[16]

The colony's enemies back in England contested its charter for their own selfish purposes (they wanted to control the territory themselves) or out of opposition to its flagrant departures from Church of England orthodoxy.[17] The allies of Massachusetts warned of the brewing threat. Winthrop himself characterized the critics as "accusing us to intend rebellion, to have cast off our allegiance, and to be wholly separate from the church and laws of England; that our ministers and people did continually rail against the state, church and bishops there, etc."[18]

Winthrop might have added that the critics had a point. The anti-Massachusetts agitation grew more serious when Archbishop Laud, the hated enemy of Puritans, assumed the leadership of the Lords Commissioners of Trade and Plantations.[19] The commission tightened up the regulations around emigration, and the king sought—without much effect—to discourage the movement of people "whose only end is to live as much as they can without the reach of authority."[20] Then the commission demanded that the charter be produced for its review.[21]

Winthrop had no inclination to give back an iota of Massachusetts' autonomy. He insisted "that which the King is pleased to bestow upon us and we have accepted is truly our owne."[22] He rejected advice from a friend in England to modulate the colony's religious policy: "What you may doe in England where things are otherwise established, I will not dispute, but our case heere is otherwise: being come to clearer light and Libertye."[23]

Fearing the imposition of a governor-general from England by force, Massachusetts Bay Colony decided for defiance and prepared for conflict. It considered a floating gun platform to protect Boston Harbor, an idea that was scrapped, but fortified Castle Island in the harbor and placed a beacon on a high point in Boston (thereafter known as Beacon Hill). It instituted an oath of loyalty to the colony's government.[24] It imposed a general levy to pay for defense and appointed a military commission. The militia began to drill in earnest.[25]

A meeting of the clergy captured Massachusetts Bay's sentiment precisely. Should a governor-general be sent from England, it declared, "We ought not to accept him, but defend our lawful possessions, (if we are able;) otherwise to avoid or protract."[26]

The commission made repeated demands for the charter, all ignored or resisted amid legal wrangling. Finally, Charles I declared that he was taking charge of New England. But the ship that was supposed to take a royal governor to Massachusetts foundered upon launch.[27] The English government didn't have the resources to enforce its will on colonists prepared, in the words of an unfriendly observer in England, "to spend their blood in maintaining their present way and humor."[28] By 1639, Massachusetts could drill a thousand militiamen in Boston, a force bigger than all the people Winthrop had brought with him in 1630.[29]

For the first time, but emphatically not the last, Englishmen living in North America had insisted on their rights and prerogatives. That attitude not only helped define America but in due course made it an independent nation-state.

We Started Out a Nation of Settlers, Not of Immigrants or Philosophers

America is not a nation of immigrants, as we are constantly told, at least it wasn't at the crucial outset; it was a nation of settlers who came here with a specific mission and whose religio-cultural attributes and commitments have helped define our national identity to this day.

Contrary to the claims of anti-nationalists, it wasn't simply ideas that mattered in establishing the American project. Culture, and the people who embodied and delineated it, mattered as much or more. This point is worth dwelling on at length because it is so often dismissed or poorly understood. Nations aren't mere intellectual constructs but accretions of history and culture, usually shaped over the long term by their beginnings.

This is as true of the United States as any other country, despite the persistent myth that the nation emerged almost out of nowhere in 1776. The truth is that an American nation existed prior to the founding of the American nation-state and had been set on its course by settlers who had braved a harrowing journey and uncertain future to create a new life on new soil.

They weren't deracinated philosophers. Their origins mattered a great deal. If America had been populated by different people from a different part of the world with different predilections, say the French or Spanish, who had their own ambitions on this continent, our national character would be very different. Instead, New England was a product of the Puritan rebellion against royal absolutism in old England and intimately connected to it.

This inheritance lent us qualities at the outset that might seem particularly American—our sense of chosenness and our broadly middle-class orientation—but came directly from the mother country.

Another quality imported, as the story of Massachusetts Bay Colony in the 1630s demonstrates, was a bullheaded resistance to arbitrary authority and a willingness to resort to force in defense of our rights. This tendency wouldn't truly make itself felt for another century and a half. As long as we were convinced that the English Crown remained committed to fighting the enemies of Protestantism, pushing France and Spain out of our way in North America, and honoring the rights of Englishmen on this continent, we were proud foot soldiers in the British Empire. As soon as those things were in doubt, we were willing to stand on our rights with all the prickly insistence of John Winthrop.

But that gets ahead of the story. For now, it's enough to emphasize that the seeds of America's wholly successful nationalist revolt derived from England's incomplete nationalist revolt. "The promise of original English nationalism," Liah Greenfeld writes, "was carried much further toward its realization, and at a much swifter pace, than could have been possible in any part of Europe, with its age-old habits of doing things and thinking, by Englishmen on the other side of the Atlantic."[30]

What East Anglia Wrought

All sorts of Englishmen emigrated here. Such was the influx that the United States today is the country in the world with the largest population of people with British ancestry, the United Kingdom included.[31] The various flows of people—including a royalist elite and indentured servants to Virginia, Quakers to Pennsylvania, border dwellers from north Britain and northern Ireland to the backwoods of Appalachia—all had their distinctive influence on America's national identity. But the settlers of Massachusetts Bay Colony mattered most.[32]

The Puritan migration was truly remarkable. It wasn't idle boasting when a colonial magistrate in 1668 said, "God sifted a whole nation that he might bring choice Grain over into this Wilderness."[33] Unlike other American colonies, Massachusetts Bay was picky about its émigrés and sometimes asked for letters of recommendation.[34] Winthrop blamed the troubles of the Virginia Company for its reliance, in contrast, on "a multitude of rude and misgoverned persona, the very scumme of the Land."[35]

Everywhere else, emigration was a young man's game given the risks, yet the settlers of Massachusetts Bay Colony tended to travel in families.[36] A typical family from Norwich, a grocer and his wife, both in their thirties, emigrated with their three children and four servants.[37] A handful of octogenarians made the voyage.[38] The transplanting of whole families lent the project an exceptional social coherence and permanence.[39]

The émigrés, by and large, weren't aristocrats or the tired and poor or servants unattached to a household—they were free and solidly middle-class yeomen, artisans, and the like.[40] One correspondent recommended to Winthrop "a carpenter and Bricklayer the most faithfull and diligent workmen in all our parts."[41] As a promoter of New England had put it, the venture needed "good Governours, able Ministers, Physitians; Souldiers, Schoolemasters, Mariners, and Mechanicks of all sorts."[42] It got them.

They tended to come from towns and were extraordinarily literate by the standards of the time; two-thirds of the adult males could sign their names, well above the rate in England.[43] Almost 100 of the migration's 130 university graduates were clergy, typically from Oxford and Cambridge.[44]

Most New England families came from East Anglia and other counties in the east of England that had formed the Eastern Association supporting the parliamentary side in the English Civil War.[45] Both Oliver Cromwell and John Winthrop came from that region. The historian Carl Bridenbaugh identified the lion's share of the migration as coming from a radius of fifty miles of Groton, Winthrop's hometown.[46]

East Anglia literally left its mark on the map of New England. The name of towns such as Braintree, Groton, Wrentham, Newton, Springfield, Hingham, and Framingham in eastern England reappeared in Massachusetts Bay. Only one town was named after the king, Charlestown, and that indirectly, from the preexisting name of the Charles River.[47]

This part of Old England lent its coloration to New England.[48] It stood apart, first, in its religion. It had been disposed to what would become known as Protestantism even prior to the advent of Martin Luther and had become the heart of Puritanism.[49] The east of England contributed a disproportionate share of martyrs under Bloody Mary and of preachers harried under the strict hand of Archbishop Laud.[50]

Settled by Angles, Danes, and Jutes, East Anglia had long outstripped the rest of England in its number of freemen.[51] The most urbanized part of England, its people were disproportionately artisans and skilled craftsmen.[52] The counties of Suffolk and Essex had the highest literacy rates in England.[53] Perhaps most important, as the historian David Hackett Fischer relates, this region long provided the seedbed for revolts against authority, going back to the Peasants' Rebellion in 1381.[54]

This country would be a very different place if, for instance, East Prussia rather than East Anglia had sent its people and cultural tropes to New England.[55]

We Imported Key Attributes of Our National Identity

East Anglia–inflected New England put an accent on three cultural attributes that took on an outsized significance in American national identity: a belief in our chosenness, the idea of the Covenant, and the King James Bible. They were all imported here from England and then eventually turned against England and made into powerful supports of American independence.

A faith in our chosenness began before the Puritan settlers left the home country. The eminent Puritan minister John Cotton preached a sermon upon the departure of the Winthrop fleet. Cotton himself would spend only a few more years in England. He ran afoul of Archbishop Laud and was forced into hiding, before fleeing what he called "Episcopal tyranny" with his wife to Massachusetts.[56] They had a child on board the ship, whom they named, appropriately enough, Seaborn. In England, Cotton had been an influential minister in Boston, Lincolnshire; across the Atlantic, he became an influential minister in Boston, Massachusetts. He preached to the departing émigrés in 1630 from Samuel II: "Also I will appoint a place for my people Israel, and will plant it, that they may dwell in a place of their own, and move no more."[57]

John Winthrop set out his interpretation of the mission to the New World in his famous sermon on Christian charity, delivered either on board the *Arbella* or just prior to the voyage.[58] In a short address that nonetheless cited verses of the Bible thirty times and made dozens of other biblical references, Winthrop rehearsed Old Testament themes familiar from Milton or Cromwell.[59] He told his listeners that obedience to God would make for a success to be emulated: "When He shall make us a praise and glory that men shall say of succeeding plantations, 'the Lord make it like that of New England.' For we must consider that we shall be as a city upon a hill. The eyes of all people are upon us."

The metaphor of the city on a hill, too, had roots in East Anglia. Puritans there often used it, drawn from the gospel of Saint Matthew, to describe the advance of the true faith. An admiring Puritan said of Colchester in the county of Essex, "the town, for the earnest profession of the gospel, became like unto a city upon a hill, and as a candle upon a candle stick."[60] So even a phrase that is taken as a token of America's universalistic mission, quoted by Ronald Reagan and his imitators, has its origins in very particular cultural and geographic soil.

The hopes expressed by Winthrop, of course, outlived the founding generation of Puritans. Cotton Mather, a grandson of John Cotton and himself an influential minister, wrote of John Winthrop as "Nehemias Americanus," after Nehemiah, who rebuilt the walls of Jerusalem and rededicated Israel to the laws of Moses.[61] Mather portrayed William Bradford, the governor of the Plymouth Colony, which predated the Massachusetts Bay Colony by a decade, as Moses himself.[62] Lest there be any doubt of the antecedents he thought appropriate, Mather called New England "A NEW-ENGLISH ISRAEL."[63]

America's faith in its chosenness would become, over time, less explicitly religious and more oriented toward the country's devotion to liberty and human rights. It would go from Jonathan

Edwards' associating America with the Reformation and therefore "the glorious renovation of the world" to John Adams' believing its settlement opened up "a grand scheme and design in Providence for the illumination and emancipation of the slavish part of mankind all over the earth."[64] This sense of a special role in the world, established at the very beginning of the Anglo-American settlement of the continent, never went away.

A hallmark of a chosen people is its covenant with God. Both Winthrop ("We are entered into Covenant with him for this work") and Bradford ("as the Lord's free people, they joined themselves by a covenant of the Lord") spoke of their ventures in these terms.[65] The idea of covenant was central to Puritan thought. It derived, as we have seen, from God's agreement with Abraham in the Old Testament.[66]

The covenant characterized the relationship of the faithful to God, as well as to one another. Churches were founded by covenanting "saints." Nearly every town in New England was established by covenant. The most famous act of covenant is, of course, the Mayflower Compact, forged aboard the iconic ship of William Bradford's Pilgrim migration.

The Pilgrims didn't land in New York, where they had intended and had permission to from the king, but in New England, on virgin soil that necessitated the establishment of a new polity. While anchored off Cape Cod, they resolved to "solemnly and mutually in the presence of God, and one of another, Covenant and Combine our selves together into a Civil Body Politick, for our better ordering and preservation and furtherance of the ends aforesaid."

This experience repeated itself over and over. Henry Steele Commager writes, "All through the colonial era Americans went from compact to compact—the Fundamental Laws of Connecticut of 1639, the 'Solemn Compact' at Portsmouth of 1638, and its successor the Charter of the Providence Plantations of 1647, the Pennsylvania Charter of Privileges of 1701 (not quite so clear a case, to be sure), and thereafter a score of compacts and agreements on one frontier after another."[67]

With its emphasis on contract and agreed-upon limits to power, the Covenant had decidedly Lockean implications. John Winthrop wrote that men shouldn't be brought under anyone's rule other "than according to their will, & Covenant." John Cotton maintained that it is appropriate that "all power that is on earth be limited." The Code of Massachusetts prohibited trials or taxation "unless it be by vertue or equitie of some expresse law of the Country waranting the same," and election sermons tended to inveigh against arbitrary rule. "The people are not for the Rulers," was a typical sentiment, "but the Rulers for the people, to minister to their welfare."

"That magistrates were limited by the compact," the eminent scholar of Puritanism Perry Miller observed, "that government should be by laws and not by men, that the covenant was annulled by any serious violation of the terms, and that the people possessed a right to resist all such infringements—these principles were declared no less emphatically in Puritan theory than in the Declaration of Independence."[68]

Of course, it'd be wrong to hold up the Puritan settlements as democracies. Massachusetts Bay might be called an elective theocracy. Only church members could vote. The Puritan fathers didn't think of liberty in the modern liberal sense but as, in the words of Winthrop, "a liberty to that only which is good, just and honest."[69]

The vision of a godly commonwealth eventually was eclipsed. Reason, always a key element of Puritan thinking, occupied a more central place until it largely stood on its own.[70] The individualistic and commercializing tendencies of the new land took a hand, as did the naturally fissiparous tendency of rival Protestant sects.[71] The attempt to establish and maintain orthodoxy always had the flaw in America that dissenters could easily pick up and move elsewhere. When the regime in Massachusetts Bay no longer suited him, Roger Williams decamped to Rhode Island and established a more religiously open polity there.

Still, the idea of covenant in America, like that of our chosenness, persisted. It predated the work of the famous thinkers associated with the social contract, such as John Locke and Thomas Hobbes, by years and decades. John Quincy Adams called the Mayflower Compact "perhaps the only instance in human history of that positive, original social compact which speculative philosophers have imagined as the only legitimate source of government."[72] Over time, a secularized version of the covenant came to undergird the country's founding documents.

Both our chosenness and the covenant depended, of course, on the Bible. Initially, the Geneva Bible favored by Calvinists dominated in America (a version of it is sometimes referred to as the "breeches" Bible for its strikingly modest version of the story of Adam and Eve, who, having discovered their nakedness, "sewed fig leaves together and made themselves breeches"). William Bradford owned a Geneva Bible.

The first copy of the King James Bible may have been brought over by the ship's carpenter on the *Mayflower*. This translation won out, and came to occupy an unparalleled place in the culture. Families often didn't own any other book. It would be passed down in wills. As the historian David D. Hall writes, "No book was read more often or in so many different ways: privately in silence, aloud in households where reading may sometimes have proceeded 'in course' through the Old and New Testaments, and in church services as the text for Sunday sermons."[73]

It wasn't until the Revolution that the Bible could be legally published in America, and the floodgates opened to an insatiable market.[74] By around 1800, the traveling Bible salesman and author Parson Weems (he gave us the story of George Washington and the cherry tree) could boast to his publisher of all the editions he was moving: "I tell you, this is the very season and age of the Bible. Bible Dictionaries, Bible tales, Bible stories—Bibles plain or paraphrased, Carey's Bibles, Collins' Bibles, Clarke's Bibles, Kimptor's Bibles, no matter what or whose, all, all will go down, so wide is the crater of public appetite at this time."[75]

The English-language Bible existed *to be read* and was thus a spur to printing and education, especially in New England. The

Puritans shipped over a printing press at the first opportunity. It arrived in 1638. John Winthrop recorded that "the first thing printed was the freemen's oath; the next was an almanac made for New England by Mr. William Pierce, mariner; the next was the Psalms newly turned into verse"—the best-selling *Bay Psalm Book*.[76]

The King James Bible suffused American oratory and literature for centuries, from Lincoln and King, to Melville and Faulkner. In 1911, upon the three hundredth anniversary of its printing, the journal *The American Review of Reviews* called it "essentially our national book." John F. Kennedy, Lyndon Johnson, and Richard Nixon all quoted it in their inaugural addresses. "The great influence of the King James Version in American history," the scholar Mark Noll has said, "came precisely because it was so widely available; because precisely its words, and what the words communicated, had entered so deeply into the consciousness of so many Americans, and particularly of otherwise voiceless Americans."

The influence of these three pillars of our national identity, dating to the first stirrings of the American nation and well before anyone had thought of establishing an American nation-state, are still profoundly felt today.

Americans Had a Limited Loyalty to the Mother Country

These pillars obviously also spoke to a deep connection with the mother country, although one with strings attached. The American experiment was, from a distance, always caught up in the fight over the nature of the British polity. In contrast to the Plymouth colonists, who simply wanted to go their own way, the Puritans of Massachusetts Bay sought to remake England in their image.[77] Their fortunes rose and fell with the struggle against an overbearing Crown that they suspected of having Catholic sympathies.

The Puritan migration ran strongest during the period when

Charles I governed England under "personal rule" without Parliament. It let up when Charles called what became known as
the Long Parliament in 1640, and fears of the worst in England
abated—at least briefly.[78]

When the English Civil War broke out in 1642, Massachusetts
Puritans sailed back to pitch in on the side of Parliament.[79] A third
of Harvard graduates crossed the Atlantic. Some of the reverse
émigrés ended up as officers in the parliamentary army or as members of the Long Parliament. A friend of Winthrop urged him to
return. He stayed put.[80] But Hugh Peter, a prominent leader in
New England active in the founding of Connecticut and Harvard
College, did indeed go back and became an influential chaplain in
the parliamentary army. His high-flying career ended badly, when
Restoration authorities had him drawn and quartered for his role
in the execution of Charles I.[81]

New England felt its own blowback from the Restoration. The
Stuart king Charles II revoked the Massachusetts charter in 1684
to tamp down the Puritan zeal of the colony. Worse, Charles II's
successor, James II, established the Dominion of New England,
consolidating the government of the New England colonies. It
abolished colonial assemblies, prohibited town meetings, threw
into doubt land titles, challenged the dominance of Puritan religi-
osity, and generally did everything to provoke the colonists with
its executive high-handedness.[82]

The colonists exulted in the Glorious Revolution, which top-
pled the Catholic James II and installed the Protestant monarchs
William and Mary, who displayed the King James Bible at their
coronation.[83] Soon after news of the rebellion reached Massachusetts, the Americans replicated it with a coup of their own. The
Boston Revolt of 1689 overthrew the governor of the dominion,
Sir Edmund Andros. The colonists succeeded in reestablishing
their provincial assemblies, a key element of their political culture
without which there might not have been a more far-reaching
revolution less than a hundred years hence.[84]

The Americans stayed loyal to the Crown, provided it remained in reliably Protestant hands and opposed the Catholic powers of France and Spain, both of which had unwelcome footholds in North America. The colonists associated what they considered the true religion, Protestantism, with true liberty. They hated the so-called Jacobites in England, who persistently attempted to restore the Stuart line to the English throne in the person of "the Old Pretender," the son of James II. They rejoiced in every setback and humiliation of the king of France, who on top of his inherent hatefulness backed the Jacobites. Cotton Mather called Louis XIV "the French Molech," "the Greatest Adversary of a Glorious Christ and of real Christianity, that ever was in the world!"[85]

Everything changed when the colonists felt the British Empire could no longer be trusted to defend Protestantism, liberty, and their interests. Then they staged the greatest and most successful nationalist revolt the world has ever known.

SECTION III

THE
AMERICAN
NATIONAL TRIUMPH

CHAPTER 7

OUR NATIONALIST REVOLUTION

O n July 9, 1776, George Washington ordered the Declaration of Independence read to his troops in New York. Officers picked up copies at the Adjutant General's Office, and brigades stood in hollow squares to listen. Washington wanted every soldier to realize "that he is now in the service of a State, possessed of sufficient power to reward his merit, and advance him to the highest Honors of a free Country."

Public readings also took place around the country, with appropriate fanfare. In Philadelphia, John Adams recounted, "the Battalions paraded on the Common, and gave Us the Feu de Joie, notwithstanding the Scarcity of Powder. The Bells rang all Day and almost all night." People marked the occasion in cities across America by trashing depictions or symbols of King George III. In New York City, a statue of George III on a horse that had been erected just a few years earlier was decapitated and melted down into 40,000 bullets. In Huntington, Long Island, patriots fashioned an effigy of George III that they, with an admirable thoroughness, "hung on a gallows, exploded, and burnt to ashes."[1]

The chief purpose of the Declaration of Independence was . . . to declare independence. As Virginia statesman Richard Henry Lee said, most important was "the Thing itself."[2]

The Declaration begins and ends with an assertion of America's nationhood. The famous first sentence says that the American "people" are going "to assume among the powers of the earth, the separate and equal station to which the Laws of Nature and of Nature's God entitle them." The last says "that these united colonies are, and of right ought to be, free and independent states."

The Declaration ran in the slipstream of the English tradition of addresses, petitions, and declarations that had long marked high politics in the mother country. As the historian Pauline Maier explains, declarations enunciated new policies or made an appeal for public support based on an alleged wrongdoing. The Americans particularly revered the Declaration of Rights of 1689, the keystone of the Glorious Revolution; it pronounced the end of the reign of James II and the beginning of the rule of William and Mary. It included a list of the abuses of James II, all deemed "utterly and directly contrary to the known laws and statutes and freedom of this realm."[3]

Throughout the revolutionary period, the Americans aped this Declaration of Rights. Thomas Jefferson's handiwork showed the influence of the English antecedent in its preamble and list of grievances. It also drew liberally from George Mason's draft of the Virginia Declaration of Rights, itself an homage to the English document.[4] The Virginia declaration insisted "That all men are born equally free & independent" and that we have a right to the "Enjoyment of Life & Liberty, with the Means of acquiring & possessing Property, & pursueing & obtaining Happiness & Safety."[5]

"Independence was new," Maier writes, "the rest of the Declaration seemed all too familiar, a restatement of what had already been said time and again." In 1822, John Adams harrumphed of the Declaration that there was "not an idea in it, but what had been hackney'd in Congress for two years before."[6]

But original thinking wasn't the point. The Declaration should be understood, Maier writes, "first and foremost not as a philosophical but, in the language of the day, as a constitutional document, that is, one that concerned the fundamental authority of government."[7] At the time, citations of the Declaration tended to focus not on the preamble that looms so large today but on the final paragraph, which does the heavy lifting of setting out our independence.[8]

As a statement of ideals, the Declaration is stirring and eloquent; as a statement of the independence of a new American nation-state, it was truly world changing.

We Launched the Revolution to Establish an Independent Nation-State

The American Revolution wasn't a primarily philosophical under taking, although obviously a great deal of thought—of grappling with history and law—went into the case for independence and into the formation of America's governing institutions.[9] But no one believed they were creating "an idea," rather than a nation-state (although initially a loosely organized one).

The rebellion didn't emerge from nowhere, disembodied from the literal and cultural soil of America. It proceeded, in part, from cold-blooded material causes, such as the push for western lands. It activated long-existing cultural predilections, including religious ones. Rather than a radical break from English tradition, it harkened back to the English Civil War and initially sought to protect the traditional rights of Englishmen. Its crucial background was a rising sense of American greatness.

Most important, Americans wanted, in the lowest-common-denominator goal of peoples everywhere, to govern themselves. They had a well-developed expectation of doing this that arose from practice rather than theory; in their colonial legislatures, not to mention their churches and town meetings, they had been operating with great independence for more than a hundred years (to the chagrin of royal governors, who had to wrestle with recalcitrant assemblies that had control of the purse strings).[10]

The Revolution established, more than anything else, our independent nationhood. Liah Greenfeld writes, "the firm conviction that the American society (every objective attribute of which—

territory, resources, institutions, and character—was as yet uncertain) was a *nation*, was the only thing that was certain." In older societies, the national idea ran up against traditional institutions and practices—monarchy, feudalism—that presented obstacles to its realization. Not in America. "It is a purer example," she adds, "of a *national* community than any other."[11]

After the Revolution, the American national project wasn't assured of success. It took the insistence of the nationalists on the Constitution and the shrewd navigation between foreign adversaries during the rocky 1790s—defended in Washington's exemplary Farewell Address—to put the new government onto a solid footing. Even then, more time would pass and blood be spilled before the heading of the Declaration, with its bold reference to the United States of America, would be fully realized.

A Rising Sense of Greatness Drove the Revolution

A fundamental constitutional dispute obviously undergirded the Revolution: the Americans argued that Parliament didn't have the power to tax or write laws for the colonies; the English wouldn't budge on the primacy of Parliament, which had been forged at such cost over the centuries, and the notorious Declaratory Act of 1766 asserted the right to legislate for the colonies in "all cases whatsoever."[12] But in the long catalogue of peoples who have sought their independence from an empire, the Americans were hardly ill used. Hans Kohn calls the colonists "the least oppressed of all peoples then on earth, politically, economically, and nationally."[13]

Americans had a heightened sensitivity to slights and less patience for commercial restraints and meddling in their internal governance as they felt their growing strength.[14] This had long been forecast. The Founders treasured a prediction by the British essayist James Harrington dating from the 1650s. He had written in his famous book *The Common-Wealth of Oceana* that the colonists were "as yet babes that cannot live without suckling the breasts of their mother-Cities, but such as, I mistake, if when they come of age they do not wean themselves."[15]

By the middle of the eighteenth century, the American economy had grown over the last century at a per capita rate twice that of Great Britain, and the population had exploded from 75,000 to more than 1.6 million.[16] This was a suckling child? "Is there not something extremely fallacious," John Adams wrote in 1765, "in the common-place images of mother country and children colonies? Are we the children of Great-Britain, any more than the cities of London, Exeter and Bath? Are we not brethren and fellow subjects, with those in Britain, only under a somewhat different method of legislation, and a totally different method of taxation?"[17]

The Americans held a sweeping view of the country's future. Timothy Dwight, a future president of Yale, gave a talk to graduating students in 1776: "You should by no means consider yourselves as members of a small neighborhood, town or colony only, but as being concerned in laying the foundations of American greatness. Your wishes, your designs, your labors, are not to be confined by the narrow bounds of the present age, but are to comprehend succeeding generations, and be pointed to immortality." Franklin wrote to the Scottish philosopher Henry Home, Lord Kames, in 1767, predicting that America "will, in less time than is generally conceived, be able to shake off any shackles that may be imposed on her, and perhaps place them on the imposers."

The shaking off would begin soon enough.

We Bristled over Limits to Our Acquisition of Land

One of the shackles was a limit to our acquisition of land. After Great Britain won a smashing success in the French and Indian War—a world war between the British and French that began in a fight over control of the Ohio Valley in North America—it enjoyed an enormous windfall of territory beyond the Appalachian Mountains.

The British sought to placate rebellious Indians on this land via the Proclamation of 1763. It established a line between the Indians and colonists running down the continent along the Appalachians, with the West constituting a vast, de facto Indian reservation.[18] Settlers on the wrong, western side of the line were ordered "forthwith to remove themselves." Lord Hillsborough, the secretary of state for the colonies, wanted, in his words, to maintain the colonists "in a just subordination to and dependence upon this kingdom."[19]

Good luck. The colonies wouldn't provide troops to garrison forts enforcing the proclamation line;[20] the British would have to do it themselves. The geopolitical obstacle to colonial settlement of the interior was no longer France, a Catholic power allied with the Indians, but Great Britain, a religiously suspect power that was protecting the Indians. That role reversal would contribute to the colonies' break with the British Empire in about a decade's time (and, in one of the great ironies of American history, the decisive alliance with none other than France during the Revolution).

George Washington was one of the land-hungry Americans checked by the proclamation. The Virginia Colony had pledged 200,000 acres of "bounty land" to the men who had fought under Washington in the French and Indian War in 1754. Granted 15,000 of those acres himself, Washington relentlessly organized to take advantage of the windfall. He lobbied in Williamsburg. He examined the lands personally, on horseback and by canoe, during a nine-week trip in 1770. He bought up the rights to more acreage from his former comrades in arms. He claimed highly desirable fertile bottomland (now in West Virginia), what he called "the cream of the country."[21]

All for naught. In 1774, he got news that Lord Hillsborough had ruled that a small exception to the proclamation for veterans of the French and Indian War applied only to British regulars, not colonial troops. Washington denounced the decision as "founded equally in Malice, absurdity, & error." In April 1775, the royal governor of Virginia moved on the basis of a technicality to wipe out

Washington's claims in the Ohio Valley, a decision Washington deemed "incredible."[22]

The edicts played into his final break with the British Empire; when he showed up at the Second Continental Congress, Washington wore the military uniform of the Fairfax Independent Militia Company.[23] In its indictment of King George III, the Declaration of Independence referred to the offense of "raising the conditions of new Appropriations of Lands," and the Revolution would efface the proclamation line and facilitate the settlement of the continent all the way to the Pacific in relatively short order.

The Revolution Replayed Old Anglo-American Divisions

When the Revolution came, it took on the aspect of a civil war within America. The denominational and regional breakdown of the two sides roughly tracked with prior Anglo-American contentions over the rights of the nation vis-à-vis the king. Except the religious terrain tilted even more in a republican direction—less than a tenth of Englishmen were members of dissenting denominations, whereas three-quarters of Americans were of this troublesome, rebellious ilk.[24]

Kevin Phillips identifies the main groups at the center of the rebellion: "two sets of dissenting Protestants, the Congregationalists and the Presbyterians, and the southern vestrymen, the Low Church Anglican gentry of the plantation states." New England, with its Puritan inheritance and true to its East Anglia heritage, was strongest for the Revolution. The Scotch-Irish and Presbyterians played a leading role in the Patriot cause in the middle colonies. The tobacco plantation owners in Virginia, Maryland, and North Carolina also buttressed the effort. Associated with the Cavaliers during the English Civil War, they were more anomalous. But their Low Church Anglicanism—the vestries ran their own churches—and their fraught relationships with British creditors inclined them toward rebellion.[25]

Lining up reliably on the Tory side were High Church Anglicans (allies of the monarchy and enemies of dissenting Protestants, who in a bygone time would have supported Archbishop Laud); Scottish merchants and clansmen (who had become loyal foot soldiers of the British Empire); and royal appointees and former British officers.[26]

The American patriots reached back to their English forebears. Thomas Jefferson recalled resorting to a history of the English Civil War by John Rushworth, former secretary to Cromwell, with colleagues in Virginia as the closing of the port of Boston loomed in 1774. They looked, according to Jefferson, "for the revolutionary precedents and form of the Puritans of that day, [and] we cooked up a resolution, somewhat modernizing their phrases, for appointing the 1st day of June, on which the Port bill was to commence, for a day of fasting, humiliation and prayer, to implore heaven to avert from us the evils of civil war."[27]

Karl Marx acerbically argued in his history *The Eighteenth Brumaire of Louis Bonaparte* that "Cromwell and the English people had borrowed speech, passions and illusions from the Old Testament for their bourgeois revolution. When the real aim had been achieved, when the bourgeois transformation of English society had been accomplished, Locke supplanted Habakkuk," a reference to the Hebrew prophet. In reality, as Mark Noll argues, Habakkuk and Locke worked in tandem in America.[28]

Most people in America at the time of the Revolution didn't suddenly start reading Locke. They were primed by their folk memory and experience toward a devotion to their rights. Decades later, a historian asked a ninety-one-year-old veteran of the Battle of Concord why he had fought that day. "I suppose," the historian ventured, "you have been reading Harrington, Sidney, and Locke about the eternal principle of liberty?" The captain replied, "I never heard of these men. The only books we had were the Bible, the Catechism, Watts' psalms and hymns and the almanacs." His interviewer wondered, "Well, then, what was the matter?" The simple answer: "Young man, what we meant in going for those Redcoats was this: we always had governed ourselves and we always meant to. They didn't mean we should."[29]

Case closed.

The Bible Buttressed the Revolution

The faith of the colonists inclined them the same way. Boston pastor Jonathan Mayhew preached in 1766 upon the repeal of the Stamp Act that we had "learned from Holy Scriptures, that wise, brave and virtuous men were always friends to liberty; that God gave the Israelites a kingdom, or absolute monarch, in his anger, because they had not sense and virtue enough to like a free commonwealth, and to have Himself for their King; that the Son of God came down from heaven to make us free indeed; and that where the spirit of the Lord is, there is liberty."[30]

The Bible pervaded the patriotic literature of the Revolution. Pastors referred often to the story of Exodus and the escape of the Hebrews from captivity in Egypt; to Judges and Israel's war against the Canaanites; and to Psalms, especially 124, wherein David praises God for delivering Israel.[31] Those themes undergirded even more secular agitation for independence.

Patrick Henry's "Give me liberty or give me death" speech of March 1775 turned again and again to biblical language, and, as Mark Noll points out, the stirring finale borrows from lines from the books of Genesis and Joshua. (So moved was the Virginia soldier and statesman Edward Carrington as he listened beneath a window outside the church where Henry spoke that he requested to be buried on the spot—and after an illustrious career in the Continental Army, he was.) The same was true of Samuel Adams rallying an embattled Continental Congress in September 1777. "In the gloomy period of adversity," he said, quoting Exodus, "we have had 'our cloud by day and pillar of fire by night.'"[32]

The old hot buttons of prior Anglo-American struggles remained in force. Talk of the Church of England sending a bishop to America (a mansion being built in Boston by an agent of the Church was said to be future lodging for a prelate) set off the alarms of Congregationalists, Presbyterians, and sundry other Protestants who associated episcopal hierarchy with tyranny.[33]

The adage "No bishop, no king" still applied. The British official William Knox regretted that "Every man being thus allowed to be his own Pope, he becomes disposed to wish to become his own King." There is a reason that King George called the Revolution a "Presbyterian War" and the parliamentarian Horace Walpole complained that "Cousin America has run off with the Presbyterian parson, and that is the end of it."[34]

In this same vein, the colonies hated the Quebec Act of 1774, which set the rules for the French-speaking province. It allowed for the free exercise of the Catholic religion; expanded the province's borders into the Ohio Country; partially returned to French civil law; and made no provision for an elected assembly. No measure could have been better designed to provoke the colonists.

They viewed it as among the Intolerable Acts passed in 1774 after the Boston Tea Party to bring Massachusetts and the colonies to heel (John Winthrop would have agreed with the designation; one of the acts revoked the charter of Massachusetts). Paul Revere made a derisive engraving of bishops dancing around the Quebec Act. The First Continental Congress in 1774 inveighed against the act for "abolishing the equitable system of English laws," and "erecting a tyranny there, to the great danger, from so total a dissimilarity of Religion, law and government of the neighboring British colonies." The Declaration of Independence repeated essentially the same charge.[35]

Despite his later authorship of the scandalous deist tract the Age of Reason, Thomas Paine, too, ran in these cultural grooves. The colonists were reluctant to make the final break with Great Britain, and Paine's Common Sense, first printed by a Philadelphia publisher on January 9, 1776, had a galvanizing effect. Heretofore

undistinguished, having bounced around doing odd jobs including corset maker, Paine had arrived in the colonies just a little over
a year earlier.

He rejected the monarchy at its root, referring to the king as
"the hardened, sullen-tempered Pharaoh of England," and imbued
the cause of American independence with the fierce urgency of
now. Not everyone was impressed. John Adams thought his
muscular, plainspoken prose, in a reference to an English jail,
"suitable for an Emigrant from New Gate, or one who had chiefly
associated with such Company." But it found an audience. Hawked
everywhere and at an affordable cost ("Common Sense for eighteen pence"), it sold roughly 150,000 copies. That didn't justify
Paine's boast of "the greatest sale that any performance ever had
since the use of letters," but it was an impressive number by any
standard, and many copies were read multiple times or read aloud
to multiple people.[36]

Paine repeatedly resorted to scripture in the section of the pam-
phlet that made a principled case against monarchy. He later told
Adams that "he had taken his Ideas in that part from Milton."
Paine called the desire of the Hebrews for a king a "national delusion," prior to which Israel had operated as "a kind of republic
administered by a judge and the elders of the tribes." He cited the
Lord's opposition to a king in 1 Samuel: "They have rejected me,
that I should not reign over them."[37]

In his hands, America's chosenness became a national destiny
of cosmic importance. With a little boldness, the Americans
could make "this continent the glory of the earth." In another
passage, he enthused, "'Tis not the affair of a City, a County,
a Province, or a Kingdom; but of a Continent—of at least one
eighth part of the habitable globe. 'Tis not the concern of a day,
a year, or an age; posterity are virtually involved in the contest,
and will be more or less affected even to the end of time by the
proceedings now."[38]

In the event, it wasn't merely inflated rhetoric.

The Founders Created a National Government Worthy of the Name

With the end of the long and costly Revolutionary War came independence and an extraordinarily generous peace settlement from the British. The borders of the new nation extended down to Florida, across to the Mississippi, and up to the Great Lakes. George III despaired over the whole business at first, then later decided that, given the ingrained "knavery" of Americans, "it may not in the end be an evil that they become aliens to this kingdom."[39]

We don't need to rehearse the details of the subsequent story, which has been well told many times, except to note that after the Revolution another nationalist project beckoned: Could the United States cohere into a single nation-state, or was it destined to split apart and become the prey of hostile powers? If it was to be the former, it needed a national government worthy of the name.

Sent to the thirteen states for ratification in 1777, the "Articles of Confederation and Perpetual Union" manifestly failed to meet the test. Congress could conduct diplomacy and wage war—and not much else. The government's weakness met with predictable contempt.

The British didn't withdraw from seven forts in the interior, as promised. Indians, under the leadership of the Miami war chief Little Turtle, prohibited white settlement north of the Ohio River. Spain, protecting its interests in the Louisiana Territory, cut off the lower Mississippi River to American watercraft, a blow to our trade meant to discourage further settlement. It seemed possible that settlers in the West could be enticed into alliances with Great Britain or Spain, while back east, Shays' Rebellion over debt relief and taxes roiled western Massachusetts.[40]

Unable to levy taxes or control the frontier enough to generate revenue by selling western land, the government floundered. George Washington wrote to Benjamin Harrison, a Virginia politician, in 1784 that he anticipated the worst "from a half-starved, limping Government, that appears to be always moving upon crutches, & tottering at every step." He wrote to the Revolutionary War officer Henry Lee III in 1786 upon the occasion of Shays' Rebellion that he believed "to be more exposed in the eyes of the world & more contemptible than we already are, is hardly possible."[41]

In four months in Philadelphia in 1787, the Framers arrived at the Constitution as the answer to the crisis of insufficient national authority. "With all its faults," Gouverneur Morris said in his final speech at the Constitutional Convention, "the moment this plan goes forth all other considerations will be laid aside, and the great question will be, shall there be a national Government or not?"[42] The question was put not to the state governments, whose deficiencies had appalled the likes of Alexander Hamilton and James Madison, but to special ratifying conventions. Madison maintained that the Constitution was nothing "until life and validity were breathed into it by the voice of the people."[43] It was an exercise of popular sovereignty worthy of the ringing opening words of the Constitution, "We the People."

George Washington's Farewell Address Is a Great Nationalist Document

After the adoption of the Constitution during the fraught 1790s, Americans had to steer between the Scylla of Great Britain and the Charybdis of France. The two powers squared off again in the aftermath of the French Revolution, and each hoped to bully and entice the United States into an alliance. The British seized American merchant ships and forced American sailors into the British navy. The French harassed American shipping, too, and plotted to stoke secessionist movements in the West and South.[44]

President Washington avoided war with both, operating on a strategy of fostering the nation's strength. As he put it in a letter to the Maryland statesman Charles Carroll in May 1796, "Twenty years peace, with such an increase of population and resources as we have a right to expect; added to our remote situation from the jarring powers, will in all probability enable us in a just cause to bid defiance to any power on earth."[45]

This is the backdrop to his Farewell Address, one of the great state papers and nationalist documents of American history, although it has lost some of the reverence in which it used to be held. As members of the Board of Visitors of the University of Virginia decades later, Thomas Jefferson and James Madison included it in a short list of essential documents for understanding the American project, recommending it "as conveying political lessons of peculiar value."[46] Lincoln issued a proclamation in 1862 urging his fellow citizens to hold meetings to "celebrate the anniversary of the birth of the Father of His Country by causing to be read to them his immortal Farewell address."[47]

Hamilton drafted the address under Washington's direction. The president closely edited it through multiple drafts and gave it a final scrub down to the punctuation marks right before its publication in a Philadelphia newspaper (the address wasn't actually an address but a written statement reprinted in newspapers around the country). It is not the isolationist statement it is remembered as and ranges far beyond foreign policy. The document sets out Washington's vision of a country needful of national unity, jealous of its sovereignty, focused on its interests, and confident in its destiny. It is addressed, in a note echoing the initial words of the Constitution, "To the PEOPLE of the United States" and opens, "Friends and Fellow-Citizens."[48]

Washington argues for the importance of a coherent national government: "The unity of government which constitutes you one people is also now dear to you. It is justly so; for it is a main pillar in the edifice of your real independence, the support of your tranquility at home, your peace abroad, of your safety, of your prosperity, of that very liberty which you so highly prize."

He makes the case for all that Americans have in common: "The name of American, which belongs to you in your national capacity, must always exalt the just pride of patriotism more than any appellation derived from local discriminations. With slight shades of difference, you have the same religion, manners, habits, and political principles. You have in a common cause fought and triumphed together. The independence and liberty you possess are the work of joint counsels and joint efforts—of common dangers, sufferings, and successes."

He has no use for undue regionalism: "In contemplating the causes which may disturb our Union, it occurs as matter of serious concern that any ground should have been furnished for characterizing parties by *geographical discriminations—northern and southern— Atlantic* and *Western*."

He defends a clear-eyed foreign policy: "The nation which indulges towards another an habitual hatred, or an habitual fondness, is in some degree a slave. It is a slave to its animosity or to its affection, either of which is sufficient to lead it astray from its duty and its interest."

He warns against allowing foreign meddling in our internal affairs: "Against the insidious wiles of foreign influence (I conjure you to believe me, fellow-citizens) the jealousy of a free people ought to be constantly awake, since history and experience prove that foreign influence is one of the most baneful foes of republican government."

He forecasts national greatness: "If we remain one people under an efficient government, the period is not far off when we may defy material injury from external annoyance; when we may take such an attitude as will cause the neutrality we may at any time resolve upon to be scrupulously respected; when belligerent nations, under the impossibility of making acquisitions upon us, will not lightly hazard the giving us provocation; when we may choose peace or war, as our interest guided by justice shall counsel."

The address implicitly endorses the nationalist program (and anti-French views) of Hamilton.

The American Nationalist Tradition
Runs through Hamilton

That program had led to a political and philosophical split between Washington and Hamilton, on the one hand, and Jefferson
and Madison, on the other.

A fiercely talented and ambitious orphaned boy from the British West Indies, Hamilton was one of the most fertile nationalist
minds in all of American history. He devoted himself to the Revolution and, in its aftermath, to creating a national government
sound enough to sustain the American order. He was a prime
mover behind the Constitutional Convention, and wrote roughly
two-thirds of the Federalist Papers, making the case for the work
product of the convention. He influenced other consequential
nationalists such as Chief Justice of the Supreme Court John
Marshall and Congressman and Secretary of State Daniel Webster.
As Washington's secretary of the Treasury, he wrote some of the
greatest state papers in our history, outlining his program for
putting the federal government onto a firm financial foundation
and fostering a thriving industrial economy.[49]

Hamilton successfully pushed to fund the national debt and
have the federal government assume the war debts of the states;
advocated tariffs to bolster the manufacturing sector; and convinced Washington to back the creation of a national bank—all
toward the goal of becoming a great power like the British.[50]

Hamilton believed, as the historian Craig L. Symonds puts it,
that the country required "all the accoutrements of world power:
a vital domestic industry, a healthy world trade, and, to protect
that trade and the national integrity, a naval fleet."[51] Hamilton
thought, as he wrote in the Federalist 11, that the United States
should "aim at an ascendant in the system of American affairs"
and "become the arbiter of Europe in America." As he put it in a
rousing finale, "Let the thirteen States, bound together in a strict
and indissoluble Union, concur in erecting one great American
system, superior to the control of all transatlantic force or influ-

ence, and able to dictate the terms of the connection between the old and the new world!"

The American nationalist tradition runs through Hamilton, and his vision of a commercial republic, buttressed by a competent state, would ultimately prevail. Yet his nemesis, Thomas Jefferson, gained the upper hand politically.

Jefferson Had His Own Vision of National Greatness

Jefferson and Madison feared that Hamilton's program entailed concentrating financial power in the hands of an elite and exceeding the bounds of the Constitution. Hamilton favored, in Madison's words, the "principles of monarchy and aristocracy."[52] This is why they styled themselves, in contrast to Hamilton and his allies, Republicans.[53]

Jefferson, though, had his own vision of national greatness. Hamilton believed that the United States constituted "the embryo of a great empire." Jefferson spoke of an "empire of liberty," which, he wrote Madison in 1801, would eventually extend across the continent. The historian Walter McDougall notes, "where Hamilton might imagine the United States an empire of commerce and industry, and Jefferson an empire of yeomen, everyone thought in terms of territorial growth."[54]

The backlash against the notorious Alien and Sedition Acts passed by the Federalists during the administration of John Adams helped propel the so-called Revolution of 1800, the election of Thomas Jefferson as president.

In preparation for his inaugural address, Jefferson simply walked from his boardinghouse to the US Capitol in plain dress on March 4, 1801 (accompanied by cannon fire, a ceremonial touch that he hadn't approved). The most famous line of the speech—"We are all Republicans, we are all Federalists"—was hardly sincere; he hoped to crush the Federalists underfoot.[55] But Jefferson offered a deeper vision of national togetherness: he

called Americans "brethren of the same principle" and urged his
fellow citizens to "unite with one heart and one mind." He believed that we enjoyed a "chosen country," our government was
"the world's best hope," and, thanks to the patriotic devotion of its
citizens, we had "the strongest Government on earth."[56]

Jefferson limned an optimistic vision that knew no bounds:
"A rising nation, spread over a wide and fruitful land, travers-
ing all the seas with the rich productions of their industry,
engaged in commerce with nations who feel power and forget
right, advancing rapidly to destinies beyond the reach of mortal
eye—when I contemplate these transcendent objects, and see
the honor, the happiness, and the hopes of this beloved country
committed to the issue and the auspices of this day, I shrink
from the contemplation, and humble myself before the mag-
nitude of the undertaking."

The country would, soon enough, justify Jefferson's awe.

CHAPTER 8

A CONTINENTAL NATION

On October 20, 1842, Commodore Thomas ap Catesby Jones, commander of the US Pacific Squadron, ordered 150 US troops ashore at Mexican-held Monterey, California. They seized a fort without resistance, and the Stars and Stripes went up over the Monterey customhouse.[1]

Earlier that year, while at Callao, Peru, Jones had gotten word that a French fleet was sailing to points unknown—perhaps to begin the occupation of Alta California, the enormous Mexican province encompassing all or parts of the modern states of California, Arizona, Utah, Nevada, Wyoming, and Colorado. He believed that British ships might be headed there, as well. And the US consul in Mazatlán, Mexico, sent him a message saying that we would soon declare war on Mexico over Texas. Jones and his officers concluded that if a state of war now existed, they should seize every port in California.

Jones ordered his flagship, *United States*, and another ship to California. When they arrived at Monterey, two Mexican officers ventured out to inform the Americans that they weren't aware of any conflict with the United States. Still, Jones made an ultimatum demanding that the Mexicans surrender the port, styling himself grandiosely "Commander-in-chief of the United States naval forces on the Pacific station and of the naval and military expedition for the occupation of Old and New California, etc."

Since the Americans had eight hundred men and eighty can-
nons and the Mexicans had nothing, it wasn't going to be a fair
fight, or any fight at all. The day after the Americans had taken
the town without a shot being fired, Jones himself went ashore
and discovered that the mails revealed no declaration of war. Yes,
the commodore had begun the conquest of California by accident.

Jones apologized, and after a warm send-off by the Mexicans,
the Americans went on their way.[2]

Nothing so starkly illustrates the American continental drive
than our immediate focus on gaining California, a territory separated by vast, unoccupied spaces from the rest of the nation.

John Quincy Adams was contending that we were rightly a
continental nation in 1819. President James Monroe's envoy to
Mexico made the case in 1822 for a border that would give us
California, Texas, and other territories in northern Mexico.
President Andrew Jackson's secretary of state instructed our
chargé d'affaires in Mexico in 1835 to explore the idea of offer-
ing $5 million to secure "within our limits the whole bay of St
Francisco."

We wanted California for many reasons, as Hunt Janin and
Ursula Carlson detail in a book on the subject. We needed California for the terminus of a transcontinental railroad. We wanted
harbors for our merchant ships trading with the East and our
Pacific whaling fleet (650 ships strong in 1844). We hoped to block
a European power, the British primarily or perhaps even the
French or Russians, from making a claim on the territory. And
we recognized the stupendous potential of that bounteous land,
even before the discovery of gold.[3]

The key thing to know about the conquest of California, when
it eventually came about in earnest in 1846–1847, is that there was
not much conquering to speak of. The province was lightly populated and barely governed. Few from Mexico settled there. At one
point, the Mexican government sent convicts to try to populate
the place, and soldiers stationed in the province were often drawn
from jails. In 1835, the Mexican army had a little more than three

hundred men in California. As of 1842, the company stationed in San Diego had all of fourteen unarmed men.[4]

FDR had it right when he wrote in an introduction to a book about the California naval battles, "Incapable of united resistance from within and devoid of any protecting power from without, the vast territory of California lay an easy prize to any strong power that might wish to seize it." Or, as a French diplomat observed at the time, California was ripe for the picking of "whatever nation chooses to send there a man-of-war and two hundred men."[5]

As it happened, that was pretty much what the United States did.

We Always Sought to Spread across the Continent

If America is an idea, it's one that has shown itself remarkably adept at eliminating threatening foreign powers from our vicinity and expanding our territory through calculation, artifice, and force. We were never content to huddle against the Eastern Seaboard thinking philosophical thoughts. We cared deeply about territorial questions and wanted to ward off geopolitical challengers and increase the extent and power of the nation. Our people ceaselessly strained against any western boundaries short of the Pacific Ocean, and almost all our statesmen—of all parties and dispositions—considered it a given that we would spread across the continent (and perhaps extend our northern and southern borders, too).

Jefferson wrote to James Monroe in 1801 in a letter regarding the ultimate fate of the Indians and Spaniards, "However our present interests may restrain us within our own limits, it is impossible not to look forward to distant times, when our rapid multiplication will expand itself beyond those limits, & cover the whole Northern, if not the Southern continent with a people speaking the same language, governed in similar forms, & by similar laws: nor can we contemplate, with satisfaction, either blot or mixture on that surface."[6]

In 1819, John Quincy Adams thought Europe should accommodate itself to "the idea of considering our proper dominion to be the continent of North America. From the time when we became an independent people it was as much a law of nature that this should become our pretension as that the Mississippi should flow to the sea."[7]

The story of our expansion was written by visionaries and statesmen such as Jefferson and Adams; by adventurers such as John C. Frémont and his sidekick in his explorations, the bullet-scarred Indian fighter and scout Kit Carson; and by warriors such as Andrew Jackson, who beat the British at New Orleans and as an Indian fighter opened up Georgia and Alabama and secured Florida, and Zachary Taylor, who won famous victories in the Mexican-American War. It is an often inspiring, always audacious, and sometimes disheartening tale. There were other people blocking us, and our means of pushing them aside could be underhanded and brutish.[8]

For anti-nationalist conservatives, much of this story is to be passed over in silence, as they effectively reduce almost a century of the nation's history to the Declaration of Independence and the Gettysburg Address. For the Left, it shows the nefariousness, even the illegitimacy, of the American nation.

There is obviously much that is regrettable, especially in our treatment of the Indians, but we should always remember the bottom line of our expansion: it was a stupendous boon to our nation, to our people, to our interests, to our wealth, and to our power. We wouldn't be nearly as affluent or influential today without it. Try to imagine an America without free navigation of the Mississippi, without New Orleans or Seattle, without Florida or Texas or California, without unified control of the Great Plains, without a secure continental base, free of foreign adversaries, from which to pursue our commerce, protect our national security, and project our power.

With the obvious and very honorable exception of Great Britain, none of the foreign nations we contended with for territory has a consistent track record of competent, liberal governance. As for the Indians, our treatment of them was often shameful, but there was an ineluctable culture clash between premodern, warlike tribal peoples, who by and large wanted to hunt and roam over vast spaces, and a technologically advanced, property-centered civilization. One way or the other, the tribes were going to give way.

Our expansion was truly a national endeavor, driven both from the bottom up, by restless settlers, and from the top down, by the highest strata of the US government. The Spanish governor in Louisiana warned in 1794, correctly, of the "unmeasured am-bition" of the Americans, this "new and vigorous people." They were "advancing and multiplying in the silence of peace," and the authorities should take note: "Their method of spreading them-selves and their policy are as much to be feared by Spain as are their arms."[9]

It was also a nationalist project, concerned with increasing both the reach and the strength of the nation. For a long time, it was a matter of consensus. But the issue of slavery always cast a shadow over the acquisition of new land: Would the resulting new states be slave or free? By the middle of the nineteenth century, the country was riven by contention over slavery, aggravated by conflict over territorial additions.

The defenders of the interests of slavery were committed anti-nationalists. They feared the rise of national institutions and the enhancement of national authority. They viewed the country as fundamentally a collection of sovereign states, and when they believed that the power of the slaveholding South was inevitably being eclipsed by the North, they launched a violent revolution to rip apart both the American nation and nation-state.

This clash gave us Abraham Lincoln, the most important American nationalist besides George Washington. Lincoln be-lieved that we were a nation, bound together by our Constitution, our common history, our ideals, and our geography, not just a compact of states. The Civil War definitively settled the question and established once and for all the standing and legitimacy of the American nation-state. What ensued was one of the foremost nationalist periods in American history, as a newly confident and powerful nation embraced its symbols and history and prepared for greatness.

Land Always Mattered to Us

It's a bit of a mystery why so many intellectuals and politicians are so reluctant to acknowledge the central role of territory in American identity and history. Perhaps they are averse to it for fear of association with the genuinely noxious blood-and-soil nationalism of dark European forces. But the fact is that this has always been a land-hungry, land-obsessed, land-enchanted country that considered itself bigger and better, more beautiful and more blessed, than anywhere else—truly a Promised Land.

In American schools, a nineteenth-century commentator related, "geography was chiefly American, and the United States was larger than all the universe beside." Size mattered. The traveler Elkanah Watson enthused, "What are called mountains in Europe, are hills in America; rivers are reduced to brooks; trees to bushes, and lakes to ponds!" And beauty mattered, too. As the book *The Scenery of the United States* put it, characteristically, "Nowhere else on the globe is Nature lovelier, grander, less austere, and more varied and picturesque, than upon this continent."[10]

Providence had set out what should be our ultimate, more expansive borders and ensured our unity via geography. The New England Unitarian minister Thomas Starr King wrote, "God grooved our noble rivers, and stretched our prairies on their level base, and unrolled our rich savannahs, and reared the prompt of our coasts with generous ocean waves, and wove all these diversities into one, to be the home of no mean people, and the theater of no paltry destiny."[11]

How to handle the West was a major sticking point at the outset of our formal existence, given the fact that Virginia, Georgia, South Carolina, and North Carolina claimed enormous swaths of western territory, whereas other states had no claims whatsoever.[12] Eventually the land got ceded to Congress. The vast Northwest Territory encompassed the future states of Illinois, Indiana, Michigan, Ohio, and Wisconsin, as well as part of Minnesota. The question was what to do with it.[13]

The Northwest Ordinance answered it in 1787. The ordinance was the most consequential congressional act under the Articles of Confederation.[14] It stipulated that once a territory reached a population of 5,000 adult males, it would have an elected assembly and, at 60,000, the chance to become a state, with equal footing as earlier states.[15] It guaranteed the rights of Americans pushing west, drawing on the English Bill of Rights of 1689 and the Massachusetts Constitution for an extensive catalogue that predated the Bill of Rights in the Constitution.[16]

The ordinance became the template for welcoming new states into the Union going forward and is one reason that the United States blew right by the timeworn axiom of Montesquieu: "It is natural for a republic to have only a small territory, otherwise it cannot long subsist."[17]

We Considered European Footholds Here a Threat

The geostrategic imperative associated with expansion was clearing out European powers on our periphery that might challenge us for power on this continent, or at the minimum cause mischief. John Quincy Adams remarked on the "physical, moral, and political absurdity that such fragments of territory, with sovereigns at 1500 miles beyond sea, worthless and burdensome to their owners, should exist permanently contiguous to a great, powerful, enterprising, and rapidly growing nation."[18]

It is in this context that we considered the Louisiana Territory west of the Mississippi. The French had given this immense, strategically vital area to Spain in 1762; then they got it back in 1800, via a secret treaty, in exchange for giving Spain duchies in Italy—a classic old-school European territorial swap.[19] During a momentary pause in his constant warfare with Great Britain, Napoleon hoped to establish a North American empire.[20]

Americans reacted with outrage.[21] Everyone agreed on the importance of access to the Mississippi for American commerce and for binding western settlers to the American nation. In a memo to Washington in September 1790, Hamilton had averred that "when we are able to make good our pretensions, we ought not to leave in the possession of any foreign power, the territories at the mouth of the Mississippi, which are to be regarded as the key to it."[22]

Congress considered sending a force of militiamen to take New Orleans.[23] With war with the British once again looming, Napoleon decided the North American gambit was more trouble than it was worth and dumped all of Louisiana for $15 million, including cash and debt relief.[24]

Jefferson blew by his constitutional qualms and his opposition to increasing the debt.[25] In a stroke, he managed to double the size of the country.[26] He called it, not unjustifiably, "one of the most fortunate events which have taken place since the establishment of our independence."[27]

So much for the French.

The faltering Spanish still held the Floridas, both west (the panhandle) and east (the peninsula).[28] Hamilton believed the United States would take over these territories "by the natural progress of things."[29] He was right, although it took a push.

American settlers rebelled in west Florida in 1810, establishing their own republic and petitioning to join the United States. American forces controlled all of it by 1813. As for east Florida, during the presidency of James Monroe, General Andrew Jackson crossed into the Spanish territory in 1818 to pacify the Seminoles.

The Spaniards objected, but they had little leverage. John Quincy Adams, then secretary of state, tartly observed, "if we should not come to an early conclusion of the Florida negotiation, Spain would not have the possession of Florida to give us."[30]

The Spanish, too, were on the way out.

Manifest Destiny Expressed an Old Nationalist Belief

The American drive west got a rubric in the 1840s, known forevermore as the age of "manifest destiny," the phrase coined by the journalist John L. O'Sullivan and initially made famous—as is often the case—by the mockery of a partisan opponent.[31]

O'Sullivan was a high-spirited man, most of whose plans didn't come to anything. One acquaintance remarked that he was "always full of grand and world-embracing schemes, which seem to him, and which he made to appear to others, vastly practicable and alluring; but which invariably miscarried by reason of some oversight which escaped notice for the very reason that it was so fundamental a one."[32]

He never made it as a businessman or got a plum political position from his exertions promoting the cause of the Democratic Party (although he became minister to Portugal under President Franklin Pierce).[33] He didn't even get historic credit for the phrase now associated with him until 1927. He died unremarked in 1895.[34] But he was a lively and talented editor and journalist.[35]

He cofounded the journal *Democratic Review* to give Jacksonianism, the populism associated with the general and president, a literary voice. It published the likes of Nathaniel Hawthorne, Henry David Thoreau, John Greenleaf Whittier, and Edgar Allan Poe.[36]

O'Sullivan used the phrase "manifest destiny" most famously in an article in a newspaper he also cofounded, the *New York Morning News*.[37] He invoked "the right of our manifest destiny to overspread and to possess the whole of the continent which

Providence has given us for the development of the great experiment of liberty and federated self-government entrusted to us."[38]

He had a vaulting view of democracy ("Christianity in its earthly aspect") and the country's mission ("her high example shall smite unto death the tyranny of kings, hierarchs, and oligarchs"). Expansion was inevitable, our future of extended borders obvious by looking at a map. It would be achieved peaceably and justly by—as he put it in the case of Texas—"The inevitable fulfillment of the general law which is rolling our population westward."[39]

This vision wasn't the least bit new, as we have seen. What O'Sullivan and his allies offered up was a somewhat secularized version of the traditional American belief—a key nationalist belief going back to ancient Israel—that we were a distinct people meant to occupy a particular land.

O'Sullivan's account of the "law" governing our expansion was overly rosy and simplistic but not completely wrong. The tide of American settlement was impossible to stop even if the US government tried, but our expansion relied on more than the peaceful movement of people. It also depended on the machinations of men such as James K. Polk.

Polk Massively Expanded the Country

Polk unexpectedly won the Democratic nomination for president in 1844. Known as "Young Hickory" after he defeated a political adversary of Andrew Jackson in a Tennessee congressional race, he was a thoroughgoing Jacksonian populist.[40] He ran on a platform in 1844 calling for the "re-annexation" of Texas and the "re-occupation" of Oregon.[41] The prefixes were a jibe at John Quincy Adams for abandoning US claims to the territories in negotiations.[42] For his part, Adams was none too impressed with Polk, whom he called "just qualified for an eminent County Court lawyer."[43]

Polk certainly lacked the charisma or eloquence of other giants of the nineteenth century.[44] Yet he added more than 1 million square miles to US territory and extended the country all the way to the Pacific, making him the most successful president not celebrated as part of the American pantheon.[45]

One flash point involved the Oregon Territory. It included the future Canadian province of British Columbia and the future US states of Washington, Oregon, and Idaho, among other territories. Both Great Britain and the United States claimed Oregon and agreed in 1818 on "joint occupancy."[46] This enormous territory didn't have more than forty Americans prior to the early 1840s.[47] Then the explorers and the settlers came, in the most characteristic covered-wagon American migration of the nineteenth century.

In 1843, the largest party yet prepared to cross. Emigrants mustered in Missouri, with 120 wagons and oxen to do the pulling (an admirer of the beasts commented, "The ox will plunge through mud, swim over streams, dive into thickets, and he will eat almost anything"). The great newspaper editor Horace Greeley caviled, "This migration of more than a thousand persons in one body to Oregon wears an aspect of insanity."[48]

That didn't deter anyone. With gunshots at 4:00 a.m. heralding a new start each morning, they traversed up to twenty miles a day across the Great Plains. It was a hard journey, but the emigrants gained in population, with births along the way outnumbering a handful of deaths. According to Steven E. Woodworth, earlier in the year, "settlers already living in Oregon had voted 52–50 to establish a provisional government. The new arrivals increased the number of American settlers in Oregon fivefold." As always, the US government wasn't far behind its venturesome settlers.[49]

Polk adopted a truculent posture towards the British in Oregon, insisting on a boundary of 54 degrees, 40 minutes north, which included everything up to the border of Russian Alaska (hence Ohio senator William Allen's famous rallying cry, "Fifty-four forty or fight!").[50] But when war with Mexico loomed, the affair was wrapped up quickly with a compromise at the 49th parallel.[51] Diplomacy prevailed, in part, because the British were willing to negotiate.[52]

Mexico was another matter.

Mexico Played a Weak Hand Badly

Around the time of its revolution against Spain in 1821, Mexico might have seemed a promising proposition.[53] In 1824, it held 1.7 million square miles and more than 6 million people, not so different from the United States at 1.8 million square miles and more than 9 million people. Three decades later, Mexico had lost more than half its territory, exceeding the extent of the Louisiana Purchase, and the population of the United States was roughly three times as large.[54]

A rot ate away at Mexico's foundations. Underdeveloped, with a vast and desperately poor population of Indians and mestizos, constantly in debt, and riven by extreme factionalism, it was beset by a cycle of coup and countercoup. One Mexican observer believed that its people couldn't demonstrate "a national spirit, for there is no nation."[55]

Our contention with Mexico began over the Mexican province of Tejas. It was supposed to have been part of the Louisiana Purchase, but Spain made a claim to it that the United States recognized in subsequent negotiations. Anglos settled in the province with the encouragement of the Spanish authorities yet never fit in comfortably (lesson: immigration policy matters).

Long estranged from the Mexican government, rebellious Anglos rose up in 1835 with other provinces against the dictatorship of Antonio López de Santa Anna.[56] He marched into Tejas promising to take no prisoners, infamously stayed true to his pledge at the Alamo, then suffered an epic defeat at San Jacinto and got captured despite trying to escape disguised as a private. He recognized Texas as an independent country with a border at the Rio Grande, but the Mexican government didn't, and he revoked his concession as soon as he managed to return home (after a near run with a Texas lynch mob).[57]

There wasn't any doubt what Texans wanted. In 1836, they passed a referendum in favor of annexation by the United States with 97 percent of the vote. Nothing happened for years because

Mexico threatened war over annexation, and the United States was divided over admitting a new slave state. After years of fits and starts and diplomatic maneuvers, including a shrewd flirtation by Texas with the British that, as intended, caught our attention, President John Tyler cut the Gordian knot with a decisive move toward annexation just prior to Polk's inauguration.[58]

Mexico was furious and insisted that its border with Texas was at the Nueces River, two hundred miles north of the Rio Grande. The acting president of Mexico, General José Joaquín de Herrera, ignored an emissary sent by Polk to negotiate, and he was deposed for not being even more harshly dismissive.[59] Polk then sent troops into the area between the Nueces River and the Rio Grande.[60] He thus took the initiative in the disputed territory and pressured Mexico to deal or fight. When 1,600 Mexican cavalry ambushed a party of 63 US dragoons north of the Rio Grande, it was a fight.[61]

And an extraordinarily foolhardy one for Mexico. Many of the officers of the Mexican army were on half pay and not on active duty (a British official considered them "as a Corps, the worst perhaps to be found in any part of the world").[62] The enlisted men were illiterate and bedraggled. They sported firearms that were castoffs from Europe. The country had no navy to speak of. Yet its newspapers pushed for a preemptive war. Mexican politicians beat the drums against America for demagogic purposes, then were unable to take a more realistic tack once in government.[63]

After repeated defeats, a US occupation of its capital, and a farcical final negotiation involving an envoy whom Polk had recalled but who stayed on in Mexico City anyway, Mexico conceded to the United States a border at the Rio Grande, running all the way to the Pacific, giving us California inclusive of San Diego, in exchange for the assumption of Mexico's debts and the price of $15 million.[64]

There's no doubt that Polk had been spoiling for a fight all along. The view of the war as simple US plunder—Ulysses S. Grant denounced the conflict as "the most unjust war ever waged by a stronger against a weaker nation"—is much too simplistic, though.[65]

The historian Robert Merry points out that the United States had a perfect right to deal with Texas once it had achieved independence via an entirely just revolution. "But Mexico said no," he writes, "withdrew its ambassador, cut off relations with the United States, and declared Texas annexation an act of war. That clearly was tempting fate by any reckoning. Then Mexico fired the first shots, inflicted the first casualties, and dared the United States to accept this bloodletting as a natural and acceptable outcome of the dispute."[66]

Then there was the matter of Mexico's debts, which weren't just a pretext. As Merry observes, the French attacked Mexico over reparations and the British threatened military action.[67]

The ultimate disposition reflected the popular will of Texans, whereas there was basically no one in California to have a popular will, although the establishment of republican government and statehood quickly ensued. The people living in these and other territories transferred at the end of the war got political stability, democracy, the rule of law, and a prosperous economic system. Polk, for his part, had done much to complete the territorial outline of the United States, an important symbol of the nation and indispensable contribution to its strength and success.

We Treated the Indians Brutally

Throughout this period, we were steadily pushing the Indians further west and circumscribing their territory, a process that didn't reach its end point until the Wounded Knee Massacre in 1890.[68]

We shouldn't have a saccharine view of the Indians. They did suffer grievously—disease may have killed up to 90 percent of the native population upon contact with whites—but they weren't the peace-loving innocents of contemporary popular imagination.[69] Tribes constantly warred among themselves and tortured captured warriors to death.[70] They fought for territory and hunting rights, for honor and revenge, over women and furs, and for captives to replenish their population.[71] They played geopolitics and allied with or opposed European forces, as they believed suited their interests.[72] To the very end, even as they were pushed against the wall in the wars of the Great Plains later in the nineteenth century, they still fought among themselves.[73]

The pattern of white encroachment was set right at the beginning. A treaty would establish a line between Indians and whites, and white settlement would soon efface it. A 1787 committee report to Congress called out the "avaricious disposition in some of our people to acquire large tracts of land and often by unfair means."[74] The settlers would inevitably have the support of western officials, and the federal government would, as a practical matter, have little choice but to back them as well. This dynamic overwhelmed even the best intentions of national policy makers.[75]

The expectation was that the Indians would steadily fade away as the whites encroached, or adopt the ways of the white man.[76] In 1808, Jefferson told the Mahican diplomat Hendrick Aupaumut, "When once you have property you will want laws & Magistrates to protect your property and persons, and to punish those among you who commit crimes. you will find that our laws are good for this purpose; you will wish to live under them, you will unite yourselves with us, join in our great Councils & form one people with us." He offered this as an alternative to "the gloomy prospect you have drawn of your total disappearance from the face of the earth which is true if you continue to hunt the Deer and buffalo & go to war."[77]

As Robert Kagan explains, Americans had a deeply embedded belief that the right to property was caught up with the improvement of that property, and therefore Indian land claims lacked legitimacy.[78] John Quincy Adams stated this view in an oration at Plymouth in 1802. He said of the Indians, "Their cultivated fields; their constructed habitations; a space of ample sufficiency for their subsistence, and whatever they had annexed to themselves by personal labor, was undoubtedly, by the laws of nature, theirs." Then he asked, "But what is the right of a huntsman to the forest of a thousand miles over which he has accidentally ranged in quest of prey?"[79]

In 1801, Indians occupied most of Tennessee and Georgia and almost all of Mississippi, Alabama, Florida, Indiana, Illinois, Arkansas, and Missouri.[80] This wasn't sustainable. Nor was it realistic for Plains Indians to roam over a vast territory, hunting buffalo, warring among themselves, and ambushing white settlers, thus permanently crimping the spread of the nation across the continent.[81]

It was understandable that the Indians fought us, to try to stop our advance and to defend their civilization. But theirs was a losing battle, militarily and culturally. Even if they had been reliably allocated major landholdings, their way of life was not going to survive competition with the dynamic, churning engine of wealth and power next to them.[82] It is a stain on our national honor that we were so often duplicitous and cruel (not to mention bigoted), yet the alternative of a continent only lightly populated by a nomadic people—as an exploding population representing the cutting edge of Western civilization limited itself to the Eastern Seaboard—wasn't realistic.

Slavery Threatened Westward Expansion and the Union Itself

The real check on US territorial expansion, at least for a time, would be slavery and the contention between the country's sections over its future. The argument over slavery also threatened American nationalism in another of its aspects: the push for a national government competent enough to command the respect of other nations and knit the country together.

This project got a boost after the War of 1812. The United States ended the war feeling a burst of pride, despite the farcical failure of an attempted invasion of Canada and the humiliation of officials having to flee Washington as the British burned down the seat of the US government.[83] We had acquitted ourselves well enough, all things considered (in other words, taking into account financial embarrassments, an utterly inadequate military, and nearly catastrophic political dysfunction as New England Federalists flirted with secession). An overriding lesson, though, was that the Jeffersonian vision of barely existent national institutions sitting atop a growing continental power was incompatible with the exigencies of government and warfare in the real world.[84] We had learned that going to war with a major European power while lacking a strong navy (the frugal Jefferson didn't want to spend money on it) was a very bad idea.[85]

The United States embarked on what became known as an "age of nationalism." According to Albert Gallatin, the Treasury secretary under presidents Jefferson and Madison, his countrymen emerged after the war with "more general objects of attachment with which their pride and political opinions are connected. They are more Americans; they feel and act more as a nation."[86]

Supreme Court justice Joseph Story enthused after the war, "Let us extend the national authority over the whole extent of power given by the Constitution. Let us have great military and naval schools; an adequate regular army; the broad foundations laid of a permanent navy; a National bank; a National system of bankruptcy; a great navigation act; a general survey of our ports, and appointments of port wardens and pilots; Judicial courts which shall embrace the whole constitutional powers; National notaries; public and national justices of the peace, for the commercial and national concerns of the United States."[87]

For about a decade, that vision held sway, and even his erstwhile opponents ended up adopting a version of the hated Alexander Hamilton's nationalizing program. What was for a time a kind of national consensus blew up with the Jacksonian revolution targeting financial and eastern interests and with the fight over slavery. The South worried that if the federal government was strong enough to do anything of much significance, it would be strong enough to act against the peculiar institution.[88]

Lincoln the Nationalist Saved the Country

Taking office in the midst of a great secession crisis in 1861, Abraham Lincoln confronted and answered three questions: Would the country survive? Would it establish, once and for all, that it was truly a unified nation-state and not a league of dozens of sovereign states? Would it pursue nationalizing policies to draw the country together economically and populate the rest of the continent with a free, educated people? Yes, yes, and yes.

A former Whig and pioneering Republican, Lincoln was a nationalist in every dimension: in his sentiment, which reflected the near ancestor worship of the American nationalist for the country's Founders; in his economic program, which always hewed to the nationalizing premises of his Whig hero Henry Clay's American System of internal improvements; and, most important, in his view of the nature of our government as an inviolable national union.

Like other Whigs, including Henry Clay, he balked at continued territorial expansion when he believed that it would only extend the ambit of slavery. He fiercely opposed the Mexican-American War as a congressman and attacked it as a partisan Democratic plot.[89] But his unionism crossed party lines and shared the same premises as that of Andrew Jackson, a figure who was anathema to the Whigs and whose politics Lincoln had otherwise opposed his entire adult life.

Prior to his first inaugural, he consulted Jackson's proclamation of 1832, a detailed, forceful, and persuasive demolition of the doctrine of nullification—South Carolina had wanted to nullify the tariff of 1828—that deserves to be remembered as one of the great state papers in American history.[90] He delivered his address from the East Portico of the US Capitol, after entering the building through a passageway specially fashioned to prevent any assassination attempt, and made the case for a deeply grounded, indissoluble union.[91]

He argued that the union was permanent by the very nature of the thing: "I hold, that in contemplation of universal law, and of the Constitution, the Union of these States is perpetual. Perpetuity is implied, if not expressed, in the fundamental law of all national governments."

He located its source in a bond more enduring than any one document: "The Union is much older than the Constitution. It was formed in fact, by the Articles of Association in 1774. It was matured and continued by the Declaration of Independence in 1776. It was further matured and the faith of all the then thirteen States expressly plighted and engaged that it should be perpetual, by the Articles of Confederation in 1778. And, finally, in 1787, one of the declared objects for ordaining and establishing the Constitution was 'to form a more perfect Union.'"

He then made a geographical case for the integrity of the nation: "Physically speaking, we cannot separate. We cannot remove our respective sections from each other, nor build an impassable wall between them."

Finally, he famously invoked a historical and cultural connection embedded in the feelings of Americans and in their land: "The mystic chords of memory, stretching from every battlefield and patriot grave to every living heart and hearthstone all over this broad land, will yet swell the chorus of the Union, when again touched, as surely they will be, by the better angels of our nature."[92]

For Lincoln, the nation always came first, even before his antislavery convictions. In 1845, he urged his fellow free soilers to leave slavery undisturbed where it already existed, for the greater good: "I hold it to be a paramount duty of us in the free states, due to the Union of the states, and perhaps to liberty itself (paradox though it may seem) to let the slavery of the other states alone."[93]

He explained in an 1854 speech, "Much as I hate slavery, I would consent to the extension of it rather than see the Union dissolved, just as I would consent to any GREAT evil, to avoid a GREATER one."[94]

This remained his hierarchy of values throughout the war. As he put it in a letter to the abolitionist newspaper editor Horace Greeley in 1862, "My paramount object in this struggle *is* to save the Union, and is *not* either to save or to destroy slavery. If I could save the Union without freeing *any* slave I would do it, and if I could save it by freeing all the slaves I would do it; and if I could save it by freeing some and leaving others alone I would do that."[95]

This wasn't quite as unsparingly tough-minded as it sounded, since Lincoln thought that an antislavery view inhered in the nation. If the Union could be preserved, eventually slavery would be eliminated. What happened over the course of the war was that Lincoln came to see abolition as a war measure that would itself help the battle to preserve the nation. This in turn, put an accent on his universalism.

Lincoln had always believed in our chosenness, although with a characteristic note of modesty that elevated his statesmanship. In a famous line in a talk to the New Jersey Senate on his way to Washington in 1861, he said he'd be happy to be an instrument "in the hands of the Almighty, and of this, His almost chosen people."[96] Lincoln wasn't an orthodox believer, but he was soaked in the Bible, and Providence figured prominently in his speeches, in terms redolent of the Israel of the Old Testament. He spoke in his first inaugural address of "Him, who has never yet forsaken this favored land."[97] As the historian Melvin Endy, Jr., archly observed, "One looks in vain for any admission on Lincoln's part that God might manage without a unified United States."[98]

Like the prophets, Lincoln believed that the nation could fall short of its obligations and suffer chastisement from God. And like the prophets, he joined the universal and the particular. The great Lincoln interpreter Harry V. Jaffa noted how he took Jefferson's Declaration and changed its iteration: "Lincoln transforms a truth open to each man as man into something he shares in virtue of his partnership in the nation."[99]

Lincoln's wartime rhetoric, especially the Gettysburg Address, is often cited by proponents of the notion that America is merely an idea. But there was a profoundly organic element to Lincoln's nationalism. He always spoke reverently of our "fathers." As president, he referred to our territory as "the national homestead." He initially favored the word *Union*, or some variant of it, when speaking of the country, but over time, he increasingly used the word *nation*. At Gettysburg, in a speech suffused with the language of birth, death, and renewal, he used only the word *nation*. At the end of the second inaugural, he spoke of binding up "the nation's wounds" and achieving "a just and lasting peace among ourselves and with all nations."[100]

In his martyrdom, Lincoln himself became part of the deeper glue of the nation. Across two weeks in seven states, from Washington, DC, to Springfield, Illinois, 1.5 million Americans saw his body and 7 million his coffin in a remarkable display of national mourning. As the train carrying his casket passed, people stood by the tracks bearing torches or doffed their hats and bowed their heads where they stood.

A speaker at the American Historical Society declared, "Before we were bound by the memories of our fathers—now the blood of the martyred president binds us."[101] Walt Whitman said in a lecture titled "Death of Abraham Lincoln": "Then there is a cement to the whole people, subtler, more underlying, than any thing in written constitution, or courts or armies—namely, the cement of a death identified thoroughly with that people, at his head, and for its sake."[102]

Also standing for our nationality was the flag, which had its apotheosis during the war. Its status at Fort Sumter was a prominent part of the negotiations with the Confederates prior to their assault. When they eventually surrendered, Union forces were allowed to hoist and salute the flag, before taking it with them. It was kept at the Metropolitan Bank in New York and borrowed by the Sanitary Commission for events around the country for fundraisers to help the troops.[103]

The firing on the flag at Fort Sumter had an electric effect in the

North. Such was the demand for flags that the price of the material used to make them, bunting, increased fourfold in New York City. "Every city, town, and village suddenly blossomed with banners," the redoubtable flag historian George Preble wrote. "On forts and ships, from church-spires and flag-staffs, from colleges, hotels, storefronts and private balconies, from public edifices, everywhere the old flag was flung out, and everywhere it was hailed with enthusiasm; for its prose became poetry, and there was seen in it a sacred value which it had never before possessed."[104]

Northerners sometimes referred to the conflict as the "War Against the Flag." Color sergeants risked life and limb carrying the flag in the battle and keeping it flying and out of enemy hands. Seven corporals of the 99th Pennsylvania Volunteer Infantry died protecting the flag at Gettysburg, right around the spot where Lincoln gave his address. At the Battle of Fredericksburg, one sergeant in the 5th New Hampshire Volunteer Infantry's color guard was wounded and handed the flag over to another sergeant, who was wounded and handed it over to yet another sergeant, who took the flag to a mortally wounded captain so he could die with it in his arms.[105]

The cult of the flag only grew in the postwar period and lives on today in the country's extraordinary devotion to its national banner.

The War Settled the Question of the Legitimacy of the American Nation-State

Much more significantly, the war settled the question of American nationhood. As Massachusetts senator Charles Sumner, a Radical Republican, declared (in an overstatement), "Among us in the earlier day there was no occasion for the word Nation, there is now. A Nation is born."[106]

The South had invented its own purported nationalism whose ultimate source was the defense of slavery. Otherwise, the region had the same history, language, Founders, and political system as the North and had no obvious, natural geographical boundaries. This Southern nationalism was strong enough to sustain a war effort for years but ultimately collapsed.

The war gave American nationalism an unmistakable northern iteration. The region's financially sophisticated, industrializing version of capitalism grew all the stronger; Congress passed a Hamiltonian program to buttress this system and encouraged the further settlement of the West (via the Homestead Act and the Land-Grant College Act, as well as plans for a transcontinental railroad); and the antislavery ideals of the North achieved ascendancy.

The historian Kevin Phillips interprets the war against the backdrop of the English Civil War and the American Revolution, which he calls the "cousins' wars"; the people who had such an outsized role in forging America's national identity in the first place prevailed yet again. "The U.S. Civil War," he writes, "was another great watershed in which victory went to a zealous, skilled, and destiny-minded minority—the principal cadre of which just happened to be descended from the intense and grasping Puritan and Yankee minority that had also been the largest single force on the two previous cousins' wars."[107]

The Civil War and its aftermath also brought—though incomplete and incompletely realized—an effort to extend rights to blacks, whose racist repression was the country's great original sin. The Reconstruction amendments abolished slavery and notionally guaranteed the vote and due process rights to blacks. Of course, the resistance of the southern states and the lagging commitment of the national government rendered much of that shamefully moot into the 1960s.

The Union Army Defended and Drew Together the Nation

At the end of the day, the Union beat the Confederacy not with its ideals (which were important in their own right) but through its superior industrial and financial might—and foremost, an army that ground its Confederate adversary to dust. The Union Army was, historian Peter Parish writes, "one of the most potent agencies of American nationalism." It not only took troops to "places and people hitherto remote, but now fixed in their minds as part of the same American nation to which they belonged." It loomed especially large at the end of the war.[108]

On May 23, 1865, two hundred thousand people crowded Pennsylvania Avenue for a grand review of the nation's victorious troops. One journalist called it "the greatest military pageant ever witnessed on this American continent," without exaggeration.[109] It took two days of parading for 150,000 Union soldiers in a twenty-five-mile-long column to file by the US Capitol, the Treasury, and a presidential reviewing stand.[110]

The blue-uniformed troops represented every place in the North. "Looking up the broad Pennsylvania avenue," an Associated Press reporter recalled, "there was a continuous moving line as far as the eye could reach of National, State, division, brigade, regiment and other flags." But they marched as one. "When I reached the Treasury-building, and looked back," General Sherman wrote in his memoir, "the sight was simply magnificent. The column was compact, and the glittering muskets looked like a solid mass of steel, moving with the regularity of a pendulum."[111]

It was a remarkable display of national power and unity, the likes of which no one had seen before. The parade itself exemplified challenges to come: black regiments were excluded, and so, of course, were Confederate soldiers. The army that had made such an impression was about to dissolve and go home. But the country had been saved and was now on the path to greatness, toward becoming an industrial juggernaut and continental nation of immense scope whose ideals and power would decisively shape the century ahead.[112]

And none of it would have been possible without an ambitious, determined, inspired American nationalism.

CHAPTER 9

THE TRIUMPH OF
THE TWENTIETH CENTURY

By George! Did you ever see such a fleet and such a day?"
Teddy Roosevelt asked the wholly rhetorical question of
his secretary of the navy, Victor Metcalf. The object of Roosevelt's
delight was the US battle fleet on December 16, 1907, in Hampton Roads, Virginia, preparing to undertake a voyage around the
world.[1] The ships were painted a gleaming peacetime white and
would be known to history as the Great White Fleet. From the
vantage point of his presidential yacht, Roosevelt watched as the
ships, in a three-mile-long line, to the traditional ditty upon setting
sail, "The Girl I Left Behind Me," steamed into the open sea and
toward Cape Horn.[2]

Tensions with Japan were the proximate cause of the movement of the fleet. Growing Japanese immigration to California
had stoked nativist opposition, including the segregation of Japanese students in the public schools. Feeling its oats after its smashing victory in the Russo-Japanese War, Tokyo objected and the
opposition party in Japan even called for war.

US naval intelligence warned that the Japanese were purchas-
ing a dreadnought from the British and other armored ships from
Europe. With all the American battleships in the Atlantic, Admi-
ral George Dewey worried that in the event of hostilities it would

take ninety days or more for the fleet to transfer to the Pacific: "Japan could, in the meantime, capture the Philippines, Honolulu, and be master of the sea."[3]

A naval enthusiast of long standing whose Harvard thesis became a book on the naval battles of the War of 1812, Roosevelt decided to send the fleet to San Francisco.[4] Did the British and Germans doubt we could pull it off? "Time to have a showdown in the matter." How many battleships should go? Why, all sixteen of them, of course. The idea, although it wasn't immediately announced, expanded from sending the fleet to the Pacific to sending it on a "practice cruise around the world."[5]

At the time, no other country had attempted a venture on the scale of the Great White Fleet, and the 43,000-mile trip, with twenty globe-spanning ports of call, came off without a hitch.[6] The fleet became a worldwide media sensation. Wherever it stopped, it made friends. Even the Japanese welcomed it (the so-called Gentleman's Agreement had reduced the flash point of immigration with the United States).[7] The cruise taught us lessons about refueling and gunnery.[8] It is regarded, as an account by naval historians relates, as "one of the greatest peacetime achievements of the U.S. Navy."[9]

Fourteen months after it had sailed, Theodore Roosevelt returned to Hampton Roads, once again in an ebullient mood, this time welcoming back the triumphant fleet. "That is the answer to my critics," he declared.[10] We'd come a long way from the Jeffersonian resistance to a strong navy.

TR Set the Stage for Twentieth-Century Nationalism

Theodore Roosevelt was the characteristic American of the early twentieth century and a thoroughgoing nationalist who exulted in his country. He loved its history, its land, and its people, and he wanted to muster its power. His venturesome self-confidence captured the mood of a nation on the verge of greatness. A big-

game hunter, boxer, ornithologist, outdoorsman, occasional cowboy, author, and journalist, TR contained multitudes.[11] He led
the Rough Riders into battle in the Spanish-American War and
wrote about forty books. He read Tolstoy while chasing down
boat thieves out west.[12] One biographer wrote that to be part of
Roosevelt's entourage "was to travel in a carnival led by a conjurer
and trailed by an idolatrous throng."[13]

The son of a patrician family, he graduated from Harvard and
plunged into politics, rising from the New York State Assembly to
become New York City police commissioner, then to the highest
office in the land at age forty-two in 1901 after an assassin killed
President William McKinley.[14]

Neither conservatives nor liberals can fully embrace him. Conservatives have no use for the way Roosevelt lurched to the left after leaving office and championed a progressive vision that would
eventually lead to an overweening administrative state. Liberals
find his hypermasculine advocacy of the strenuous life ridiculous
and offensive to PC sensibilities. Roosevelt partook of the preju-
dices of his time and reflected some of its worst intellectual influences, particularly Social Darwinism. But he understood the
appeal and the importance of the nation.

"There are philosophers," he wrote in 1894, "who assure us
that, in the future, patriotism will be regarded not as a virtue at
all, but merely as a mental stage in the journey toward a state of
feeling when our patriotism will include the whole human race
and all the world." He found that fantastical: "It may be, that in
ages so remote that we cannot now understand any of the feelings
of those who will dwell in them, patriotism will no longer be regarded as a virtue, exactly as it may be that in those remote ages
people look down upon and disregard monogamic marriage."
(Little did he know.) But for now, and for thousands in years in the
past and thousands in the future, he insisted, "the words *home* and
country mean a great deal."[15]

Roosevelt set the stage for the American nationalism that defined much of the twentieth century. As a newly potent force in

the world, the United States took an outsized role in preserving and creating the international system of nation-states as we know it, first under Woodrow Wilson and then under FDR. It mustered every ounce of its unity and power to beat the Nazis and imperial Japan in World War II and worked to loosen the grip of western colonialism. Confronted with a new totalitarian empire in the form of the Soviet Union, it pushed relentlessly for the self-determination of the captive nations held by Moscow. Across the decades, a democratic nationalism was one of the baselines of US foreign policy.

Our nationalism at home, buttressed not just by government but by popular culture, didn't create the hellscape one would expect if the critics of nationalism are correct. There were grievous injustices (the internment of the Japanese) and anti-Communist excesses (the Joseph McCarthy investigations), but the pressure of war has, unfortunately, led to abuses of civil liberties throughout our history. In the broadest sense, the mid–twentieth century in America was a golden age, with a consensus nationalism providing the foundation for our cohesion and dynamism.

Some of the proudest achievements of the era were nationalistic. The moon shot was a national challenge, undertaken in part as a matter of national pride, festooned with national symbols. The civil rights movement leveraged the country's nationalism to finally, fully extend the rights and privileges of American citizens to blacks.

The beginning of our discontent wasn't nationalism but its breakdown in the 1970s. The power of Ronald Reagan in the 1980s was tapping into nationalistic sentiments (and, obviously, pursuing successful policies) to restore a sense of national pride. That both FDR and Reagan could access the American nationalist tradition and make use of it for their own purposes shows how broad and mainstream that tradition is, even if we are told by anti-nationalists on both the left and the right that we must turn our back on it.

Conservation Preserved the Nation's Natural Patrimony

TR's nationalism can be seen starkly, and admirably, in his push for the conservation of our natural wonders, insistence on assimilation of immigrants, and consistent advocacy of military preparedness.

Roosevelt loved the West. A spell in the Badlands of the Dakota Territory as a young man had been formative for him, and he wrote a series of books on ranching and hunting.[16] He didn't lose his taste for outdoor adventure as president. He loved climbing and swimming along Rock Creek in Washington, DC, warning those he invited along to bring their "worst clothes."[17] On a trip to the Oklahoma Territory, he thrashed to death a rattlesnake that lunged at him, using an eighteen-inch quirt for the task.[18] On a trip to Yellowstone National Park, he desperately wanted to shoot a cougar, courting a public backlash, until friends talked him out of the plan.[19]

The Yellowstone visit was a leg of his famous "Great Loop Tour" in 1903 to promote his conservation agenda. He toured the park with the renowned naturalist John Burroughs, who said of Roosevelt, "Nothing escaped him, from bears to mice, from wild geese to chickadees, from elk to red squirrels; he took it all in."[20] Literally nothing escaped him; at one point TR jumped from a sled to capture a vole that he thought might be a new species. He stuffed it and sent it to the Smithsonian.[21]

The president gave a speech at the north entrance to the park upon laying the cornerstone for an archway inscribed FOR THE BENEFIT AND ENJOYMENT OF THE PEOPLE. He called the park "a great natural playground" and argued, "The only way that the people as a whole can secure to themselves and their children the enjoyment in perpetuity of what the Yellowstone Park has to give, is by assuming the ownership in the name of the nation and by jealously safeguarding and preserving the scenery, the forests, and the wild creatures."[22]

On the south rim of the Grand Canyon, he gave a talk to Arizonans that touched on similar themes. "I hope you will not have a building of any kind, not a summer cottage, a hotel, or anything else, to mar the wonderful grandeur, the sublimity, the great loneliness and beauty of the canyon," he said. "Leave it as it is. You cannot improve on it; not a bit. The ages have been at work on it, and man can only mar it. . . . keep it for your children and your children's children and for all who come after you, as one of the great sights which every American if he can travel at all should see."[23]

In Yosemite, he toured the sequoias with naturalist John Muir. Roosevelt ditched a dinner in his honor at the Wawona Hotel to camp under the well-known tree called Grizzly Giant. The next night they camped out again and it snowed. TR approved—"We were in a snowstorm last night," he told people the next day, "and it was just what I wanted."[24]

Altogether, Roosevelt had conserved more than 230 million acres by the end of his presidency. He established six national parks, created eighteen national monuments, including the Grand Canyon, set aside fifty-one federal bird preserves, and designated or expanded one-hundred fifty national forests.[25] He didn't oppose development. But he believed that the nation is not merely a collection of individuals in the present; its natural treasures, the jewels of its landscape, should be held in trust for future generations.

TR Realized the Importance of Assimilation

Roosevelt also had a view of immigration that emphasized what we held in common. He believed deeply in assimilation and a cohesive culture at a time when America was roiled by a historic influx of new immigrants, especially a wave from Germany that became particularly large in the run-up to World War I.

He wasn't immune to the bigotry of the time. He supported the 1882 Chinese Exclusion Act, explaining that "the Chinaman is kept out because the democracy, with much clearness of vision, has seen that his presence is ruinous to the white race."[26] But he wasn't, despite such terrible blind spots, a nativist. "Let us remember that the question of being a good American," he declared in his fourth annual message as president in 1904, "has nothing whatever to do with a man's birthplace."[27] Nor did he disdain immigrant communities.

As New York City police commissioner, he angered German Americans with strict enforcement of laws against Sunday drinking (not that he was against drinking, but he felt that he had to enforce the law on the books). The German Americans held a protest march and whimsically invited the offending police commissioner. He gladly accepted and enjoyed himself in a position of prominence on the reviewing stand, delighting the crowd by replying to a passing marcher who asked, "Wo ist der Roosevelt?" with the exclamation "Hier bin ich!"[28]

He was adamant, nonetheless, that we, not the immigrants, set the terms of entry and life in this country. He called for "Americans, pure and simple," and advocated an "intense and fervid Americanism" as the "one quality which we must bring to the solution of every problem."[29]

He set out his views at length in an essay published in a magazine called *The Forum* in April 1894.[30] "We must Americanize them in every way," he wrote of newcomers, "in speech, in political ideas and principles, and in their way of looking at the relations between Church and State."[31]

"We welcome the German or the Irishman who becomes an American," he averred. "We have no use for the German or Irishman who remains such." He continued, "We believe that English, and no other language, is that in which all the school exercises should be conducted." (In another context, he called English the "language of Washington and Lincoln.")[32]

"He must revere," he said of the immigrant, "only our flag; not only must it come first, but no other flag should even come second. He must learn to celebrate Washington's birthday rather than that of the Queen or Kaiser, and the Fourth of July instead of St. Patrick's Day."[33]

In short, he declared, if immigrants "remain alien elements, un-assimilated, and with interests separate from ours, they are mere obstructions to the current of our national life, and, moreover, can get no good from it themselves."[34]

This is a strong, principled, high-toned voice for what the historian John Fonte has called *patriotic assimilation*.[35] It remains highly relevant today (more about that in a subsequent chapter), and should stand as a guide for how to think about immigration for anyone who believes we are a people and not an abstraction.

TR's Foreign Policy Outlined the Duties of a Great Power

On foreign policy, too, Roosevelt's views weren't for the faint of heart. He partook of the renewed post–Civil War push for Manifest Destiny that called for overseas possessions and led, notably, to a poorly justified and brutal war in the Philippines (nationalism should never justify ruling another people). His robust views could fade into militarism. He flirted with the belief that war in and of itself is a good thing, declaring in 1897, "No triumph of peace is quite so great as the supreme triumph of war."[36]

Whatever his excesses, though, he was ultimately a realist in the Hamiltonian tradition. He believed, rightly, that conflict is endemic among nations and that military strength is necessary to deter it or, should it come to that, win it.

He blamed Jefferson's opposition to a strong, capable navy for the onset of the War of 1812.[37] He took as his axiom a line of George Washington, "To be prepared for war is the most effectual means to promote peace."[38] The ultimate goal, as he put it in his famous 1901 "big stick" speech, was "that self-respecting peace, the attainment of which is and must ever be the prime aim of a self-governing people."

As president, he enhanced the country's role on the world stage, and not just with the Great White Fleet. He brokered the peace in the Russo-Japanese War, becoming the first US president to win a

Nobel Prize. He also negotiated a settlement of a dispute between France and Germany over control of Morocco. He extended the 1823 Monroe Doctrine from its original formulation that warned against European intervention with a corollary that made the United States the "policeman" of the Western Hemisphere and asserted the right to intervene in the affairs of Latin American countries so misgoverned that they might invite European meddling.[39]

In 1906, he became the first president to travel out of the country, to visit Panama at the time of the construction of the canal that he had done so much to promote, taking the controls of a steam shovel for a jaunty photograph. The largest building project in US history, the canal linked the Atlantic and Pacific oceans, boosting commerce and easing US naval operations by cutting the trip from San Francisco to New York by eight thousand miles. It was yet another sign of the arrival of the United States as a world power.[40]

Roosevelt clearly understood the role of America in the twentieth century. "Whether we wish it or not," he said in his "big stick" speech, "we cannot avoid hereafter having duties to do in the face of other nations. All that we can do is to settle whether we shall perform these duties well or ill."

His nationalism inclined him to want to do them well.

The Progressive Welfare State Was Fundamentally about Statism

Roosevelt left office in 1909. He eventually became disenchanted with his handpicked successor, William Howard Taft, and split from him under the banner of "the New Nationalism." The phrase was associated with the journalist Herbert Croly, who wrote a seminal document of progressivism, *The Promise of American Life*, and cofounded the magazine *The New Republic* as its tribune.

The progressivism that Croly outlined had little respect for the Founding Fathers or American traditions, hoping to take a leap beyond them and the system of government they had created. It hoped to perfect human nature and to establish an enlightened administration of experts and redistribute the nation's wealth, enhancing federal power along the way. This program traveled under the banner of neo-Hamiltonianism, although it went well beyond Hamilton's project of building a nation-state strong enough to provide public goods and instead sought the creation of a regulatory behemoth and sprawling federal welfare state.

Croly's book pointed to TR as the figure who could take up the progressive charge, and Roosevelt, who had already dabbled in this agenda as president, rose to the challenge.[41] Croly helped draft Roosevelt's famous New Nationalism speech in Osawatomie, Kansas, declaring war on his own party and Taft's conservatism.[42]

Running for president as the nominee of the Progressive Party, Roosevelt split the Republican vote in 1912, paving Woodrow Wilson's path to victory. The former Princeton University president adopted much of the Roosevelt agenda once in office, and federal power increased vastly under the pressure of World War I. Most of it washed out again when the war ended and Republicans regained power, only to be picked up by FDR during the Great Depression.[43]

Franklin D. Roosevelt used nationalist symbols to try to boost support for his program, especially the blue eagle for the misbegotten National Recovery Administration, which was struck down by the Supreme Court. Yet, tellingly, the welfare and regulatory state that emerged would be defended decades later by cosmopolitan progressives strenuously opposed to nationalism— for them, it is the sheer statism that truly matters.

Both Wilson and FDR Supported National Self-Determination

Wilson and FDR had something else in common besides their progressive domestic policies: both took the country to war in a global conflict, and both hewed to an anti-imperialist agenda of national self-determination. In this regard, both Wilson and Roosevelt were nationalists in the best sense, recognizing the importance of peoples governing themselves free of outside impositions.

Wilson enunciated his Fourteen Points, his program for peace after World War I, in an address to Congress in January 1918. He elaborated on the concept of self-determination in a subsequent congressional speech. "Peoples," he said, "are not to be handed about from one sovereignty to another by an international conference or an understanding between rivals and antagonists. National aspirations must be respected; peoples may now be dominated and governed only by their own consent."[44]

The vaulting idealism of Wilson's vision was a secularized form of the age-old belief in American chosenness, transported to the international stage and supplemented with Wilson's signature lack of realism. "America is the only national idealistic force in the world," he believed, "and idealism is going to save the world. Selfishness will embroil it."[45] Wilson thought this was the role America had been preparing for ever since the Founders "set up a new nation in the high and honorable hope that it might in all that it was and did show mankind the way to liberty." It was, he maintained, "the hand of God who led us into this way."[46]

Wilson hoped to bring forth an international system indistinguishable from domestic civil society. The unachievability of this and much else in his program occasioned eye-rolling from Wilson's peers. French leader Georges Clemenceau observed archly, "God gave us his Ten Commandments and we broke them. Wilson gave us his Fourteen Points—we shall see."[47]

Wilson arrived in Europe in December 1918 as a conquering hero, with peasants kneeling in prayer besides the tracks of his train in France and 2 million people cheering him in Paris.[48] His concept of self-determination foundered nonetheless. It was too vague (his own secretary of state wondered, "What unit has he in mind? Does he mean a race, a territorial area, or a community?").[49] The European and Japanese empires weren't going anywhere, regardless of what Wilson said or believed.[50] And the welter of ethnicities in central Europe weren't neatly demarcated by any national boundaries.

Wilson's project was also undone by his own rigidity and moralism. He couldn't abide domestic interference in his international handiwork, the Treaty of Versailles and the accompanying League of Nations. He considered opposition to be "disloyalty."[51]

Teddy Roosevelt died in January 1919, before the Senate debate over the League reached a conclusion later in the year, but he had opposed it in favor of the alliance with Great Britain and France. He didn't want the United States to become "an international Meddlesome Matty" and declared, "I am insisting upon Nationalism against Internationalism."[52] The influential Republican senator Henry Cabot Lodge believed that the treaty substituted "an international state for pure Americanism."[53] Lodge objected to Article X, which committed signatories to defending the territorial integrity of all members of the League. He bogged down consideration of the treaty—he spent two weeks reading its text aloud—and proposed reservations, including, most importantly, that the United States wouldn't go to any other member state's defense without congressional approval.[54] Lodge wasn't an isolationist, and this reservation constituted a basic protection of American sovereignty.[55] Rather than accept an amended treaty, though, Wilson preferred to have no treaty at all.

That's what he got.

Wilson's influence was still profound. Thereafter, the international mission of the United States was expressed in terms of spreading not white Christian civilization but democracy and human rights.[56] Wilsonianism became the argot of US foreign policy, although not without a cost in idealistic overreaching. Wilson's program roughly foreshadowed what would become the norm later in the twentieth century in much of the developed world, namely national self-determination and respect for the sovereignty of the world's nation-states.

Franklin Roosevelt didn't have any more use for imperialism

than Wilson did. FDR insisted in 1942, "The colonial system means war." He told his son that Americans wouldn't be dying in the Pacific "if it hadn't been for the shortsighted greed of the French and the British and the Dutch."[57] His opposition to colonialism was a constant flash point with Winston Churchill, who the president believed was "mid-Victorian" on the question.[58]

Yet Roosevelt forged a close relationship with Churchill and, in a shipboard meeting off Newfoundland in 1941 before the United States was in the war, agreed with him on eight points that became known as the Atlantic Charter. The statement oriented the Allied war aims around a democratic nationalism. It swore off "aggrandizement, territorial or other," and opposed "territorial changes that do not accord with the freely expressed wishes of the peoples concerned." It made clear its respect for "the right of all peoples to choose the form of government under which they will live" and stipulated its "wish to see sovereign rights and self government restored to those who have been forcibly deprived of them."

The Charter referred to a "wider and permanent system of general security," the seed of the United Nations. The new organization would resemble the League of Nations, except that it didn't attempt to short-circuit the constitutional processes of its members.[59] Notably, the United Nations would prove to be almost worthless as an institution. Its pretensions to world government were ridiculous, and its ability to act in any true crisis that divided the great powers nonexistent. A poisonous ideological hostility to the Western nations most jealous of their sovereignty, namely the United States and Israel, would pervade much of its work.

But that was in the future.

World War II Brought an Era of Consensus Nationalism

Uncharacteristically in American history, World War II didn't occasion roiling dissension and protest. FDR didn't impose the shameful repressive measures on domestic dissent that Wilson had in World War I, with the hideous exception of his internment of Japanese Americans. The war was a time of great common national purpose.

As FDR said of himself, Dr. New Deal gave way to Dr. Win the War. He no longer inveighed against "economic royalists" or brayed for economic warfare.[60] He became the voice of national determination and ideals in a confrontation with foreign aggression and evil.

His third inaugural address in January 1941 was a meditation on the American nation under the threat of a looming war. "On each national day of Inauguration since 1789," he said, "the people have renewed their sense of dedication to the United States. In Washington's day the task of the people was to create and weld together a nation. In Lincoln's day the task of the people was to preserve that nation from disruption from within. In this day the task of the people is to save that nation and its institutions from disruption from without."

"Lives of nations," FDR observed, "are determined not by the count of years, but by the lifetime of the human spirit. The life of a man is three-score years and ten: a little more, a little less. The life of a nation is the fullness of the measure of its will to live." He extended the argument: "A nation, like a person, has something deeper, something more permanent, something larger than the sum of all its parts. It is that something which matters most to its future—which calls forth the most sacred guarding of its present."

"If," he continued, "we lose that sacred fire—if we let it be smothered with doubt and fear—then we shall reject the destiny which Washington strove so valiantly and so triumphantly to establish. The preservation of the spirit and faith of the nation does, and will, furnish the highest justification for every sacrifice that we may make in the cause of national defense."[61]

In a radio address on June 6, 1944, as American troops were storming Normandy, FDR delivered a stirring prayer that is one of the rhetorical highpoints of American nationalism: "Almighty

God: Our sons, pride of our nation, this day have set upon a mighty endeavor, a struggle to preserve our Republic, our religion, and our civilization, and to set free a suffering humanity." He explained that "Many people have urged that I call the nation into a single day of special prayer. But because the road is long and the desire is great, I ask that our people devote themselves in a continuance of prayer." Near the end, he implored, "And, O Lord, give us Faith. Give us Faith in Thee; Faith in our sons; Faith in each other; Faith in our united crusade. Let not the keenness of our spirit ever be dulled."[62]

Roosevelt spoke for his countrymen, who united around the cause of preserving, in his phrase, the sacred fire. Americans purchased 85 million war bonds, at a time when the adult population was about 95 million people, raising more than $185 billion. Everyone from individuals to corporations to trade unions pitched in, including the full spectrum of ethnic groups. In 1944, purchases by black Americans may have accounted for more than $1 billion.[63]

The rate of naturalization spiked. About 40 percent of the alien population became citizens during the war.[64]

The sense of unity began, if slowly, to erode the system of racial discrimination. "The new nationalism," Lewis A. Erenberg and Susan E. Hirsch write, "not only had to include African Americans because of that group's growing political power, but also encouraged blacks and other minorities to demand their birthright as Americans and to resist attempts to suppress their awakened American identity."[65] Demonstrators outside a segregated Washington, DC, restaurant captured the attitude, with signs declaring WE DIE TOGETHER. LET'S EAT TOGETHER.[66]

The great civil rights leader A. Philip Randolph planned a march of 100,000 blacks down Pennsylvania Avenue in 1941 to protest employment segregation and demand the integration of the military. FDR wanted to avoid the march and so signed Executive Order 8802 banning discrimination in defense industries.[67] Compared to the vast sea of injustice suffered by blacks in America, the order was a drop in the bucket, but it was something. The desegregation of the military would have to await the end of the war and finally occurred in 1948 under Harry Truman.[68]

Pop culture supported the national effort on all fronts. In the movies, old class and ethnic conflicts were put aside. The now-clichéd geographically and ethnically mixed military unit appeared in films such as *Bataan, Sahara,* and *The Fighting 69th.*[69] In the 1944 Alfred Hitchcock film *Lifeboat,* diverse survivors from a luxury liner sunk by a German submarine struggle to cohere and eventually succeed, in a metaphor of a pluralistic society pulling together.[70]

Comics became populated with red, white, and blue–clad characters who fought the Axis and domestic subversives. The first such character spawned in this era was the Shield, an FBI agent ("G-man Extraordinary") unveiled in 1940. Captain America followed shortly thereafter and punched out Hitler on the cover of his first number. Wonder Woman debuted around the same time, wearing her star-spangled skirt and riding a white horse into battle. Lesser characters included a combative Uncle Sam and Major Liberty, who battled for righteousness while communing with the spirits of past American heroes.[71]

Glenn Miller gave up his profitable swing orchestra to enlist—in fact, to beg to be accepted into the military given his relatively advanced age. Swing was considered particularly important to the cause, because the troops loved it and the jazz-averse Nazis hated it.[72] Miller worked to make traditional military music snazzier and, via his Army Air Force Band, to unify the country and inspire the troops. One of the band's tunes, "There Are Yanks," described the makeup of US forces: "There are Okies there are crackers/Every color every creed/And they talk the only language/That the master race can read."

Miller and the band traveled and performed tirelessly, and in 1944, he was killed in a plane crash over the English Channel. At the end of the war in Europe, the band played for 40,000 troops in Nuremberg Stadium, in a statement of military and artistic triumph.[73]

The Moon Shot and Civil Rights Movement
Were Nationalist Triumphs

After the war, the United States enjoyed a period of consensus nationalism for the next few decades. This doesn't mean that there weren't hard-fought political issues and domestic contention, but a lowest-common-denominator patriotism and belief in our national goodness, especially vis-à-vis our Cold War adversary, the Soviet Union, undergirded public life. John F. Kennedy, who famously implored, "Ask not what your country can do for you, ask what you can do for your country," spoke for the liberal element of this consensus and initiated one of the signature national accomplishments of the mid-twentieth century.

His legendary "We choose to go to the moon" speech at Rice University in 1962 is shot through with national pride. He said, "This city of Houston, this State of Texas, this country of the United States was not built by those who waited and rested and wished to look behind them. This country was conquered by those who moved forward—and so will space." He cited William Bradford for the proposition that great actions come with formidable difficulties. He called space exploration "one of the great adventures of all time, and no nation which expects to be the leader of other nations can expect to stay behind in the race for space."

What ensued was a massive, sustained, intense national effort to meet JFK's challenge to get a man on the moon by the end of the decade. It drew on American ingenuity, derring-do, and treasure. At its height, NASA accounted for 4.4 percent of the federal budget, and almost 400,000 people worked on Apollo 11, the lunar mission.[74]

Everyone knows Neil Armstrong's famous words upon descending the ladder onto the surface of the moon in 1969: "That's one small step for man, one giant leap for mankind." But the stirring universalist gloss obscured the true nature of the venture. The moon landing was driven by a competition between the United States and the Soviet Union that implicated our national prestige and the reputation of our economic and political system. The Apollo program wasn't so much about the brotherhood of man as it was about outpacing a national enemy.

Apollo 11 was wrapped in American symbols. The mission's well-known seal had an impressively spread-winged eagle landing on the moon. The lunar module itself was dubbed *Eagle* (hence, "the *Eagle* has landed"), and the command module *Columbia*. One idea had been to put the UN flag on the moon's surface, but it was cast aside in favor of Old Glory.[75]

As live video streamed back to Earth, Neil Armstrong and Buzz Aldrin struggled to get the flag planting right. They hadn't been able to practice. First they had trouble fully extending the horizontal telescoping arm that kept the flag extended, which was why it ended up having a perpetual wave. Then they worried that they wouldn't be able to get the staff far enough into the lunar soil to make it stand up. But it all worked, and Armstrong took the famous picture of Aldrin saluting the flag.[76] (After all that, the flag blew over when Armstrong and Aldrin took back off.)[77]

The other mid-twentieth-century triumph happened closer to home. One reason the civil rights movement under the leadership of Martin Luther King, Jr., succeeded was that it had such ready access to our national identity and made such a compelling appeal to it.

King's touchstone as a Baptist preacher was that bedrock of American culture, the Bible. His biographer David Garrow explains, "The writers who had the greatest formative influence on King were named Amos, Jeremiah and Matthew."[78] In particular, King returned again and again to the central story of the Ancient Israelites, Exodus, which had such influence on Anglo-American history. His people were in the Egypt of oppression and had to cross the Red Sea and march through the wilderness to the land of freedom, the Promised Land.[79] In his first famous sermon in 1955, months before the Montgomery boycott, he preached from Exodus 14:30 ("And Israel saw the Egyptians dead upon the seashore").[80] In his very last, in 1968, he evoked Moses on the mountaintop, looking over at the Promised Land.[81]

King joined his prophetic voice, honed in the Protestant oral tradition, to an appeal to patriotism in the cause of social and political reform. The historian Scott Sandage writes that "it was precisely the unrelenting nationalism that reigned from the 1930s to the 1960s that finally offered black activists a cultural language to speak to white America and to elicit support. The black church and Gandhian non-violence were not the movement's only well-springs of unity and strength, the stories and values of American history were equally vital resources. The famous picket sign 'I AM A MAN' may have been morally compelling, but winning political and legal rights for blacks required a more focused message: I AM AN AMERICAN."[82]

King soaked his rhetoric in the symbols of America and its creed. In 1961, he praised lunch counter protestors for "taking our whole nation back to those great wells of democracy which were dug deep by the Founding Fathers in the formulation of the Constitution and the Declaration of Independence. In sitting down at the lunch counters, they are in reality standing up for the American dream." His historic speech at the March on Washington in 1963 evoked a national hymn in one of its famous riffs. He spoke of "the day when all of God's children will be able to sing with new meaning: 'My country, 'tis of thee, sweet land of liberty, of thee I sing. Land where my fathers died, land of the pilgrims' pride.'"[83]

King's victory was a nationalist achievement, although he himself was a Christian universalist who issued a prophet's stinging rebukes of the failings of his own country. His movement won the battle over patriotism. "In an era obsessed with defining Americanism," Sandage writes, "activists successfully portrayed their adversary as un-American."[84] In the Cold War ideological struggle with the Soviets, vindicating the rights of blacks became a way to save our national honor. More fundamentally, the civil rights legislation of the mid-1960s was the final spasm of the Civil War. Defenders of segregation advanced a bogus, swollen version of states' rights to defy national authority and to deny blacks the rights guaranteed in the Constitution, the nation's foundational law. They finally lost.

The 1970s Brought a Nationalist Crack-Up

The postwar nationalist consensus began to break down in the late 1960s, in the turbulence of the protests against the Vietnam War, political assassinations, urban violence, and economic stagnation. The counter to the patriotic pieties and nonviolence of Martin Luther King was the aggrieved voice of black nationalism. With ideological support from parts of the white Left, it gained more traction than it had in its past iterations.[85] The fundamental critique of America it advanced came, over time, to characterize a swath of elite American opinion.

Malcolm X, the charismatic disciple of the lunatic Nation of Islam, was King's alter ego. He launched a high-octane attack on America. He considered the American Revolution to have been an exercise in "white nationalism." At a 1964 event, he thundered, "No, I'm not an American. I'm one of the 22 million black people who are the victims of Americanism. One of the 22 million black people who are the victims of democracy, nothing but disguised hypocrisy. So, I'm not standing here speaking to you as an American, or a patriot, or a flag-saluter, or a flag waver—no, not I. I'm speaking as a victim of this American system. And I see America through the eyes of the victim. I don't see any American dream. I see an American nightmare."[86]

Soon enough, groups central to the civil rights movement, the Student Nonviolent Coordinating Committee and the Congress of Racial Equality, expelled their white members and began appealing not to America's civic nationalism but to black power.[87]

Reagan Renewed Our National Self-Confidence

The discontents and humiliations of the 1970s opened the way to the presidency of Ronald Reagan. He always maintained that he'd never stopped being a devotee of FDR, for whom he had voted four times. Reagan remembered the fireside chats fondly: "His strong, gentle, confident voice resonated across the nation with an eloquence that brought comfort and resilience to a nation caught up in a storm and reassured us that we could lick any problem."[88] He recalled seeing Roosevelt in 1936 at a campaign parade in Des Moines, Iowa, with "a familiar smile on his lips, jaunty and confident."[89]

Reagan sometimes remarked on both Presidents Roosevelt when he spoke to groups in the Roosevelt Room of the White House. According to Reagan, "both understood the vital importance of keeping America strong," and "there was one subject on which they saw eye to eye: that from Tierra del Fuego to the upper reaches of Baffin Bay, we are all Americans, brothers and sisters with a shared history and a common birthright— freedom."[90]

Reagan understandably emphasized these qualities in FDR, since he shared them in abundance. He was a creature of the era of consensus nationalism and, like Roosevelt, a master of the twentieth-century media technologies that buttressed the consensus; Reagan had appeared in movies as an actor, did radio commentaries both out of office in the 1970s and as president, and owed much of his political success to TV. But he obviously believed that the key to national revitalization was rowing in the opposite policy direction from FDR: "With the same energy that Franklin Roosevelt sought Government solutions to problems, we will seek private solutions."[91]

Although he was an inveterate optimist who was open-handed on the issue of immigration, Reagan shared a slogan with Donald Trump: "Let's make America great again." His presidential announcement speech in 1979 lamented national weakness and self-doubt. "I don't agree," he declared, "that our nation must resign itself to inevitable decline, yielding its proud position to other hands. I am totally unwilling to see this country fail in its obligation to itself and to the other free peoples of the world."

Reagan uttered his signature phrase hearkening back to the beginnings of the nation in this same speech: "We who are privileged to be Americans have had a rendezvous with destiny since the moment in 1630 when John Winthrop, standing on the deck of the tiny *Arbella* off the coast of Massachusetts, told the little band of Pilgrims, 'We shall be a city upon a hill. The eyes of all people are upon us so that if we shall deal falsely with our God in this work we have undertaken and so cause Him to withdraw His present help from us, we shall be made a story and a byword throughout the world.'"

A belief in our chosenness resounded throughout Reagan's rhetoric. In his acceptance speech at the Republican Convention in 1980, he expressed a vaulting faith in America: "It is impossible to capture in words the splendor of this vast continent which God has granted as our portion of His creation. There are no words to express the extraordinary strength and character of this breed of people we call Americans."[92]

In a debate with independent presidential candidate John Anderson that year, he pointed out, "Our government, in its most sacred documents—the Constitution and the Declaration of Independence and all—speak of man being created, of a Creator; that we're a nation under God."

Once in office, a central element of his program of national renewal was a vast, across-the-board military buildup, including the TR-esque goal of a 600-ship navy (it peaked at 594). He sold his foreign policy in terms of America's ideals but was cautious and hard-headed in its execution. He had no compunction about insisting on the nation's interest, even vis-à-vis allies, as he did in contention with the western Europeans over a Soviet gas pipeline. He distrusted supranational institutions such as the United

Nations and worked to vindicate the nationhood—and traditional religion—of Poland in the struggle with the Soviets. In his farewell address, he cited "the resurgence of national pride that I called the new patriotism" as "one of the things I'm proudest of in the past 8 years."[93]

His foremost intellectual supporters recognized Reagan's nationalistic appeal. After his election, the influential editor of *Commentary* magazine, Norman Podhoretz, hailed the "new nationalist spirit" in the land. He noted the passing of "the self-doubts and self-hatreds" of the post–Vietnam War era and a turn "toward what some of us have called a new nationalism." Irving Kristol wrote in 1983 of Reagan representing a different kind of Republican: "He came 'out of the West,' riding a horse, not a golf cart, speaking in the kind of nationalist-populist tonalities not heard since Teddy Roosevelt, appealing to large sections of the working class."[94]

Reagan's warning in his farewell address was of losing the foundations of our patriotism. "Those of us who are over 35 or so years of age," he observed, "grew up in a different America. We were taught, very directly, what it means to be an American. And we absorbed, almost in the air, a love of country and an appreciation of its institutions. If you didn't get these things from your family you got them from the neighborhood, from the father down the street who fought in Korea or the family who lost someone at Anzio. Or you could get a sense of patriotism from school."

Then there was a final backstop, according to Reagan: "And if all else failed you could get a sense of patriotism from the popular culture. The movies celebrated democratic values and implicitly reinforced the idea that America was special. TV was like that, too, through the mid-sixties."

But things had changed. "Younger parents," he lamented, "aren't sure that an unambivalent appreciation of America is the right thing to teach modern children. And as for those who create the popular culture, well-grounded patriotism is no longer the style. Our spirit is back, but we haven't reinstitutionalized it."

To do that, according to Reagan, "We've got to do a better job of getting across that America is freedom—freedom of speech, freedom of religion, freedom of enterprise. And freedom is special and rare. It's fragile; it needs protection. So, we've got to teach history based not on what's in fashion but what's important— why the Pilgrims came here, who Jimmy Doolittle was, and what those 30 seconds over Tokyo meant." He feared "an eradication of the American memory that could result, ultimately, in an erosion of the American spirit." Reagan advocated starting "with some basics: more attention to American history and a greater emphasis on civic ritual."[95]

It is advice as sound as—and even more urgent than—it was thirty years ago. If we ignore it, as discussed in the following section, we put at risk the handiwork of the great twentieth-century nationalists.

THE

THREAT

TO THE

NATION

CHAPTER 10

THE TREASON OF THE ELITES

In the late 1970s, a little-known left-wing professor and activist decided to embark on a three-year-long project to balance the alleged patriotic bias in American historical writing.[1]

His name was Howard Zinn, and his project became the book *A People's History of the United States*, a desecration of American memory that is the single most destructive act in the annals of American historiography.

Not much was expected of the fifty-something historian, whose prior books were out of print and whose work had largely consisted of attending protests. His agent sought a $20,000 advance, but Harper & Row coughed up only $10,000. The publisher initially printed just 5,000 copies. At first sales didn't amount to much, although the book got a nomination for an American Book Award.

It gained renown from pop culture. The Matt Damon character in *Good Will Hunting* tells his therapist, played by Robin Williams, "If you want to read a real history book, read Howard Zinn's *A People's History of the United States*. That book will [expletive] knock you on your ass." In the HBO show *The Sopranos*, A.J., the dim-witted son of the mob boss Tony, implausibly reads Zinn at the breakfast table in an episode about Christopher Columbus: "It's the truth, it's in my history book." The references boosted the work into orbit.

Its sales increased year over year, until it had sold more than two million copies and been translated into at least twenty languages.[2]

Zinn was born in the 1920s to poor eastern European immigrants who lived in a miserable cold-water flat in Brooklyn. The family didn't have an interest in books, but Howard did (he first read a tattered copy of *Tarzan and the Jewels of Opar* he found on the street). When, as a teenager, he was knocked unconscious by police during a Communist protest in Times Square, he instinctively knew his politics: "I was no longer a liberal, a believer in the self-correcting character of American democracy. I was a radical, believing that something fundamental was wrong in this country . . . something rotten at the root."

Embarking on an academic career after serving in World War II, he went for undergraduate studies to New York University, and on to Columbia for his graduate work. He got teaching postings at Spelman College in Atlanta and Boston University, both marked by political acrimony. His radicalism associated him with a splinter of the history profession.[3]

Zinn supported an anti–Vietnam War resolution at the 1969 convention of the American Historical Association that identified the war with racism and domestic repression and sympathized with the Black Panthers.[4] The resolution was soundly defeated. Despite this setback, radical history steadily gained ground, and Zinn himself came to occupy an outsized place in the American historical mind.

Originally confined to journals such as *Studies on the Left*, started by students of the left-wing scholar William Appleman Williams at the University of Wisconsin, and *Radical America*, founded by Students for a Democratic Society (SDS), a highly politicized, fragmentary, identity politics–driven approach to history took over the discipline.

A critique of the radicals published in *The American Historical Review* in 1967 warned that the most prominent figures were only the tip of the iceberg: "Beneath the surface still lies the main mass of young radical scholars just now completing their training at the major cosmopolitan graduate schools." This proved prescient. Plus, distinguished historians such as Richard Hofstadter, David Potter, and C. Vann Woodward lost confidence in the old historical consensus. By 1980, the journal *Marxist Perspectives* listed 125 editors and organizational secretaries in academic institutions around the country, "the clearest measure," the historian Jonathan Wiener wrote in an account of this period, "that the boundary separating Marxism from the history profession had disappeared."[5]

Zinn did more than his share, rendering the American story as an unremitting tale of greed and oppression, a monstrous scam perpetuated on the masses by a parasitical and self-interested ruling class.

This was his gloss on every major event in American history. The migration across the Atlantic? "Behind the English invasion of North America, behind their massacre of Indians, their deception, their brutality, was that special powerful drive born in civilizations based on private property."[6]

The Revolution? "Around 1776, certain important people in the English colonies made a discovery that would prove enormously useful for the next two hundred years. They found that by creating a nation, a symbol, a legal unity called the United States, they could take over land, profits, and political power from favorites of the British Empire. In the process, they could hold back a number of potential rebellions and create a consensus of popular support for the rule of a new, privileged leadership."[7]

The Civil War? "It was money and profit, not the movement against slavery, that was uppermost in the priorities of the men who ran the country."[8]

And so on, all built on a tendentious or partial account of events, not to mention outright falsehoods. He neglected to include Washington's farewell address and Lincoln's Gettysburg Address, and D-Day and Gettysburg.[9] Reviewing the book when it first appeared, Harvard University professor Oscar Handlin noted that "Zinn is a stranger to evidence bearing upon the peoples about whom he purports to write" and slammed "the deranged quality of his fairy tale, in which the incidents are made to fit the legend, no matter how intractable the evidence of American history."[10]

Much of the American Elite Seeks to Deconstruct the Nation

But evidence be damned. Zinn's work is a go-to book on college campuses—for nearly everything. It shows up in courses not only in history but in political science, economics, literature, and—of course—women's studies. A course at Evergreen State College stipulated, typically, "This is an advanced class and all students should have read Howard Zinn's *A People's History of the United States* before the first day of class, to give us a common background to begin the class."[11]

When Zinn died, *The Guardian* called him a great man and the Russian TV network RT gushed that he had "limitless depth."[12] The novelist Dave Eggers wrote in *The New Yorker* that he "was the embodiment of the term 'living legend,' and his effect on how we see and teach history is immeasurable."[13] True enough, to his and our shame.

As we have seen, poets, novelists, lexicographers, and historians have, over the centuries, been central to excavating and delineating the identities of nations, toward the goal of establishing proud, self-governing peoples. In the United States, this class has turned its back on a nation-buttressing role and instead embraced a hostility to the American nation as such, to its cultural supports, its traditions, and its history.

The clerisy has often been abetted in this project by leaders of the country, including in government, who were robustly nationalist until the latter half of the twentieth century. "Then in the 1960s and 1970s," Samuel Huntington writes, "they began to promote measures consciously designed to weaken America's cultural and creedal identity and to strengthen racial, ethnic, cultural, and other subnational identities. These efforts by a nation's leaders to deconstruct the nation they governed were, quite possibly, without precedent in human history."[14]

We live in their ongoing anti-national experiment.

Cosmopolitanism Inevitably Involves Estrangement from Your Own

Just as nationalism, or at least loyalty to the nation-state, is very old, so is the impulse to move beyond mere local or national attachments. The word *cosmopolitan* has its root in the Greek word *kosmopolites*, or citizen of the cosmos or world.[15]

The fourth-century BC Cynic philosopher Diogenes lived in Athens after his exile from his native Sinope and rejected all convention in favor of a life of virtue, making a barrel into his home in the Athenian marketplace.[16] He is the first recorded person to use what has now become a cosmopolitan cliché: it is reported that "when he was asked where he came from, he replied, 'I am a citizen of the world.'"[17] This was a radical, even senseless, statement since the Greeks considered citizenship possible only through the *polis*, or city.

The Stoics took the cosmopolitan baton from the Cynics. We exist in a local community by an "accident of birth," according to the first-century Roman philosopher Seneca, but the world beyond is "truly great and truly common." We should "measure the boundaries of our nation by the sun."[18]

This tradition was recovered during the Enlightenment. In his 1753 work *Le Cosmopolite*, the widely traveled Louis-Charles Fougeret de Montbron maintained that "All the countries are the same to me" and boasted that he changed "my places of residence according to my whim."[19] The cosmopolitan idea was expressed in the Enlightenment notion of *Weltbürger*, or world citizen.[20] The great German philosopher Immanuel Kant posited a "cosmopolitan right" to participate in the free exchange of ideas in the global community and urged the adoption of a league of nations as a means of achieving "perpetual peace."[21]

Cosmopolitanism came in different flavors, some more robust than others. It could refer merely to someone who traveled frequently and had a keen interest in the world. Or it could denote a desire for a world state. The eighteenth-century Prussian nobleman Anacharsis Cloots wanted to eliminate nations and establish a "republic of united individuals," based on the principle of one sovereign for all people. He was fired by enthusiasm for the French Revolution, which he considered a step toward that glorious outcome. He led a delegation of foreigners to the French National Constituent Assembly to declare the world's fealty to the Revolution's Declaration of the Rights of Man. The self-styled *citoyen de l'humanité*, or citizen of mankind, was eventually guillotined by his fellow revolutionaries when they falsely accused him of being part of, yes, a foreign plot.[22]

What's behind all cosmopolitanism is what the British writer Paul Gilroy has called "the principled and methodical cultivation of a degree of estrangement from one's own culture and history."[23] This tendency has been given stark expression by the likes of the novelist Virginia Woolf, who urged the rejection of "pride of nationality" (as well as "religious pride, college pride, family pride, sex pride and those unreal realities that spring from them"), and Leo Tolstoy, who despite his powerful literary evocations of Russian culture was a Christian anarchist who thought it "obvious that patriotism as a sentiment is bad and harmful; as a doctrine it is stupid."[24]

As such, cosmopolitanism has always been open to the charge that—whatever its broad-mindedness or idealism—it cultivates a contempt for what's near, immediate, and tangible, in favor of what's far off. Charles Dickens skewered the character Mrs. Jellyby in his novel *Bleak House* for being so consumed with a humanitarian project in Africa that she neglected all around her, including her own children. She "had a curious habit of seeming to look a long way off" as if she "could see nothing nearer than Africa!"[25]

Getting at the same point, Rousseau commented that cosmopolitans "boast that they love everyone, to have the right to love no one."[26]

Whether this indictment is fair regarding any particular cosmopolitan figure or not, it gets at the natural drift. This is all the more important in the contemporary context. It used to be that cosmopolitanism was largely the attitude of philosophers and critics of society—outsiders. Diogenes, while he was eating and masturbating in public to outrage the bourgeoisie, never imagined governing Athens. Now a broadly cosmopolitan sensibility infuses our elite in government, academia, and business.

America's Self-Conception Changed—First for the Better, Then for the Worse

Our view of ourselves as a nation has changed over time, and much of this is to the good. The conception of America as an ethnic nation, dominated first by British American Protestants, then more broadly by white Christians, and buttressed throughout by a racial caste system, wasn't sustainable and shouldn't have been sustained. Throughout the twentieth century, the American ethnic archetype of the WASP slowly gave way. First Germans, Scandinavians, and Irish Catholics gained acceptance; then Jews and a broader range of Europeans; finally, non-Europeans.

The seeds of the underlying intellectual shift began, as the scholar Eric Kaufmann notes, with the Anglo-Protestant elite itself, which embraced a cosmopolitanism that disdained the Anglo-Protestant ascendancy. Progressive activists and thinkers such as Jane Addams and John Dewey led the way. They were then joined by mainline Protestant elites, the urban avant-garde, and New York intellectuals associated with journals such as *Partisan Review*. They eventually won over the university, corporate, and governmental establishment.[27]

Insofar as the ferment contributed to a more open and just

society, it was healthy. But the potential was always there for the new cosmopolitanism to give way to something more extreme, namely, to an opposition to the unity of the American people as such and the very basis of the American nation.

In a 1915 essay in *The Nation*, the scholar Horace Kallen attacked standard notions of assimilation as a plot by the Anglo-Saxons for continued dominance. "The 'American race' is a totally unknown thing," he wrote, arguing instead for "a democracy of nationalities." The common tongue of this democracy is still English, "but each nationality expresses its emotional and voluntary life in its own language." The country merely serves as a platform for multiple nations living within its borders: "As the foundation and background for the realization of the distinctive individuality of each *natio* that composes it."[28]

Randolph Bourne picked up the theme in *The Atlantic* in a 1916 essay titled "Trans-national America." He saw immigration as an opportunity to create "the first international nation," a "cosmopolitan federation of national colonies."[29]

Radical at the time, this point of view steadily insinuated itself into the mainstream. Horace Kallen took a bow in 1972 as a ninety-year-old, with multiculturalism on the rise. "It takes about 50 years for an idea to break through and become vogue," he stated. "No one likes an intruder, particularly when he is upsetting the commonplace."[30]

Multiculturalism Rejected *Unum* for *Pluribus*

Fueled by the rise of ethnic pride movements in the 1960s and critiques of America as fundamentally racist and corrupt, the intellectual tide of multiculturalism swelled in the 1990s. In a typical expression of the worldview, the academic Amy Gutmann, who eventually became president of the University of Pennsylvania, wrote in favor of "public recognition and preservation" of "discrete ethnic, linguistic, and other cultural groups." She insisted that our schools "must move beyond the morally misguided and politically dangerous idea of asking us to choose between being, above all, citizens of our own society or, above all, citizens of the world. We are, above all, none of the above."[31]

It became in vogue, as John Fonte explains in his book *Sovereignty or Submission: Will Americans Rule Themselves or Be Ruled by Others?*, for curricula and standards to refer to the American "peoples."[32]

The title of the New York State social studies curriculum in 1991 was "One Nation, Many Peoples: A Declaration of Cultural Interdependence." States such as Colorado and Maryland recommended a similar emphasis, and controversial United States History Content Standards, even after revisions to remove their worst bias, adopted the "many peoples" framework of the United States. The historian of education Diane Ravitch reported that textbooks under the influence of the standards had "nearly buried the narrative about the ideas and institutions that made our national government possible."[33]

The liberal political philosopher Richard Rorty argued in the mid-1990s that there was much to admire in the academic Left's focus on underrepresented groups. "But there is a problem," he wrote, "with this left: it is unpatriotic. In the name of 'the politics of difference,' it refuses to rejoice in the country it inhabits. It repudiates the idea of a national identity, and the emotion of national pride."[34]

The destructive trend met resistance from old-school liberals. In a book-length polemic, the liberal lion Arthur Schlesinger, Jr., court historian to the Kennedys, made a traditionalist case against multiculturalism. He called it an "ethnic upsurge," not a "revival" because it was something completely new. It had begun "as a gesture of protest against the Anglocentric culture" and became "a cult." He warned that "today it threatens to become a counterrevolution against the original theory of America as 'one people,' a common culture, a single nation."[35]

But the intellectual momentum behind this poisonously fissiparous view of America was too strong. It is deeply embedded in academia, in corporate America via the diversity industry, and in our politics, which is more openly racialized than at any time since the days of segregation.

Relatedly, the end of the Cold War engendered a newly potent transnationalism, contemptuous of national boundaries and supportive of institutions of global governance.

Strobe Talbott, a *Time* magazine columnist turned high-level Clinton official, forecast that "nationhood as we know it will be obsolete; [and] all states will recognize a single global authority."[36] This was presumed to be the inexorable drift of the future and, as John Fonte notes, differed from mere internationalism and its system of sovereign nation-states. John Ruggie of the Harvard Kennedy School of Government explained that postwar institutions such as the United Nations were created "for an *international* world, but we have entered a *global* world." Thus, we need "to devise more inclusive forms of global governance."[37]

The old loyalties were not just anachronistic but morally unsupportable. The social critic Richard Sennett wrote of "the evil of a shared national identity."[38] Professor of law and ethics Martha Nussbaum warned of the "morally dangerous" dictates of "patriotic pride," commending instead a commitment to the "worldwide community of human beings."[39]

In a speech to the Organization of American Historians, University of Iowa academic Linda Kerber asked, "Do we need citizenship? We are embedded in postnational and transnational relationships that may be changing the meaning of citizenship beyond recognition."[40]

And it's not just the intellectuals.

America's Elites Became Transnational

American elites are enmeshed in the world of globalization—the enhanced travel and contacts, the multinational corporations, the NGOs. This inclines them to the view that the world is and should be ever more interconnected, often fired by a near-messianic certitude that this trend is associated with the spread of all that is true and good. As Huntington points out, in the nineteenth century, the growing sophistication and continental scale of American business promoted the nationalism of American elites over and against localism; now they promote the transnationalism of American elites over and against nationalism.[41]

These elites spend an inordinate amount of time flying into and out of international airports, attending conferences and business meetings in foreign capitals, often at the same top-notch hotels, interacting with Western-educated elites from other countries who all speak English and the globalized argot of markets and inevitable progress. They are more truly "citizens of the world" than anyone who used the phrase in past centuries could have imagined, their territory a globe-spanning metropolitan archipelago that takes no account of mere national borders.[42]

They ate up Thomas Friedman's 2005 book *The World Is Flat: A Brief History of the Twenty-first Century*, which sold more than 4 million copies based on the argument that the world was becoming more interconnected, or flatter. Its supporting evidence marshaled from overseas travels and conversations with CEOs, Friedman's tome was, in effect, by and for the transnational elite, and reinforced its comforting assumptions. In a withering and prescient review at the time, the contrarian academic John Gray associated Friedman's simplistic, overly confident neo-liberalism with the most flaccid aspects of Marxism, especially "its consistent underestimation of nationalist and religious movements and unidirectional view of history."[43]

Globalization is real and the market a powerful force, but utopianism about trade and technology—supposedly driving us toward a borderless world and inevitable progress—has proven as facile and wrong as any other utopianism.

No, trade with China didn't radically transform its regime. The general secretary of the Communist Party of China, Xi Jinping, has effectively made himself president for life, centralizing power

and writing authoritarian "Xi Jinping thought" into the constitution. The country has no rule of law and depends on state-led,
rather than market-led, capitalism. It has poured its windfall from
globalization into a military it is using to challenge American
power.

No, social media haven't promoted liberalization. Once upon
a time, leaders in tech boasted that, in the words of Facebook
founder Mark Zuckerberg in 2015, the internet is a "force for
peace" in the world.[44] That was before it became clear that tech
was a powerful tool in the arsenal of Russia and China, that
Facebook had played a role in ethnic cleansing in Myanmar, and
that white nationalists and other extremists use social media
platforms as a tool of radicalization.[45]

And no, the nation isn't fading away, as has been constantly
predicted by observers who wish it were so.

No matter. The transnational elite still exists in a gigantic
bubble removed from the concerns and emotional attachments of
the citizenry of nation-states. "Elites are cosmopolitan," the sociologist Manuel Castells writes, "people are local." One way or the
other, more or less consciously, a significant slice of the intelli-
gentsia and business elite takes it as a given that nationalism and
patriotism are atavistic and must be steamrolled by the forces of
History.[46]

The History Profession Turned Its Back on the Nation

The people who write down and teach our nation's story share
this attitude. They have reversed the traditional role of historiography. For the longest time, the bounds of historical writing were
set by the nation, which was the natural subject of historians. At
the same time, in telling the nation's story, historians provided a
cultural glue that helped it to cohere. In the nineteenth century,
the modern nation-state and professional historiography literally
grew up together.[47]

In America, as the New York University historian Thomas Bender remarks, the very first histories focused on localities and states. The first national work, *The History of the American Revolution*, didn't appear until 1789, the year of the adoption of the Constitution. Americans still struck most observers as not very historically minded.[48]

John Adams plaintively asked a correspondent in 1813, "Can you account for the Apathy, the Antipathy of this Nation to their own History? Is there not a repugnance to the thought of looking back? While thousands of frivolous Novels are read with eagerness and got by heart, the History of our own native Country is not only neglected, but despised and abhorred?"[49]

Alexis de Tocqueville remarked of the America he experienced in the early 1830s, "No one cares for what occurred before his time. No methodical system is pursued; no archives are formed; and no documents are brought together when it would be very easy to do so. Where they exist, little store is set upon them." He believed that "in fifty years it will be more difficult to collect authentic documents concerning the social condition of the Americans at the present day than it is to find remains of the administration of France during the Middle Ages."[50]

Actually, about that time, a more rigorous effort to document the country's founding and history was just getting under way. Key debates and documents were published, including in a series of books called *American Archives*. It proudly announced, "The undertaking in which we have embarked is, emphatically, a National one: National in its scope and object, its end and aim."[51]

And then there was George Bancroft. A prodigious scholar and politically active Democratic statesman (as James Polk's secretary of the navy, he ordered what became the Conquest of California), he wrote the magisterial *History of the United States, from the Discovery of the American Continent*, published beginning in 1844.

The work stretched across ten volumes, written over the course of four decades, and eventually covered the years 1492 to 1789. Bancroft started his research by devoting a page of a blank book to each day of the year, then, based on his extensive reading, filled the page with every possible fact that occurred on that date. His volumes became best sellers and earned him a fortune.[52]

Hans Kohn situated him within the great tradition of nationalist historians: "Bancroft, who occupies the same place in the development of American historiography and of the American national consciousness as Palacký does among the Czechs, Michelet among the French, Munch among the Norwegians, and Treitschke among the Germans, was a national historian not only because he saw national history in as favorable a light as possible but because he tried to formulate and document some of the most prominent traits of American national self-identification. He helped delineate the image that Americans formed of themselves."[53]

Bancroft was unembarrassingly, unabashedly, pro-American. While studying in Germany as a young man, he marked July 4 with another American student, toasting everything about our country, including its government, "watered by the dews of Heaven and quickened by the genial warmth of freedom—the nurseries of enlightened patriots."[54]

He had a providential view of America that infused his *History* and believed in the essential beneficence of the American project: "The government by the people is in very truth the strongest government in the world. Discarding the implements of terror, it dares to rule by moral force, and has its citadel in the heart."[55]

Bancroft's work may not meet contemporary professional standards, but America's historians have eschewed his approach and point of view entirely. They have turned their backs on the nation as a subject and, to the extent they take account of it, portray it as a vehicle of rapacity and misrule, as Howard Zinn did.

"If love of the nation is what drove American historians to the study of the past in the nineteenth century," the Harvard historian Jill Lepore writes, "hatred for nationalism drove American historians away from it in the second half of the twentieth century."[56] The discipline became obsessed with microtopics dictated by identity politics, dismissive of the lay reader, and, of course, hostile to the nation as such. In the words of the historian John Higham, "The insistent pluralism of our post-Marxist era rejects any claim to centeredness in the forms of experience. In short, postmodernism calls for destabilizing and decentering an integrated national history."[57]

And so it has.

The Schools Have Been Divested of Patriotic History

The schools have run the same course. In the nationalist period after the Civil War, the teaching of American history flourished after a sustained push to emphasize it in curricula. Before the war, only a handful of states required history instruction; by the turn of the century, a majority of states did. And it was explicitly patriotic.

According to the historian Merle Curti, the schools "emphasized the importance of presenting vividly and attractively to children the glorious deeds of American heroes, the sacrifices and bravery of our soldiers and sailors in wartime, the personalities of presidents, who might properly be regarded as symbols of the nation in the manner in which royal personages of Europe were regarded. By the 1890s, state after state was requiring by law that subjects deemed peculiarly fitted to inculcating patriotism, such as American history and civics, be taught on every educational level below the college."[58]

As the long nationalist era after the Civil War faded, so did the emphasis on patriotism in instruction. Patriotic themes disappeared from school readers steadily throughout the twentieth century, and history itself has begun to vanish from our education system.[59]

Less than a fifth of colleges and universities require their students to take an American history or government course.[60] Of the top colleges and universities in the country, only a fraction require even *history majors* to take a course in American history, although they often have geographic distribution requirements (which helpfully exclude the United States).[61] Gender, racial, class, and environmental history have captured the heart of the academy. So it's no surprise that colleges are turning out historical illiterates—more than three-quarters of college graduates can't identify James Madison as the "Father of the Constitution," or place the phrase "government of the people, by the people, and for the people" in the Gettysburg Address.[62]

Worse, of course, there has been a deliberate effort to trash America's statesmen and heroes as exemplars of racism, sexism, and classism. By the 1980s, one survey found that textbooks portrayed America as "exploitative, unequal, and almost unredeemable in its general nastiness."[63]

In 2014, a firestorm erupted over the College Board's new curriculum for Advanced Placement United States History. It didn't mention James Madison or Martin Luther King but did manage to name check Chief Little Turtle and Mercy Otis Warren. It had a hostile view of the American experience, noting, for instance, that the British legacy here was "a rigid racial hierarchy" and minimizing the importance of the American Revolution.

A group of more than a hundred scholars wrote a letter complaining that the new framework imposed "an arid, fragmentary, and misleading account of American history," in addition to downplaying "American citizenship and American world leadership in favor of a more global and transnational perspective." In sum, they wrote, the curriculum was "so inattentive to the sources of national unity and cohesion, that it is hard to see how students will gain any coherent idea of what those sources might be."

After denouncing its critics as chauvinistic hacks, the College Board reversed course and modified the curriculum. But the spirit that animated the effort in the first place is dominant in US education and eating away at the foundations of our national project.[64]

A Nation Needs a Common Memory to Survive

Memory is what gives a nation its self-image and its sense of unity and coherence. It plays the same role in a country as it does in an individual, providing, in the words of Ralph Waldo Emerson, "the cement, the bitumen, the matrix in which the other faculties are embedded."[65]

The great historian William H. McNeill puts it well: "A people without a full quiver of relevant agreed-upon statements, accepted in advance through education or less formalized acculturation, soon finds itself in deep trouble, for, in the absence of believable myths, coherent public action becomes very difficult to improvise or sustain."[66]

McNeill cites the example of the British in World War II, who were fortified by what they had learned from their schoolbooks, namely that they had lost the initial battles in European conflicts but always prevailed in the end.[67]

Arthur Schlesinger explains, "As the means of defining national identity, history becomes a means of shaping history."[68]

What historic challenges do the race, gender, and class obsessions of American historiographers prepare us for today? To win a campaign against heteronormativity? To beat ourselves up endlessly and dethrone historical figure after historical figure, over white privilege? To be constantly watchful for the baleful effects of toxic masculinity?

An anti-national history is, on top of everything, profoundly ungrateful. It fails to credit our ancestors for achievements on an epic scale. It denies the continuities of our history and our dependence on men and women who didn't know us but bequeathed us the marvel of America. It runs counter to the inscription that John Adams wrote on the tombstone of his forebear Henry Adams: "This stone and several others have been placed in this yard, by a great great grandson from a veneration of the piety, humility, simplicity, prudence, patience, temperance, frugality, industry and perseverance of his Ancestors, in hopes of recommending an imitation of their virtues to their Posterity."[69]

We have traveled a long way down from that sentiment, which is impossible to improve on more than two centuries later. If centuries of adventure, drama, striving, and achievement aren't to be wiped away in a "great forgetting," the country needs an Americanizing campaign of civic and history education, suffused with a belief in the country's uniqueness and greatness.

And it should be grounded in the fact that we are a people.

CHAPTER 11

ONE NATION, ONE PEOPLE

At a dinner party at his retreat near Versailles in 1865, the law professor Édouard René Lefèbvre de Laboulaye exulted at the passage of the Thirteenth Amendment to the US Constitution, abolishing slavery. He told the gathering of prominent political and literary friends that if a monument should be erected to mark the centennial of American independence, he thought it should be a joint French-American project, given the historic ties between the two countries.[1] The conversation left an impression on one of his guests, the sculptor Frédéric Auguste Bartholdi.

At the time, the artist was working on a project for a gigantic torch-bearing, draped female figure at the entranceway to the Suez Canal, called *Egypt Carrying the Light to Asia*. When that went nowhere, he turned his attention to the idea of a colossal statue in America, scouting out locations and settling on a small island in New York Harbor as best. He reported back to his French associates, including Laboulaye, and they began to undertake the organizing and fund-raising.[2]

The project, which blew by its original centennial deadline, would never have come off without the tireless promotion of Bartholdi. When interest was slow to build in France, he commissioned a thirty-six-foot-tall painting of New York Harbor with the proposed statue looming over it to dramatically illustrate its awesome scale.[3]

He used his progress to keep up the fund-raising momentum. He sent the right hand holding the torch, the first part completed, to the Centennial International Exhibition in Philadelphia in 1876 (it was then displayed in Madison Square Park in New York for years).[4] The head went to the Universal Exposition in Paris in 1878.[5]

It seemed for a while that America wouldn't be able to deliver on its end of the bargain: raising the money for the completed statue's pedestal. But New York felt an added incentive to deliver upon reports that Boston might swoop in as the home for the statue.[6] A New York newspaper objected, "This statue is dear to us, though we have never looked upon it, and no third rate town is going to step in and take it from us."[7]

When everything had fallen into place and the statue was built and finally ready to be unveiled in New York Harbor on October 28, 1886, perhaps a million people watched the celebratory parade that morning, which, for the first time, featured stock traders throwing ticker tape out of windows.[8]

They all gathered to celebrate a monument to liberty. The sculptor Bartholdi based his work on the symbols of American freedom, Columbia, the female personification of the United States, and Libertas, the Roman goddess of freedom. He considered depicting her wearing a pileus, the cap associated with freed Roman slaves, but gave her a crown instead. Rather than put a broken chain into her hand, which he thought might be too stark a reference to chattel slavery right after the Civil War, he depicted her stepping on a broken chain and holding a tablet symbolizing the law in her arm.[9]

The speeches the day of the dedication emphasized French-American friendship and liberty. President Grover Cleveland averred, "We will not forget that liberty has here made her home; nor shall her chosen altar be neglected. Willing votaries will constantly keep alive its fires, and these shall gleam upon the shores of our sister republic in the East. Reflected thence and joined with answering rays, a stream of light shall pierce the darkness of ignorance and man's oppression, until liberty enlightens the world."[10]

There were references to immigration, although no one thought it central to the statue's meaning. The orator Chauncey M. Depew spoke of "the rays from this beacon, lighting this gateway to the continent." He stipulated that "there is room and brotherhood for all who will support our institutions and aid in our development; but that those who come to disturb our peace and dethrone our laws are aliens and enemies forever."[11]

In the course of the fund-raising effort in New York, the poet Emma Lazarus had been asked to contribute something about the statue. At first she waved off the request; then, inspired by her experience with Jewish refugees, wrote her famous lines, which were read aloud at an art exhibition raising money for the project.[12] Not until 1903 was the poem added to a plaque, now displayed in an exhibition within the statue's pedestal and occupying an outsized space in the public understanding of Lady Liberty.

Immigration Policy Is Central to the Nation

The legend of the statue as a statement about openness to immigration gained a hold in the 1930s, at a time when—as noted in the prior chapter—cosmopolitan ideas were in the ascendancy.[13] Soon enough, we were calling ourselves a "nation of immigrants," the title of a 1958 book by then senator John F. Kennedy that advocated liberalizing our immigration laws.[14]

Today, anything other than a latitudinarian approach is taken as an offense against the statue and especially against the Lazarus poem. Few topics in our public life are so heavily encrusted with clichés and saccharine myth and so resistant to reality and rational analysis. Everything is geared to ruling out of bounds the view that we need less immigration, and indeed, bipartisan "comprehensive" immigration reforms invariably propose more.

The issue of immigration involves questions central to the nature and standing of the American nation. Are we a people with a coherent culture as opposed to an abstraction or a collection of "peoples"? Do we have borders that can and should be meaning-fully enforced (including by a wall, if necessary)? Is it legitimate to put the interests of people already here, both the native-born and legal immigrants, over and above all the would-be immigrants who would like to come here? The answers to all the above should be in the affirmative.

There is no doubt that the cause of immigration restriction has often been tainted by racism, anti-Catholicism, and hostility to immigrants as such. Today, it has tawdry allies such as Iowa Republican congressman Steve King, rebuked by his own party for repeatedly making white nationalist–tinged statements. That said, we shouldn't unthinkingly accept the status quo based on a flawed understating of our history and national project.

It is in the nation's interest to have fewer, and better-skilled, immigrants coming here. Such a change would promote the eco-nomic prospects of Americans *and* the assimilation of immigrants, both important goals for our national health.

This more restrictive approach wouldn't be "un-American," as supporters of a liberal immigration policy allege, but best suited to preserving the "unum" in "E pluribus unum." Moreover, we should hope that America's racial and ethnic lines blur, rather than harden, under the benign influence of intermarriage, perhaps the best friend of national unity over the long term.

The Founders Worried about the Effects of Unchecked Immigration

Contrary to the conventional wisdom, there has never been a period in the history of the United States when the vast majority of people in this country weren't native born, and levels of immi-gration have ebbed—even stopped—and flowed over time.[15]

The Founders weren't hostile to immigration, but they weren't starry-eyed about it, either. They tended to worry about the effects of unassimilated blocs of immigrants and suggested moderating the numbers admitted and ensuring that they dispersed among the general population and adopted our mores.

In a 1753 letter, Benjamin Franklin stated all his worries about German immigration before stipulating, "Yet I am not for refusing entirely to admit them into our Colonies: all that seems to be necessary is, to distribute them more equally, mix them with the English, establish English Schools where they are now too thick settled, and take some care to prevent the practice lately fallen into by some of the Ship Owners, of sweeping the German Gaols to make up the number of their Passengers."[16]

"The United States have already felt the evils of incorporating a large number of foreigners into their national mass," Alexander Hamilton opined in a pseudonymous newspaper article in 1802, "by promoting in different classes different predilections in favor of particular foreign nations." Hamilton didn't call for "closing the door altogether," instead advocating that a "reasonable term ought to be allowed to enable aliens to get rid of foreign and acquire American attachments; to learn the principles and imbibe the spirit of our government; and to admit of at least a probability of their feeling a real interest in our affairs."[17]

In 1794, George Washington wrote a letter to John Adams that struck a similar note: "My opinion with respect to emigration is, that except of useful mechanic's—and some particular descriptions of men—or professions—there is no need of extra encouragement: while the policy, or advantage of its taking place in a body (I mean the settling of them in a body) may be much questioned; for by so doing they retain the language, habits & principles (good or bad) which they bring with them; whereas, by an intermixture with our people, they, or their descendants, get assimilated to our customs, manners and laws: in a word, soon become one people."[18]

James Madison, too, believed that immigration policy had to suit our interests. He said in a congressional speech in 1790, "I should be exceeding sorry, sir, that our rule of naturalization excluded a single person of good fame, that really meant to incorporate himself into our society; on the other hand, I do not wish that any man should acquire the privilege, but who, in fact, is a real addition to the wealth or strength of the United States."[19]

A little more than two hundred years later, this commonsensical sentiment would be considered radical, in part because we have become accustomed to a deeply flawed account of the country's history on immigration.

Immigration Numbers Have Gone Up and Down

In the late eighteenth century, about 80 percent of the free population was of British descent.[20] For almost the first hundred years of the country's existence, we didn't have immigration restrictions and saw major influxes of Germans and Irish in the mid-nineteenth century.[21] After an 1875 Supreme Court decision struck down a California levy meant to discourage immigration from China and made it clear that immigration policy was a federal responsibility, the federal government started to tighten up.[22]

Since the late nineteenth century, immigration levels have waxed and waned: up in the 1880s, down in the 1890s, up before World War I, down during the war, up in the aftermath. The 1924 immigration law, the so-called national origins quota system that granted visas overwhelmingly to people from Great Britain, Germany, and Ireland and sought to preserve the existing ethnic balance of the country, put immigration on a lower trajectory that lasted forty years. In 1965, the United States admitted fewer than 300,000 immigrants.[23]

That drastically changed with the 1965 Immigration and Nationality Act, which threw out the national origins quotas and put a new emphasis on family connections.[24] We have been at elevated levels ever since and now admit about 1 million legal immigrants a year. Asia and especially Latin America became vastly more important sources of immigration, with Mexico contributing even more through illegal immigration.[25]

Today, the United States has the largest immigrant population in the world and is home to 20 percent of all the world's immi-grants. A majority of US population growth since 1965 has been produced by immigrants and their children and grandchildren: 72 million people total.[26] The overall share of the population that is foreign born is projected to exceed the previous high of 15 per-cent from around the turn of the twentieth century, when newly inexpensive transatlantic transport, political unrest overseas, and a booming industrial economy in the United States created a massive influx.[27]

So what's the problem now?

Our Immigration Policy Runs Heedless of Consequences

The current, historic increase in immigration has proceeded heedless of the economic consequences.

There is a small economic benefit to the current wave, perhaps $50 billion annually, which comes from lower wages and prices.[28] The benefit tends to be redistributed upward to capital and con-sumers, while the cost is borne by lower-wage workers (especially immigrants who were already here).[29] It's not clear that there's an overall net economic benefit because of the fiscal costs associated with welfare, health care, and schooling for immigrants.[30]

More important is the strain that this long wave of immigration is putting on the cultural fabric and the assimilative capacity of the United States.

Conditions were much better for assimilation a hundred years ago. Immigrants arrived into a robust manufacturing economy, and the overall skill gap between immigrants and natives was smaller than it is currently. It was much harder to travel to and communicate with the home country.[31] The world wars were a force for cohesion and created an incentive for ethnic groups to demonstrate their loyalty.[32] The consensus for assimilation was still very strong, astonishingly so by the standards of today.[33]

The Americanization Movement Insisted on Assimilation

Consider: On July 4, 1918, in the midst of World War I, a parade clogged Fifth Avenue in New York City for ten hours. Seventy thousand people marched on a beautiful summer day, including thousands of immigrants in national contingents, from a tiny band of Haitians, who brought up the rear, to a throng of 10,000 Italians, who had to be pared back from the 35,000 who had wanted to participate. The committee behind the event organized it, in the words of the *New York Times*, as "a demonstration of the loyalty of Americans of foreign birth to their adopted country."[34]

And so it was. The Lithuanians carried a banner that declared, UNCLE SAM IS OUR UNCLE. Three hundred Italians sported red, white, and blue umbrellas in the shape of an American flag. New York City's only Zoroastrian Parsee, marching with his little son, held a banner boasting AMERICA ALWAYS.[35]

The parade represented perhaps the very peak of the Americanization movement. Catalyzed by a combative strike in Lawrence, Massachusetts, led by restive immigrant workers in 1912, the movement sought to fully integrate new immigrants via English-language classes, instruction and lectures in American civics and history, and patriotic rituals, fanfare, and pamphlets.[36]

The future Supreme Court justice Louis Brandeis memorably defined Americanization in a 1916 speech: "It manifests itself, in a superficial way, when the immigrant adopts the clothes, the manners and the customs generally prevailing here. Far more important is the manifestation presented when he substitutes for his mother tongue, the English language as the common medium of speech." But that wasn't all. "However great his outward conformity, the immigrant is not Americanized unless his interests and affections have become deeply rooted here," he continued. "He must be brought into complete harmony with our ideals and aspirations and cooperate with us for their attainment. Only when this has been done, will he possess the national consciousness of an American."[37]

It's hard to exaggerate the reach of the movement, which was felt in every place in America that had an immigrant community. "By 1916," John J. Miller writes, "millions of posters, pamphlets, and curriculum guides on English, naturalization, and citizenship were in circulation."[38] This period gave us the phrase "the melting pot," courtesy of a 1908 play by Israel Zangwill celebrating the intermarriage of a Russian immigrant couple, one Jewish, the other Christian: "Yes, East and West, and North and South, the palm and the pine, the pole and the equator, the crescent and the cross—how the great Alchemist melts and fuses them with his purging flame!"[39]

Institutions across American society supported the Americanization effort, something unimaginable today.

Private organizations did their part, beginning with the YMCA, which provided evening classes in English and civics.[40] The North American Civic League for Immigrants, founded in 1907, sponsored lectures, printed pamphlets, and helped immigrants establish themselves; it had prominent backers in business.[41] The Carnegie Foundation sponsored books on "Americanization Studies."[42]

Now, in contrast, ethnic organizations encourage the racial self-consciousness of immigrants.[43] The Ford Foundation, for instance, provided the seed money for the Mexican American Legal Defense and Educational Fund, which encourages Latinos to consider themselves an oppressed minority.[44]

Back then, the schools chipped in. In Lawrence, Massachusetts, they came up with an "American Plan for Education in Citizenship."[45] The New Jersey State Board of Education actively encouraged local districts to offer Americanization classes, as did other educational bodies across the country.[46]

Now schools are intensely multiculturalist vehicles for students retaining or acquiring a group identity.[47]

Corporate America was on board, with Ford Motor Company a leading advocate. "I am a good American" was the first sentence taught in the company's English classes (immigrants made up three-quarters of its workforce in 1914).[48]

Now corporate America embraces the new multicultural consensus. When the gadfly Ralph Nader puckishly requested that CEOs open their shareholder meetings with the Pledge of Allegiance, he got rebuffed. Ford replied, "We do not believe that the concept of 'corporate allegiance' is possible."[49]

Back then, states around the country established immigration agencies to push Americanization, as did the federal government through the Division of Immigrant Education, under the auspices of the federal Bureau of Education. The federal outfit supported localities that wanted to start English-language and citizenship classes and relentlessly boosted the Americanization cause.[50]

Now the governmental focus on Americanization is gone, replaced by affirmative action and other group preferment. "The United States government," Samuel Huntington writes, "is probably alone in the extent to which it encourages immigrants to hold on to the language, culture, and identity of their birth country."[51]

The Sources of Immigration Have Become Imbalanced

On top of all this, the current level and composition of immigration make assimilation harder. The prior wave in the twentieth century was distributed across different nationalities, preventing any one group, speaking a single foreign language, from predominating. Germans, Italians, Russians, Poles, Canadians, and British each made up about 10 percent of the foreign-born population in 1920.[52] Now Mexico alone accounts for 28 percent of the foreign-born population. Four of the other top ten sending countries are also from Latin America.[53]

The great boost to the melting pot in the twentieth century was the pause on new arrivals that began after 1924.[54] "The ensuing, four-decade interruption in steady, large-scale immigration virtually guaranteed that ethnic communities and cultures would be steadily weakened over time," Richard Alba and Victor

Nee write.[55] People left the immigrant communities where they had originally settled, and newcomers didn't replace them.[56] With fewer ethnic reinforcements, intermarriage among their children and grandchildren with members of other groups increased.[57] The policy expert Reihan Salam explains the effect on Italian Americans. "The result," he writes, "is that Italian American identity is largely symbolic and optional, and Italian Americans are perceived as no different from other white Americans. When Italians stopped arriving in America, Italian Americans had little choice but to marry non–Italian Americans. The Mexican American ethnic community, in contrast, was until recently constantly being replenished by new Mexican arrivals, which in turn has sharpened the distinctiveness of Mexican identity."[58]

Immigrants who join large numbers of ethnic compatriots already here tend to assimilate less quickly, to learn English at a slower rate, and to advance more slowly economically.[59]

The conventional wisdom says that worries about assimilation are disproven by the steady economic progress of immigrants. It's not clear, though, that this trend is as robust as it once was. Economically, immigrants are starting at a lower place than natives and not gaining as quickly.[60]

The immigrants who experience the most economic assimilation tend to have the highest levels of education, but immigrants from Latin America lag badly on this metric.[61] Fifty percent or more of immigrants from Guatemala, Mexico, and Honduras lack a high school diploma. Roughly 60 percent of households of immigrants from those countries use a means-tested welfare program. Nearly half of these immigrants, when asked on Census Bureau surveys, indicate that they don't speak English at all or well. And roughly two-thirds are in or near poverty.[62]

The risk is that they are assimilating into a culture of poverty and an associated politics of ethnic grievance, rather than the American mainstream. The answer here is relatively simple, if anathema to ethnic pressure groups and our denationalized elite:

we should reduce immigration overall, put a greater emphasis on skills in the immigrants we take, and insist on a renewed focus on assimilation, especially the acquisition of English.

As we have seen, few things are as important to national identity and cohesion than unity in language. Yet we are seeing some erosion in it. Encouragingly, by the third generation, immigrants generally aren't speaking the native langue of their forebears anymore.[63] On the other hand, about a third of Hispanics in the United States don't speak English very well, and new immigrants are acquiring English proficiency less quickly.[64] A National Academy of Sciences study noted that Spanish-speaking immigrants are acquiring English more slowly than other immigrant groups: "A major reason is the larger size and frequent replenishment of the Spanish-speaking population in the United States."[65]

The broader culture, and the government, aren't as focused on English acquisition as they should be. The country has two Spanish-language TV networks. Although the percentage of Hispanics getting some of their news in Spanish has ticked down, from 78 percent in 2006, it was still 68 percent as of 2012.[66]

Immigrants who become citizens are supposed to demonstrate a basic knowledge of English. Yet the Voting Rights Act mandates foreign-language ballots, and federal rules require that federal services be provided in foreign languages. The focus of so-called bilingual education in the schools is preserving the native language and culture as much as teaching English.[67] In 2016, the state of California voted to return to bilingual education after it had been rolled back in the 1990s—and despite the clear evidence of the success of insisting that native Spanish speakers be taught English.[68]

Intermarriage Is the Answer

What we want to guard against, in our immigration policy and more broadly, is the continued rise of identity politics. The notion that people can be reduced to their race or ethnicity and are not otherwise susceptible to reasoned persuasion is inimical to democratic deliberation, and subnational identities are the enemy of national cohesion. In the United States, white nationalism or any other ethnic nationalism should be a contradiction in terms. We should be doing everything possible to break down tribal group loyalties rather than build them up.

A powerful tool for doing that is racial and ethnic intermarriage. The assimilative potential of intermarriage has long been recognized, if it was only a brave few who openly advocated it at a time when fierce prejudice and the force of law were arrayed against it.

The abolitionist Wendell Phillips spoke of its marvels in an 1863 speech: "Remember this, the youngest of you: that on the 4th day of July, 1863, you heard a man say, that in the light of all history, in virtue of every page he ever read, he was an amalgamationist, to the utmost extent. I have no hope for the future . . . but in that sublime mingling of races, which is God's own method of civilizing and elevating the world."[69] The sociologist Calvin C. Hernton wrote a century later of how assimilation "has been going on throughout the entire span of human history. Not once, to my knowledge, has it happened without intermarriage ultimately taking place. In fact, intermarriage is perhaps the crucial test in determining when a people have completely won their way into the mainstream of any given society."[70]

We've come a long way since interracial marriages were still banned fifty years ago. Public sentiment has become steadily more open to them. In 2013, 15 percent of marriages were interracial or interethnic, a marked increase from 7.4 percent in 2000.[71] Ten percent of babies in a two-parent household were biracial in 2013, and almost 20 percent of cohabiting couples were interracial or interethnic in 2015, according to the Census Bureau.[72]

The trend will blur racial and ethnic lines and help avoid the entrenchment of hostile subnational groups. In the 2010 census, 53 percent of Hispanics identified themselves as white. About 1.2 million people had shifted from a designation of "some other race" on the 2000 census to "white" in 2010.[73]

THE CASE FOR NATIONALISM

This shows how fluid supposed racial categories can be (ideally, the government wouldn't categorize people by race at all).[74] According to the Pew Research Center, "About three-in-ten adults with a multiracial background say that they have changed the way they describe their race over the years."[75]

The more, the better.

Assimilation Itself Is under Attack

There's an enormous question, though, if blending people together is still considered a desirable goal.

A telling episode in early 2019 had the venerable news anchor Tom Brokaw saying on the Sunday morning political program *Meet the Press* that "the Hispanics should work harder at assimilation." The world immediately crashed in on him. Brokaw's long history as a beloved figure in the media and chronicler of the achievements of "the greatest generation" proved no defense.

The political organization Latino Victory thundered that Brokaw had given "credence to white supremacist ideology." The president of the National Association of Hispanic Journalists denounced assimilation as such, for the offense of "denying one culture for the other." Democratic congressman Joaquin Castro accused Brokaw of xenophobia.[76] This was all ridiculous. First, white supremacists are concerned with maintaining racial supremacy, hierarchy, and purity, not assimilating immigrants into a common culture. Second, denying one culture for another—namely the one that immigrants have voluntarily joined by coming here in the first place—is the least we can ask as the price of entry to our country. Finally, wanting immigrants to become fully part of us is not xenophobia but the opposite. It reflects a belief that our culture can and should be embraced by people from varied backgrounds.

This gets to what should be the bottom line of a contemporary nationalist agenda: the preservation of the American cultural nation.

CHAPTER 12

THE IMPORTANCE OF CULTURAL NATIONALISM

In 1903, the black musician W. C. Handy waited for a late train in the small Delta town of Tutwiler, Mississippi.

He later recounted that a "lean, loose-jointed" man, with ragged clothes and a look betraying "some of the sadness of the ages," started playing a guitar while Handy tried to sleep.[1]

The man repeatedly sang the line, "Goin' where the Southern cross' the Dog." Handy found that "the effect was unforgettable" and considered it "the weirdest music I had ever heard." He asked what the line meant. Amused at Handy's ignorance, the singer explained that it referred to a train crossing at the city of Moorhead, where the Southern Railway crossed the Yazoo-Delta Railroad, nicknamed the "Yellow Dog."[2]

"This was not unusual," Handy wrote. "Southern Negroes sang about everything. Trains, steamboats, steam whistles, sledge hammers, fast women, mean bosses, stubborn mules—all became subjects for their songs. They accompany themselves on anything from which they can extract a music sound or rhythmical effect, anything from a harmonica to a washboard."[3]

By his own account, Handy, the "father of the blues," discovered that day the musical style that would enjoy a nationwide boom a couple of decades later. Like any origin story, it is surely encrusted with legend (the "mother of the blues," Ma Rainey, had her own story dating from a 1902 tent show in Missouri). Nonetheless, the tale hit on a truth about a most American art form, and one that shows our culture at its syncretic best.[4]

The blues arose in the Delta in roughly the 1890s. With roots ultimately in West Africa, it evolved from group work songs with their call and response—sung in the fields, on the railroads, or in lumber gangs—and field hollers, described by the landscape architect and social critic Frederick Law Olmsted as a "long, loud, musical shout, rising and falling and breaking into falsetto."[5]

The cultural context that gave us the blues was the rich, racially mixed musical tapestry of the American South. The banjo was derived from Africa but quickly jumped racial bounds: slaves taught whites how to play, and the instrument became a key part of the folk culture of rural whites.[6] Likewise, everyone played the fiddle—as many as half of southeastern fiddle songs may have African roots. Both whites and blacks performed in minstrel shows.[7]

Black musicians played whatever white audiences wanted to hear. The Delta blues guitarist Sam Chatmon explained, "Mighty seldom I played for colored—they didn't have nothing to hire you with." Meanwhile, white artists freely borrowed from black musicians. In the end, as the music historian Elijah Wald writes, "it is often impossible to trace a given style or tune specifically to African or European sources."[8]

The blues, from its lowly origins, perhaps including that ill-kempt man with a guitar overheard by Handy, came to have a major influence on our nation. It's extraordinary, the jazz critic Francis Davis writes, that "the music of a people regarded as worthless except as cheap labor could turn out to be this nation's source music—the yeast that gave rise to rhythm 'n' blues, rock 'n' roll, and a style of popular song unshackled by the restraints of Viennese operetta."[9]

But so it was.

We Should Defend the Nation's Sovereignty and Culture

The blues is as good a demonstration as any other of the glories of American culture, which is neither fully white nor black, neither rich nor poor, and binds us tighter than and sets us apart from people in the rest of the world.

We have seen in the prior two chapters the importance of historical memory and of immigration policy to the nationalist project. We will conclude by emphasizing a defense of the core of the nation: its sovereignty and especially its culture—inclusive, yet bounded and distinct; suffused by our values but deeper than any ideology; a wellspring of our greatness.

It is given its shape by those things that are characteristically American: the festivals Thanksgiving and Christmas (as well as, one might add, Super Bowl Sunday) and the official patriotic holidays the Fourth of July and Memorial Day; the manners— open, familiar, straightforward—that are instantly recognizable to foreigners; a common stock of knowledge about our history and culture, from the Bible to Elvis; and the bourgeois virtues of self-discipline, diligence, and honesty.[10]

The American creed is an important expression and pillar of this, our cultural nation. But that creed isn't the sum total of what makes us Americans. Mores, institutions, and ideals are all important, and they influence and support one another.

We are not in the position of Massimo d'Azeglio, starting from scratch in the project of making Italians after the establishment of national unity. But the making of Americans is a continuous work in progress. It depends, as the editors of the patriotic reader *What So Proudly We Hail: The American Soul in Story, Speech, and Song* argue, "partly on explicit instruction, partly on habituation in character-shaping activities—in homes, schools, houses of worship, community organizations, youth groups, voluntary associations, branches of military service, and the like." The goal is nothing less than "the shaping of the central attitudes, sensibilities, and concerns of their being."[11]

How we do that is a question that implicates our national character—and perhaps ultimately our national survival.

The National Interest Must Be Paramount

There are many policy mixes and approaches to government that fit into a broad nationalist framework. A socialist cosmopolitanism obviously doesn't, nor does a libertarianism that dreams of dispensing with the national government altogether. The federal government doesn't need to be sprawling and expansive, but it does need to be strong and capable, powerful enough to muster the nation in a great cause (the Civil War, World War II) or in response to one (the civil rights movement).

There are several other obvious imperatives: We need to unabashedly make the interests of American citizens the test of government policy. We need to maintain the world's foremost military, to defend the homeland and our interests overseas. We need to stand up for national sovereignty, our own foremost, and that of our European allies who are subsuming themselves (willingly or under threat) in the European Union superstate.

The final priority involves the defense of what John Fonte calls Philadelphian sovereignty. Its foundation is obviously the US Constitution.[12] The Supreme Court stated the matter simply and sharply in a 1957 case: "The United States is entirely a creature of the Constitution. Its power and authority have no other source. It can only act in accordance with all the limitations imposed by the Constitution."[13]

The United States isn't confronting any threat to its sovereignty on a par with that of the European Union, but it still should be extremely jealous of its prerogatives.

This means remaining a cussed global outlier and not ratifying treaties such as the UN Convention on Elimination of All Forms of Discrimination Against Women and the UN Convention on the Rights of the Child. The UN committees monitoring compliance with these treaties are intrusive. Although they have no direct mechanism for coercion and rely on political pressure, their most fervent supporters want eventually to give them the force of domestic law.

This means preserving the "reservations" we've stipulated to the UN conventions that we've already joined, making clear our objections to provisions that are incompatible with the US Constitution.[14]

This means staying out of the International Criminal Court, a permanent, supranational tribunal that claims the right to prosecute citizens of countries around the globe.[15]

This means opposing the concept of a "customary" international law that seeks to take supposed global norms established by the United Nations and other multilateral institutions and impose them on sovereign states.[16]

This means resisting the citation of foreign law in US legal decisions, which should be based solely and entirely on the US Constitution and US law.[17]

Outside of exceptional cases, the focus of US policy should be the national interest. We can (and should) know about the world, we can (and should) forge international alliances, we can (and should) trade with the rest of the world. But the animating goal of our government should be promoting the interests of its own citizens. On trade, it shouldn't be enough to say that it has lifted hundreds of millions of Chinese out of poverty, not if there's been a substantial cost to Americans.

All of this is important, but in the grand scheme it just creates the parameters and conditions for the defense of the national culture.

Culture Is at the Root of Our National Identity and Way of Life

The overarching priority of American nationalists has to be protecting and fostering the cultural nation, as a source of coherence and belonging and the foundation of our way of life.

No less an authority than Alexis de Tocqueville remarked in *Democracy in America* on the essential role of our mores in making this country what it is. "The customs of the Americans of the United States are, then," he wrote, "the peculiar cause which renders that people the only one of the American nations that is able to support a democratic government." He insisted, "If I have hitherto failed in making the reader feel the important influence of the practical experience, the habits, the opinions in short, of the customs of the Americans upon the maintenance of their institutions, I have failed in the principal object of my work."[18]

As Michael Lind argues in his brilliant book *The Next American Nation: The New Nationalism and the Fourth American Revolution*, our culture—the language, the holidays, the national symbols and mores—provides a source of national identity that doesn't depend on citizenship or government recognition of any sort, nor on doctrinal tests. It is organic and open.

Lind quotes the historian Tzvetan Todorov on how one learns a culture: "By mastery of the language above all; by familiarization with the country's history, its landscapes, and the mores of its original population, governed by a thousand invisible codes (it would obviously be a mistake to identify the culture with what is found in books)." Todorov added that "we do not have to have been born into a culture to acquire it: blood has nothing to do with it, nor even genes. Furthermore, not all native-born citizens necessarily possess the culture of their country."[19]

In an 1869 speech on immigration, Frederick Douglass set out his exuberant vision of cultural unity: "We shall spread the network of our science and civilization over all who seek their shelter whether from Asia, Africa, or the Isles of the sea. We shall mold them all, each after his kind, into Americans; Indian and Celt; negro and Saxon; Latin and Teuton; Mongolian and Caucasian; Jew and Gentile; all shall here bow to the same law, speak the same language, support the same Government, enjoy the same liberty, vibrate with the same national enthusiasm, and seek the same national ends."[20]

Our national culture isn't endlessly flexible, but it does change. The Harvard social scientist Orlando Patterson writes that it is "an ever-evolving national process which selects, unrepresentatively, from the market-place of raw, particular identities those that everyone finds it useful and gratifying to embrace and transform into their own."[21]

Even when America has fallen short of its ideals, its culture has absorbed the influences of all its people. Lind calls our culture "a unique blend of elements contributed by Algonquian Indians and Midwestern Quakers and black Americans and Mexican mestizos and New England patricians." As it happens, "black Americans have shaped it far more than the most numerous white immigrant group, German-Americans."[22]

This is a point worth dwelling on.

Our Culture Is Neither White nor Black

An American cultural nationalism is an inclusive nationalism. As we saw in the early history of the blues, we shouldn't believe the lie perpetrated by white nationalists that our culture is in any meaningful sense "white" or the countervailing lie perpetrated by black nationalists that blacks are anything other than fully American. The emphasis in the phrase "African American" should decidedly be on *American*.

According to the earliest US census, blacks made up about a fifth of the population in 1790.[23] Even then, most of them were native born.[24] Fewer slaves were imported here than elsewhere in the Americas (roughly 400,000, compared to 4 million to the Caribbean and 5 million to Brazil), and subsequently, the racial bias of US immigration policy prevented the entry of new blacks, not to mention the inherent difficulties of African émigrés traveling here on their own prior to the jet age.[25]

All this means that the average African American probably has a longer lineage in this country than the average European

American white nationalist marcher in Charlottesville (owing to the large European immigrant influxes after this country's black population had been long established—not of its own volition, of course).

This is just one of the ironies of race in America. The economist and social scientist Thomas Sowell directs us to another, which is that southern blacks were, over time, more affected by what he calls southern redneck culture than by the African cultures from which they had been long removed.[26]

This included ways of talking that southern blacks took with them when they migrated to northern cities in the twentieth century. So-called black English, Sowell notes, "followed dialects brought over from those parts of Britain from which many white Southerners came, though these speech patterns died out in Britain while surviving in the American South."[27]

Despite the worst efforts of white majorities over the centuries, despite the repression, dispossession, and segregation of blacks, we are one people, inextricably bound up together and so profoundly influenced by one another we might not be fully aware of it.

Ralph Ellison, the novelist, wrote a brilliant and compelling essay on this theme in *Time* magazine in 1970. He, too, emphasized language. According to Ellison, "the American nation is in a sense the product of the American language." And "whether it is admitted or not, much of the sound of that language is derived from the timbre of the African voice and the listening habits of the African ear."

"Whitman," he continues, "viewed the spoken idiom of Negro Americans as a source for a native grand opera. Its flexibility, its musicality, its rhythms, freewheeling diction and metaphors, as projected in Negro American folklore, were absorbed by the creators of our great nineteenth-century literature even when the majority of blacks were still enslaved."

In the absence of it, Mark Twain wouldn't have written *Huckleberry Finn* and given us the American novel as we know it, and there would have been no William Faulkner.

"Without the presence of Negro American style," Ellison added, "our jokes, tall tales, even our sports would be lacking in the sudden turns, shocks and swift changes of pace (all jazz-shaped) that serve to remind us that the world is ever unexplored, and that while a complete mastery of life is mere illusion, the real secret of the game is to make life swing."[28]

The twentieth-century critic Albert Murray wrote in a similar key (not coincidentally, like Ellison, he was an aficionado of jazz, another musical style that arose from rich cross-racial sources). "American culture," he insisted, "even in its most rigidly segregated precincts, is patently and irrevocably composite. It is, regardless of all the hysterical protestations of those who would have it otherwise, incontestably mulatto. Indeed, for all their traditional antagonisms and obvious differences, the so-called black and so-called white people of the United States resemble nobody else in the world so much as they resemble each other."[29]

That is a truth that should buttress a healthy nationalism and not be forgotten in the contention over racially divisive issues, from affirmative action to reparations.

Thanksgiving Represents the Heart of the Cultural Nation

The richness of our national culture isn't simply a matter of its varied sources but of the historical resonances of rites as old as, nay, older than, the republic. Consider that most American holiday, Thanksgiving.

It doesn't have ideological content. It dates from before the establishment of the American nation-state and harkens back to our original settlers. Although the official holiday was formally established by the government and is marked by US presidents, it has acquired its layers of meaning through religious faith, informal culinary and social customs, and a centuries-old vein of tradition—in other words, from the heart of the cultural nation.

After their brutal first winter in the New World, the Pilgrims—

all fifty-three of them were survivors from the original *Mayflower* voyage—shared a feast with Wampanoag Indians in 1621. It wasn't quite the picture-perfect gathering depicted in the famous, delightfully anachronistic Jennie Brownscombe painting of 1914 (complete with what looks like a golden-brown Butter Ball Turkey at the end of the table), but notable all the same.[30]

Their meal was very different from ours, with seafood and venison occupying an important place (the Indians killed five deer). They also certainly ate birds. One of the participants in the feast, Edward Winslow, wrote a letter to a friend describing how the "harvest being gotten in, our governor sent four men on fowling, so that we might rejoice together." Turkey wasn't necessarily on the menu, although the Plymouth Colony governor, William Bradford, made a reference in his journal to the "great store of wild turkeys, of which they took many."[31]

Technically, the Pilgrims' celebration was a harvest feast, rather than what they would have understood as a day of thanksgiving, which would have involved fasting and supplications to God. In time, the New England colonies established annual general thanksgiving days not occasioned by any specific event, although they, too, were solemn occasions. From these sources, as Melanie Kirkpatrick explains in her book on the holiday, Thanksgiving as we know it arose.[32]

It is a thread that runs throughout American history. In 1778, the Continental Congress designated December 30 "to be observed as a day of public thanksgiving and praise, that all the people may, with united hearts, on that day, express a just sense of his unmerited favors."[33] George Washington made the first presidential proclamation in 1789, urging gratitude, among other things, "for the signal and manifold mercies, and the favorable interpositions of his providence, which we experienced in the course and conclusion of the late war—for the great degree of tranquillity, union, and plenty, which we have since enjoyed."[34]

In 1863, Abraham Lincoln declared a national day of Thanksgiving—designating it as the last Thursday of November—and every president has done the same since with some occasional deviations as to the exact day.[35]

Even the connection of the holiday to football stretches back to a Princeton-Yale game in 1873, which became an annual tradition in New York City. Long before the Detroit Lions and Dallas Cowboys made playing on Thanksgiving one of their signatures, colleges and high schools scheduled rivalry games for the day.[36]

The holiday is associated in the American imagination—and in fact—with the ingathering of family and with warmth and plenty. The widely reproduced George Durrie painting from 1863, *Home to Thanksgiving*, depicts a couple returning to a snow-covered farm for the holiday and getting greeted by an older couple at the door of the house, welcoming them back to hearth and home. The even more famous Norman Rockwell painting from eighty years later, *Freedom from Want*, might as well be the continuation of the Durrie scene, now indoors. An elderly couple serves a big, juicy bird to a beaming family conversing around the table. (Rockwell painted the turkey from a real model, soon consumed, on Thanksgiving Day.)

For most Americans, the day functions as the great nineteenth-century promoter of the holiday, Sarah Josepha Hale, hoped it would on the cusp of the Civil War. "Such social rejoicings," she wrote in 1857, "tend greatly to expand the generous feelings of our nature, and strengthen the bond of union that finds us brothers and sisters in that true sympathy of American patriotism."[37]

Old Rites and Symbols Delineate Our Nationhood

Obviously, other American holidays and traditions have much more of an ideological charge than Thanksgiving does. But it'd be a mistake to see them as merely expressions of our universal creed. They fill out and enrich our shared national life, which is much more real to the vast majority of people than any abstractions. "National identity is unavoidable; it is also desirable," write the editors of *What So Proudly We Hail*. "For the plain truth of the matter is that, for the vast majority of human beings, human life *as actually lived* is lived parochially and locally, embedded in a web of human relations, institutions, culture, and mores that define us and give shape and meaning to our lives."[38]

Among them are the symbols, civic rites, holidays, songs, and heroes that give concrete expression to Lincoln's mystic chords of memory. We don't have fewer of these cultural tropes and practices than other countries—as one might expect if our nation was merely a set of ideals—but perhaps more, and we certainly adopted some of them earlier and with more fervor than people anywhere else did.

They are the grace notes of our national life. They point to what unites us. They elicit and express devotion to, and gratitude for, the nation in all its dimensions and the contributions to it from those who came before us. Some of them are so much taken for granted that they have faded to part of the American backdrop; others are vital elements of our civil religion. All of them delineate and enliven our nationhood.

There are the symbols. The Great Seal of the United States, predating the Constitution and adopted after six years of deliberation by three different committees. It still graces the back of the $1 bill and gave us the red, white, and blue shield that is ubiquitous in our culture (not least as a signature accoutrement of Captain America). The seal's designers invested every aspect of it with meaning. To wit, "The Escutcheon is born on the breast of an American Eagle without any other supporters to denote that the United States of America ought to rely on their own Virtue," i.e., its own power.[39]

The eagle itself. The bird of prey hadn't been prominent in the colonies before the seal took a traditional totem of empires and made it an emblem of our republic. Majestic and bespeaking a fierce, yet stately independence, it spread all over the landscape, into homes, and onto every imaginable commercial product. Some Union regiments carried live eagles into battle in the Civil

War. (Herman Melville wrote a poem about one: "Though scarred in many a furious fray,/No deadly hurt he knew;/Well may we think his years are charmed—/The Eagle of the Blue.") The historian Marshall Smelser writes, "Probably no modern civilized nation has venerated its national emblem as much as Americans."[40]

The onmipresent flag, flown from government buildings and, often in huge, honking style, from car dealerships, from fire trucks and ships at sea, from homes and churches, and from a vast array of other establishments. Its roots go back to before the Revolution, perhaps to a Sons of Liberty banner with white and red stripes. An offshoot of our devotion to the flag is the irresistibly charming, if unsupported, legend of Betsy Ross. The etiquette for handling the banner is set out in elaborate and loving detail in the federal code, which states, "The flag represents a living country and is itself considered a living thing."[41]

There are the civic rites. The Pledge of Allegiance, recited by schoolchildren across the country, saluting the flag and pledging their fealty to it. There is no similar practice in other advanced democracies.[42] Adults often recite the Pledge, too, at the start of meetings and other events. "I would hazard the guess," the cultural geographer Wilbur Zelinsky observes, "that in no other country do schoolchildren and other civilians pay obeisance to the flag so regularly and so often."[43]

The national anthem may be the unsingable composition of a possibly tone-deaf lawyer, Francis Scott Key, but it is sung frequently at all sorts of occasions nonetheless.[44] Lest we have only one national song, "God Bless America" has attained informal anthem status, getting the same hats-off respect as "The Star-Spangled Banner."

There are the patriotic holidays. Of course, the Fourth of July: Independence Day, the Glorious Fourth, the National Sabbath. "Clear evidence of the sanctification of American nationalism," John F. Berens writes, "the Fourth of July became literally the holy day of obligation for American patriots." As with practices around honoring the flag, we led the way and other countries followed to make their own independence days into holiday festivals, too.[45]

Memorial Day, with its roots going back to the ancient practice of placing flowers on the graves of the war dead and arising from spontaneous local ceremonies around the time of the Civil War, so widespread that it's hard to determine who went first or spawned the idea of a national holiday. The decorating of military graves connects the living to the dead and their sacrifice in a profoundly organic ritual.[46]

There is the veneration of our heroes, George Washington foremost among them. By the early nineteenth century, his image was everywhere, prompting a Russian diplomat to remark that apparently every American "considered it his sacred duty to have a likeness of Washington in his home just as we [have] images of God's saints." By his second year as president, celebrations of his birthday had become the norm across the country. "This," Zelinsky writes, "may well be the earliest instance of such a commemorative holiday honoring anyone other than a religious figure or monarch."[47]

Sympathy with all this, together with the embrace of other basic norms of speech, dress and cuisine, and a basic familiarity with American pop culture and history, marks someone out as culturally American, part of the broad mainstream of the country, united at its roots whatever our political, ethnic, or religious differences.

This is a precious quality and one that should be fostered and preserved as our foremost national glue.

A Campaign of Cultural Vandalism Threatens the Nation

Yet the nation is under threat. A heedless vandalism seeks to tear down pillars of the cultural nation for the offense of association, or purported association, with the nation's sins.

This drive is waxing rather than waning. Already wide ranging, it has no limiting principle and conceivably may not be sated until the Jefferson Memorial is repurposed or razed.

The singer who gave us our second national anthem, Kate Smith, has been tested and found wanting. She performed a couple of songs with racially offensive lyrics in the early 1930s, so must be anathematized. Never mind that one of the songs was a satire, also performed by Paul Robeson. Never mind that she denounced racism in the 1940s on her radio broadcast or had the black singer Josephine Baker for a groundbreaking appearance on her TV program in 1951. Never mind her extraordinary place in American pop culture, recording nearly three thousand songs, including more than a thousand new ones, six hundred of which were hits. Never mind her service to the nation, helping sell more than $600 million worth of bonds during World War II and traveling extensively to perform for the troops.[48]

And never mind, of course, her transcendent performances of "God Bless America" that made it a national treasure. On the twentieth anniversary of the armistice ending World War I, her manager reached out to the songwriter Irving Berlin for a new patriotic number. Berlin came up empty but remembered a song he'd never done anything with that he'd written while in the army during World War I. Kate Smith performed it on the radio, and the rest is history. For a time, she owned the rights, but then she realized that the song properly belonged to the American people as a whole and gave them up. Neither she nor Berlin ever took royalties, giving the proceeds instead to the Boy Scouts and Girl Scouts.[49]

No, no, pay none of that any heed. Instead damn her to the outer darkness for a couple of offensive songs from eighty years ago. This is what the New York Yankees and the Philadelphia Flyers, neither of them college campuses or otherwise politically progressive organizations, did in early 2019. The Yankees had played Kate Smith's rendition of "God Bless America" during the seventh-inning stretch since after the September 11 attacks, but no more. The Flyers were more egregious. Kate Smith had

become a good-luck charm for the team when it had won cham-
pionships in the 1970s, performing before key games. The franchise
had erected a statue of her outside its arena as a gesture of gratitude after she died. But it immediately forswore the playing of
her rendition of "God Bless America" and covered up and carted
off her statue.[50]

The Kate Smith test, as established by the Yankees and Flyers
without much public backlash, is that anyone who has ever said or
done anything offensive by contemporary standards—no matter
how attenuated—must be banished. If applied across the board,
it would cut a swath through our cultural life and leave very few
historical figures untouched.

As it is, the official national anthem has been accused, as well.
As the website The Root explained, "It is one of the most racist,
pro-slavery, anti-black songs in the American lexicon, and you
would be wise to cut it from your Fourth of July playlist."[51]

The California chapter of the NAACP has called for dumping
the anthem, and a couple of years ago a Baltimore monument in
honor of Francis Scott Key, a slave owner who favored colonizing
American blacks, was defaced with red paint and spray-painted
with the words RACIST ANTHEM.[52]

His supposed offense is the anthem's seldom-heard third verse:

No refuge could save the hireling and slave
From the terror of flight or the gloom of the grave,
And the star-spangled banner in triumph doth wave
O'er the land of the free and the home of the brave.

The charge is that Key was braying for the blood of black troops
fighting with the British, the so-called Colonial Marines. There's
nothing to suggest that this hostile reading is accurate, though.
The Colonial Marines were a minor force that didn't loom large
in anyone's consciousness. The word "hireling" surely referred
to British mercenaries, and "slave" was likely an insult hurled at
the comparatively unfree British, subjects of a monarchy.[53] Francis

Scott Key's handiwork will nonetheless come under continued pressure.

John Wayne has been targeted, and so has Thanksgiving. The holiday is allegedly tainted by the mistreatment of the Indians and white supremacy.[54] A piece for Al Jazeera rehearsing these arguments was titled "Thanksgiving: The Annual Genocide Whitewash."[55]

This is not to say that we shouldn't occasionally review our cultural—and statuary—landscape. Certainly, American nationalists should have no particular brief for honoring Robert E. Lee. The Confederate general obviously wasn't a Nazi, and his postwar emphasis on reconciliation was a great service to the country. Presented with a momentous choice between his nation and his native state of Virginia, though, he chose the latter and nearly brought our national government to its knees. Often, statues of him were erected after the war to try to sugarcoat the cause of the Confederacy. They can be removed to battlefields and museums without rending our cultural fabric (rather, mending it for African Americans, for whom the statues are an understandable affront).

The problem is we obviously don't live at a time of careful distinctions. After the Charlottesville protests, a historic Episcopal church in Alexandria, Virginia, decided to remove plaques in its sanctuary of both Robert E. Lee *and* George Washington, who had both worshipped there. The plaques had hung there since 1870. The church explained that the plaques might "create an obstacle to our identity as a welcoming church and an impediment to our growth and to full community with our neighbors."[56] This is a perhaps legitimate concern with Lee, but Washington?

At his namesake George Washington University, students voted in March 2019 to ditch the school's nickname, "The Colonials." A student petition complained that the name "has too deep a connection to colonization and glorifies the act of systemic oppression."[57] It didn't occur to the objecting students, evidently, that in the context of the American Revolution, *we* were the colonials, in the sense of being subjects of a great empire, until we determined to make our exit under the leadership of the man the school is named after.

The founding and the instruments created by it are vulnerable to this rampaging spirit of destruction. The Electoral College and the US Senate—the design of which is deemed unamendable in the US Constitution—have been condemned as racist, both because they involved compromises with slave states and because they supposedly dilute black political power today. Given the sweeping nihilism of this ongoing campaign, it's going to be tricky for a figure such as Thomas Jefferson, a slave owner who wrote racist things and stands accused of raping Sally Hemings, to survive the onslaught.

Culture Unites Us as Americans

All of this is a grievous mistake. Our national sins should be acknowledged and repented of but not weaponized in an unyielding attempt to ransack our heritage and shoot holes in our common culture.

We should have a more capacious and merciful self-understanding. We all are Thomas Jefferson and W. C. Handy, the Pilgrims and Frederick Douglass, British and African, black and white, sitting at a vast Thanksgiving table within sight of an enormous flat-screen tuned to a Lions or Cowboys game under the watchful gaze of a red, white, and blue–bedecked Eagle, sharing, laughing, squabbling, commiserating, and doing it all loudly, in the distinct, instantly recognizable American style that makes its indelible imprint on us all.

In short, our culture is the warp and woof of the American nation. Throw it away, and we will lose ourselves as a people and lose a country that is the most glorious jewel in the millennia-long history of nations.

EPILOGUE:
THE ANTI-NATIONALIST TEMPTATION

In a 2015 interview with Bernie Sanders, the editor of the progressive explainer website Vox, Ezra Klein, found to his astonishment that the Vermont socialist still took the nation-state and its obligations to its own citizens seriously.

Klein broached the subject of immigration, and the two had this exchange:

KLEIN: You said being a democratic socialist means a more international view. I think if you take global poverty that seriously, it leads you to conclusions that in the US are considered out of political bounds. Things like sharply raising the level of immigration we permit, even up to a level of open borders. About sharply increasing . . .

SANDERS: Open borders? No, that's a Koch brothers proposal.

KLEIN: Really?

SANDERS: Of course. That's a right-wing proposal, which says essentially there is no United States. . . .

KLEIN: But it would make . . .

SANDERS: Excuse me . . .

KLEIN: It would make a lot of global poor richer, wouldn't it?

SANDERS: It would make everybody in America poorer—you're doing away with the concept of a nation-state, and I don't think there's any country in the world that believes in that.[1]

The Sanders view represented not just common sense but a long-standing vein of thinking on the Left that the welfare state depends on a sense of national solidarity. It's why Sweden's socialists made nationalistic appeals in the twentieth century: "Embracing concepts such as 'people' and 'nation' that the radical right was exploiting successfully elsewhere," the political scientist Sheri Berman writes, Sweden's Social Democrats were "able to claim the mantle of national unity and social solidarity during the chaos of the early 1930s."[2] It's why FDR made use of nationalist symbols and appeals to unity and Americanism even as he excoriated the rich.

All of that was a long time ago, before the Left lost touch with patriotic feeling. Even clear-sighted progressives recognize as much. Writing in the left-wing journal *Dissent*, Michael Kazin describes the problem: "Antiwar activists view patriotism as a smokescreen for U.S. hegemony, while radical academics mock the notion of 'American exceptionalism' as a relic of the cold war, a triumphal myth we should quickly outgrow. All the rallying around the flag after September 11 increased the disdain many leftists feel for the sentiment that lies behind it. 'The globe, not the flag, is the symbol that's wanted now,' scolded Katha Pollitt in the *Nation*."[3]

So it was that Bernie Sanders got beaten about his head and shoulders for his allegedly retrograde sentiments in his interview with Klein. A piece on Vox faulted him for his moral lapse: "he's wrong in treating Americans' lives as more valuable and worthy of concern than the lives of foreigners."[4] Sanders had to back down and get with the cosmopolitan program.

The rise of Donald Trump has pushed the Left even further in this direction: away from respect for nationalistic attitudes and even patriotic symbols (it was heresy for Democrats to suggest that perhaps extremely well-paid athletes should stand for the national anthem) and toward an ever-more-elaborate and arcane identity politics of "intersectionality" and obsession with supposed "white privilege."

Democrats—and the country—would be much better served if they countered Trump's nationalism with a version of their own. Their iteration would presumably emphasize national solidarity as a reason for across-the-board federal activism, and national unity and ideals as the rationale for their preferred immigration policies and international posture.

On his own side of the aisle, Trump has made Republicans more nationalistic. Still, much of the party is quietly uncomfortable with its new nationalism. It's unclear how the Trump phenomenon will ultimately turn out. If it goes badly, the party's establishment may try to snap back to its pre-Trump disposition of relative indifference to nationalism. This, too, would be bad for the party and bad for the country.

Republicans should be considering how to learn the lessons of Trump and in particular how to thoughtfully integrate his nationalism into the party's orthodoxy.

In sum, this hasn't been an explicitly political book. But if there's one clear political lesson from the long history of nationalism in this country and elsewhere—which underlines its obvious potency and staying power—it is that anyone interested in moving people and selling a program should make an appeal to it.

Nationalism shouldn't be a dirty word, especially in this country, where it has been an indispensable element in the success of our extraordinary, centuries-old, and still vital and ongoing national project.

ACKNOWLEDGMENTS

Writing a book is a solitary activity, but unless you are a desert monk, it still involves a group effort. It takes the forbearance and support of lot of people. I'm grateful, first and foremost, to my wife and family, who allowed me the time to go off and work for hours every weekend. I'd trudge out the door with a tote bag full of books, and when I'd explain to one of the kids I needed to go and write, the question often would be, "But why?" My wife never asked that, but could have been forgiven for thinking it, as she was left juggling things—once again—on her own. She's the most tireless person I know, who keeps us all on track with her incredible care, attention to detail, and boundless love.

I'm grateful to friends who acted as sounding boards and gave thoughtful advice and feedback, including Michael Lind, Yoram Hazony, and Yuval Levin. The book grew out of a piece I co-authored with my longtime friend and colleague, Ramesh Ponnuru, who writes and thinks with the precision of a dagger.

My research assistants, Justin Shapiro and Grayson Logue, were energetic, smart, and careful. By the end, Justin had read the entire manuscript multiple times and knew it about as well as I did.

I appreciate all those people who read the book or portions of it, including Victor Davis Hanson, Matthew Continetti, Charlie Cooke, Andrew Stuttaford, Steven Camarota, Reihan Salam, Matthew Franck, John O'Sullivan, Deroy Murdock, Elliott Abrams, Rob Thomas, and John Fonte.

Of course, all mistakes are mine.

My assistant, Mary Spencer, provided all sorts of indispensable editorial support.

My brilliant, endlessly interesting colleagues are a constant source of pride and were, as always, encouraging. My thanks especially to the one and only Jack Fowler.

My agent and friend Keith Korman is hilarious and wise.

Eric Nelson and Hannah Long and everyone else at Broadside and HarperCollins were devoted to the project and made the book better.

I benefited from the acute work of the countless historians cited throughout the text.

My good friends at my "third place," LPQ, weren't annoyed that I spent hours perched at my favorite spot but regaled me with free coffee and foodstuffs.

Christian and Melia were generous as always and even provided business services in a pinch.

Finally, I'm thankful beyond words to my angel mother, Sue, whose devotion to me and my pal Robert can never be adequately repaid. The word *privilege* is fashionable these days. I'm well aware of our "Sue and Ed privilege," the unmerited gift of being raised by parents who never put themselves first and provided sterling examples of what a mother and father, nay, what a person, should be. The older I get, the more grateful I am.

NOTES

Introduction: What Trump Realized

1. Jennifer Rubin, "Three Interpretations of Trump's 'Nationalist' Rhetoric," *Washington Post*, October 24, 2018, https://www.washingtonpost.com/news /opinions/wp/2018/10/24/three-interpretations-of-trumps-nationalist -rhetoric/?utm_term=.a84cfc497fb2.

Chapter 1: America the Nation

1. Sally Jenkins, "How the Flag Came to Be Called Old Glory," *Smithsonian Magazine*, October 2013, https://www.smithsonianmag.com/history/how-the -flag-came-to-be-called-old-glory-18396/.
2. Quoted in ibid.
3. *The Essex Institute Historical Collections* (Salem: The Essex Institute, 1911), 100.
4. Marc Leepson, *Flag: An American Biography* (New York: St. Martin's Griffin), 117.
5. Samuel P. Huntington, *Who Are We?: The Challenges to America's National Identity* (New York: Simon & Schuster, 2004), 126–27.
6. Scot M. Guenter, *The American Flag, 1777–1924: Cultural Shifts from Creation to Codification* (Cranbury, NJ: Associated University Presses, 1990), 22–23.
7. Quoted in Huntington, *Who Are We?*, 46.
8. Quoted in Michael Lind, *The Next American Nation: The New Nationalism and the Fourth American Revolution* (New York: Simon & Schuster, 1995), 220.
9. Quoted in ibid., 3.
10. Hagen Schulze, *States, Nations and Nationalism*, translated by William E. Yuill (Malden, MA: Blackwell Publishers, 1998), 96.
11. Jonah Goldberg, "The Trouble with Nationalism," *National Review*, February 7, 2017, https://www.nationalreview.com/2017/02/nationalism-patriotism-donald -trump-response-national-review-cover-story/.
12. Ilya Somin, "Against Nationalism," The Volokh Conspiracy, December 1, 2009, http://volokh.com/2009/12/01/against-nationalism/.
13. Elizabeth Bruenig, "Trump's Solution to America's Crisis: Nationalism,"

Washington Post, January 30, 2018, https://www.washingtonpost.com/opinions
/trumps-solution-to-americas-crisis-nationalism/2018/01/30/db5f15f4–062f
-11e8–94e8-e8b8600ade23_story.html?utm_term=.4189172527eb.

14.   Michael Brendan Dougherty, "Confiscating the Nation," *National Review*, March
      2, 2018, https://www.nationalreview.com/2018/03/national-identity-made-up
      -not-fast/.

15.   Quoted in Gregory Jusdanis, *The Necessary Nation* (Princeton: Princeton University
      Press, 2001), 20.

16.   Anthony D. Smith, *Nationalism* (Cambridge, UK: Polity Press, 2010), 20.

17.   G. K. Chesterton, *The Collected Works of G. K. Chesterton* (San Francisco: Ignatius
      Press, 2001), 597.

18.   Azar Gat, *Nations: The Long History and Deep Roots of Political Ethnicity and
      Nationalism* (Cambridge, UK: Cambridge University Press, 2013), 26.

19.   Anthony D. Smith, *Nationalism in the Twentieth Century* (Canberra: Australian
      National University Press, 1979), 2.

20.   Lind, *The Next American Nation*, 5.

21.   Quoted in Bernard Yack, "The Myth of the Civic Nation," in *Theorizing
      Nationalism*, edited by Ronald Beiner (Albany: State University of New York
      Press, 1999), 104–05.

22.   Ibid., 117.

23.   Eugen Weber, *Peasants into Frenchmen: The Modernization of Rural France*
      (Stanford, CA: Stanford University Press, 1976), 67.

24.   Quoted in ibid., 113.

25.   George Washington Parke Custis, *Recollections and Private Memoirs of Washington
      by His Adopted Son* (New York: Derby & Jackson, 1860), 443.

26.   Gat, *Nations*, 272.

27.   Quoted in Anthony D. Smith, *The Nation in History* (Hanover, NH: University
      Press of New England, 2000), 11.

28.   Schulze, *States, Nations and Nationalism*, 260.

29.   Gat, *Nations*, 318.

30.   Emilie Ashurst Venturi, *Joseph Mazzini, A Memoir by E. A. V.* (London: Henry S.
      King & Co., 1875), 28.

31.   Roger Eatwell, "Fascism and Racism," in *The Oxford Handbook of the History of
      Nationalism*, edited by John Breuilly (Oxford: Oxford University Press, 2013), 573.

32.   Ibid., 581–83.

33.   Konrad H. Jarausch, "Illiberalism and Beyond: German History in Search of a
      Paradigm," *The Journal of Modern History* 55, no. 2 (June 1983): 268–84.

34.   Smith, *Nationalism in the Twentieth Century*, 13.

35.   Edward J. Goodman, "Spanish Nationalism in the Struggle Against Napoleon,"
      The Review of Politics 20, no. 3 (July 1958): 330–46; Dror Zeevi, "Back to
      Napoleon? Thoughts on the Beginning of the Modern Era in the Middle East,"
      Mediterranean Historical Review 19, no. 1 (June 2004): 73–94.

36.   Daniel Walker Howe, "Why the Scottish Enlightenment Was Useful to the
      Framers of the American Constitution," *Comparative Studies in Society and
      History* 31, no. 3 (July 1989): 572–87.

37.   Quoted in Hans Kohn, *The Idea of Nationalism* (New York: Macmillan, 1961),
      300–301.

38. Anatol Lieven, *America Right or Wrong* (New York: Oxford University Press, 2012), 16–19.

39. Steven Grosby, *Biblical Ideas of Nationality: Ancient and Modern* (Winona Lake, IN: Eisenbrauns, 2002), 208.

40. Quoted in Lloyd Kramer, *Nationalism in Europe and America: Politics, Cultures, and Identities Since 1775* (Chapel Hill: University of North Carolina Press, 2011), 72–73.

41. Merle Curti, *The Roots of American Loyalty* (New York: Columbia University Press, 1946), 43–44.

42. John Thornton Kirkland, *An Oration Delivered at the Request of the Society of Φ. B. K.* (Boston: John Russell, 1798), 13–14.

43. Alexander Hamilton, "The Examination Number VIII, 12 January 1802," in *The Papers of Alexander Hamilton*, vol. 25, *July 1800–April 1802*, edited by Harold C. Syrett (New York: Columbia University Press, 1977), 495–97.

44. Kohn, *The Idea of Nationalism*, 308.

45. Quoted in Henry S. Randall, *The Life of Thomas Jefferson* (New York: Derby & Jackson, 1858), 432.

46. Quoted in Curti, *The Roots of American Loyalty*, 46.

47. Mark Twain, *Life on the Mississippi* (London: Chatto & Windus, 1883), 5–7.

48. Lind, *The Next American Nation*, 225.

49. Kevin Phillips, *The Cousins' Wars: Religion, Politics, and the Triumph of Anglo-America* (New York: Basic Books, 1999), 5.

50. Lind, *The Next American Nation*, 225.

Chapter 2: Love, Not Hate

1. Kathryn Harrison, *Joan of Arc: A Life Transfigured* (New York: Doubleday, 2014), chap. 1, Kindle.

2. Julien Théry, "How Joan of Arc Turned the Tide in the Hundred Years' War," *National Geographic*, March 2017, https://www.nationalgeographic.com /archaeology-and-history/magazine/2017/03–04/joan-of-arc-warrior-heretic -saint-martyr/.

3. Quoted in Deborah McGrady, "Joan of Arc and the Literary Imagination," in *The Cambridge Companion to French Literature*, edited by John D. Lyons (Cambridge, UK: Cambridge University Press, 2016), 25.

4. Quoted in Harrison, *Joan of Arc*, chap. 6.

5. Théry, "How Joan of Arc Turned the Tide in the Hundred Years' War."

6. Harrison, *Joan of Arc*, chap. 1.

7. Quoted in Daniel Hobbins, *The Trial of Joan of Arc* (Cambridge, MA: Harvard University Press, 2005), 110.

8. Théry, "How Joan of Arc Turned the Tide in the Hundred Years' War."

9. Aviel Roshwald, *The Endurance of Nationalism: Ancient Roots and Modern Dilemmas* (Cambridge, UK: Cambridge University Press, 2006), 52.

10. Schulze, *States, Nations and Nationalism*, 99.

11. Quoted in Azar Gat, *Nations: The Long History and Deep Roots of Political Ethnicity and Nationalism* (Cambridge, UK: Cambridge University Press, 2013), 47, 215–17.

12.   Benedict Anderson, *Imagined Communities* (London: Verso, 2016), 143.
13.   Quoted in Lloyd Kramer, *Nationalism in Europe and America: Politics, Cultures, and Identities Since 1775* (Chapel Hill: University of North Carolina Press, 2011), 106.
14.   Anderson, *Imagined Communities*, 141–42.
15.   G. K. Chesterton, *The Collected Works of G. K. Chesterton* (San Francisco: Ignatius Press, 2001), 597.
16.   Gat, *Nations*, 8.
17.   Peter Burke, "Nationalisms and Vernaculars, 1500–1800," in *The Oxford Handbook of the History of Nationalism*, edited by John Breuilly (Oxford: Oxford University Press, 2013), 22.
18.   Anderson, *Imagined Communities*, 18.
19.   Quoted in Anthony D. Smith, *National Identity* (Reno: University of Nevada Press, 1991), 71.
20.   Quoted in Gat, *Nations*, 131.
21.   Ibid., 85–87, 93, 104–06.
22.   Quoted in ibid., 215–16.
23.   Ibid., 161.
24.   Quoted in Hagen Schulze, *States, Nations and Nationalism*, translated by William E. Yuill (Malden, MA: Blackwell Publishers, 1998), 108.
25.   Anthony D. Smith, *Chosen Peoples* (Oxford, UK: Oxford University Press, 2003), 107.
26.   Quoted in Gat, *Nations*, 200.
27.   Ibid., 218–19.
28.   Schulze, *States, Nations and Nationalism*, 114–15.
29.   Ibid., 112.
30.   Burke, "Nationalisms and Vernaculars, 1500–1800," 42.
31.   Gat, *Nations*, 180.
32.   Ibid., 278.
33.   Ibid., 199.
34.   Ibid., 165.
35.   Anderson, *Imagined Communities*, 144–45.
36.   John Hutchinson, "Cultural Nationalism," in *The Oxford Handbook of the History of Nationalism*, edited by John Breuilly (Oxford, UK: Oxford University Press, 2013), 81–82.
37.   Smith, *National Identity*, 92; Hutchinson, "Cultural Nationalism," 82.
38.   Joep Leerssen, *National Thought in Europe: A Cultural History* (Amsterdam: Amsterdam University Press, 2006), 192.
39.   Ibid., 195.
40.   Roger Scruton, *England and the Need for Nations* (London: Civitas, 2006), chap. 4, Kindle.
41.   Quoted in Gregory Jusdanis, *The Necessary Nation* (Princeton: Princeton University Press, 2001), 47; Gat, *Nations*, 158.
42.   Quoted in ibid., 72.
43.   John H. Wuorinen, *A History of Finland* (New York: Columbia University Press, 1965), 138–39.
44.   Gat, *Nations*, 159.
45.   Jusdanis, *The Necessary Nation*, 78–79.
46.   Quoted in Richard White, "Herder: On the Ethics of Nationalism," *Humanitas*

18, nos. 1 and 2 (2005): 166–81, https://pdfs.semanticscholar.org/2de2/c1dceb5609f2111821debfbed3d72c6781b0.pdf.

47. Quoted in Gat, *Nations*, 256.
48. Ibid., 250.
49. Quoted in Yoram Hazony, *The Virtue of Nationalism* (New York: Hachette, 2018), 136.
50. Gat, *Nations*, 249.
51. Ibid., 256.
52. Krishan Kumar, *Visions of Empire: How Five Imperial Regimes Shaped the World* (Princeton: Princeton University Press, 2017), 176, 184, 206.
53. Ibid., 173–74, 206.
54. Gat, *Nations*, 190.
55. Quoted in Kumar, *Visions of Empire*, 196, 206.
56. Ibid., 76; Gat, *Nations*, 253.
57. Kumar, *Visions of Empire*, 83, 110.
58. Ibid., 125–27; Gat, *Nations*, 251–52.
59. Quoted in Bertram D. Wolfe, *Three Who Made a Revolution: A Biographical History of Lenin, Trotsky, and Stalin* (New York: Rowman & Littlefield, 2001).
60. Kumar, *Visions of Empire*, 217–18, 241; Gat, *Nations*, 254.
61. Kumar, *Visions of Empire*, 290; Sergei Maksudov and William Taubman, "Russian-Soviet Nationality Policy and Foreign Policy: A Historical Overview of the Linkage Between Them," in *The Rise of Nations in the Soviet Union: American Foreign Policy and the Disintegration of the USSR*, edited by Michael Mandelbaum (New York: Council on Foreign Relations Press, 1991), 15–41.
62. Kumar, *Visions of Empire*, 291–99.
63. Quoted in White, "Herder: On the Ethics of Nationalism," 172.
64. Gat, *Nations*, 255.
65. Ibid., 319–20.
66. Kumar, *Visions of Empire*, 390–91.
67. Ibid., 459–63.
68. Ibid., 314, 372.
69. Rudyard Kipling, *The Writings in Prose and Verse of Rudyard Kipling*, vol. 11 (New York: Charles Scribner's Sons, 1898), 42.
70. Quoted in Kramer, *Nationalism in Europe and America*, 175.
71. Quoted in Jusdanis, *The Necessary Nation*, 36–37.
72. Gat, *Nations*, 287–91.
73. Jonathan Power, "Africa: Tribalism Lives, for Better and for Worse," *New York Times*, May 25, 2006, https://www.nytimes.com/2006/05/25/opinion/25iht-edpower.html.
74. Craig Calhoun, *Nations Matter: Culture, History and the Cosmopolitan Dream* (New York: Routledge, 2007), 164.
75. Scruton, *England and the Need for Nations*, chap. 2.

Chapter 3: The Smear Against Nationalism

1. Norman M. Naimark, *Genocide: A World History* (Oxford, UK: Oxford University Press, 2017), 21.

2. W. B. Bartlett, *The Mongols: From Genghis Khan to Tamerlane* (Stroud, UK: Amberley Publishing, 2012), chap. 3, Kindle.

3. Naimark, *Genocide*, 17–18.

4. Brian Handwerk, "An Ancient, Brutal Massacre May Be the Earliest Evidence of War," *Smithsonian Magazine*, January 20, 2016, https://www.smithsonianmag.com/science-nature/ancient-brutal-massacre-may-be-earliest-evidence-war-180957884/.

5. Bartlett, *The Mongols*, chap. 2.

6. Quoted in Naimark, *Genocide*, 12.

7. Ibid.

8. Quoted in ibid., 26–27.

9. Thomas Fleiner and Lidija R. Basta Fleiner, *Constitutional Democracy in a Multicultural and Globalized World*, translated by Katy Le Roy (Fribourg, Germany: Springer-Verlag, 2009), 425.

10. Steven Pinker, *The Better Angels of Our Nature: Why Violence Has Declined* (New York: Penguin, 2012), 316.

11. Quoted in ibid., 49, 325.

12. Azar Gat, *Nations: The Long History and Deep Roots of Political Ethnicity and Nationalism* (Cambridge, UK: Cambridge University Press, 2013), 318.

13. Pinker, *The Better Angels of Our Nature*, 250–51.

14. Ibid., 237.

15. Hagen Schulze, *States, Nations and Nationalism*, translated by William E. Yuill (Malden, MA: Blackwell Publishers, 1998), 155.

16. Michael Rowe, "The French Revolution, Napoleon, and Nationalism in Europe," in *The Oxford Handbook of the History of Nationalism*, edited by John Breuilly (Oxford, UK: Oxford University Press, 2013), 128.

17. Ibid., 134–38, 144.

18. Pinker, *The Better Angels of Our Nature*, 243.

19. Quoted in Schulze, *States, Nations and Nationalism*, 251, 261.

20. Adrian Hastings, *The Construction of Nationhood: Ethnicity, Religion and Nationalism* (Cambridge, UK: Cambridge University Press, 1997), 130–31.

21. G. J. Meyer, *A World Undone: The Story of the Great War, 1914 to 1918* (New York: Random House, 2006), 11–12.

22. Friedrich Naumann, *Central Europe*, translated by Christabel M. Meredith (New York: Alfred A. Knopf, 1917), 192.

23. Quoted in Yoram Hazony, *The Virtue of Nationalism* (New York: Hachette, 2018), 39.

24. Robert O. Paxton, *The Anatomy of Fascism* (New York: Random House, 2004), chap. 1, Kindle.

25. Roger Eatwell, "Fascism and Racism," in *The Oxford Handbook of the History of Nationalism*, edited by John Breuilly (Oxford: Oxford University Press, 2013), 580.

26. Anthony D. Smith, *Nationalism in the Twentieth Century* (Canberra: Australian National University Press, 1979), 48.

27. Eatwell, "Fascism and Racism," 575–79.

28. Ibid., 574.

29. Paxton, *The Anatomy of Fascism*, 345.

30. Smith, *Nationalism in the Twentieth Century*, 58.

31. Ibid., 56–57.

32.   Ibid., 82–84.

33.   Ibid., 66.

34.   Paxton, *The Anatomy of Fascism*, chap. 2.

35.   Quoted in Douglas R. Holmes, *Integral Europe: Fast-Capitalism, Multiculturalism, Neofascism* (Princeton, NJ: Princeton University Press, 2000), 212.

36.   Paxton, *The Anatomy of Fascism*, chap. 2.

37.   David McCullough, *Mornings on Horseback: The Story of an Extraordinary Family, a Vanished Way of Life, and the Unique Child Who Became Theodore Roosevelt* (New York: Simon & Schuster, 1981), 352.

38.   Smith, *Nationalism in the Twentieth Century*, 70–72.

39.   Paxton, *The Anatomy of Fascism*, chap. 2.

40.   Eatwell, "Fascism and Racism," 579.

41.   Paxton, *The Anatomy of Nationalism*, chap. 2.

42.   Ibid., chap. 4.

43.   Smith, *Nationalism in the Twentieth Century*, 74–76.

44.   Hazony, *The Virtue of Nationalism*, 200.

45.   Smith, *Nationalism in the Twentieth Century*, 79–80.

46.   Pinker, *The Better Angels of Our Nature*, 321.

47.   Ibid., 322–36.

48.   Hastings, *The Construction of Nationhood*, 121–22.

49.   Benjamin Isaac, "Proto-racism in Graeco-Roman Antiquity," *World Archaeology* 38, no. 1 (2006): 32–47.

50.   Smith, *Nationalism in the Twentieth Century*, 91.

51.   Ali Rattansi, *Racism: A Very Short Introduction* (Oxford, UK: Oxford University Press, 2007), 13–14.

52.   Ibid., 23.

53.   Robert Palter, "Hume and Prejudice," *Hume Studies* 21, no. 1 (April 1995): 3–23, http://www.humesociety.org/hs/issues/v21n1/palter/palter-v21-n1.pdf.

54.   George M. Fredrickson, *Racism: A Short History* (Princeton, NJ: Princeton University Press, 2002), 28.

55.   Quoted in Rattansi, *Racism*, 32.

56.   Smith, *Nationalism in the Twentieth Century*, 89.

57.   Rattansi, *Racism*, 4–15; Fredrickson, *Racism*, 21.

58.   Smith, *Nationalism in the Twentieth Century*, 59.

59.   Rattansi, *Racism*, 4.

60.   Smith, *Nationalism in the Twentieth Century*, 90–93.

61.   Ibid., 92–103.

Chapter 4: The Exemplar of Ancient Israel

1.   Simon Sebag Montefiore, *Jerusalem: The Biography* (New York: Penguin Random House, 2011), 140.

2.   Lindsay Powell, *The Bar Kokhba War* (Oxford, UK: Osprey Publishing, 2017), chap. 1, Kindle.

3.   Montefiore, *Jerusalem*, 140.

4.   Quoted in Powell, *The Bar Kokhba War*, chap. 1.

5. Ibid., chap. 2.
6. Ibid., chap. 3.
7. Montefiore, *Jerusalem*, 142.
8. Powell, *The Bar Kokhba War*, chap. 5.
9. Steven Grosby, *Biblical Ideas of Nationality: Ancient and Modern* (Winona Lake, IN: Eisenbrauns, 2002), 106.
10. Quoted in Powell, *The Bar Kokhba War*, chap. 5.
11. Montefiore, *Jerusalem*, 143.
12. Powell, *The Bar Kokhba War*, chap. 6.
13. Ibid.
14. David K. Shipler, "Israel Buries Bones of Ancient Warriors," *New York Times*, May 12, 1982, https://www.nytimes.com/1982/05/12/world/israel-buries-bones -of-ancient-warriors.html.
15. Grosby, *Biblical Ideas of Nationality*, 108–13; Yoram Hazony, *The Virtue of Nationalism* (New York: Hachette, 2018), 19.
16. Aviel Roshwald, *The Endurance of Nationalism: Ancient Roots and Modern Dilemmas* (Cambridge, UK: Cambridge University Press, 2006), 16.
17. Smith, *Chosen Peoples*, 14.
18. Grosby, *Biblical Ideas of Nationality*, 24.
19. Roshwald, *The Endurance of Nationalism*, 15.
20. Grosby, *Biblical Ideas of Nationality*, 15–17.
21. Smith, *Chosen Peoples*, 52.
22. Paul Johnson, *A History of the Jews* (New York: HarperCollins, 1987), 15–19.
23. Max I. Dimont, *Jews, God and History* (New York: Signet Classics, 1990), chap. 2, Kindle.
24. Jonathan Kirsch, *Moses: A Life* (New York: Random House, 1998), 1–11.
25. Johnson, *A History of the Jews*, 26–27.
26. Ibid., 28, 34–35.
27. William Barclay, *The Ten Commandments* (Louisville, KY: Westminster John Knox Press, 2001), 5.
28. Grosby, *Biblical Ideas of Nationality*, 16–17.
29. Johnson, *A History of the Jews*, 28.
30. Grosby, *Biblical Ideas of Nationality*, 23.
31. Ibid., 59–65.
32. Israel Finkelstein and Neil Asher Silberman, *David and Solomon: In Search of the Bible's Sacred Kings and the Roots of the Western Tradition* (New York: Free Press, 2007), chap. 1, Kindle.
33. Johnson, *A History of the Jews*, 55–59.
34. Azar Gat, *Nations: The Long History and Deep Roots of Political Ethnicity and Nationalism* (Cambridge, UK: Cambridge University Press, 2013), 90, 110.
35. Anthony D. Smith, *The Ethnic Origins of Nations* (Oxford, UK: Blackwell Publishers, 1988), 117.
36. Grosby, *Biblical Ideas of Nationality*, 108.
37. Roshwald, *The Endurance of Nationalism*, 99.
38. Ibid., 98; Finkelstein and Silberman, *David and Solomon*, chap. 1.
39. Montefiore, *Jerusalem*, 145.

40. Shlomo Avineri, *The Making of Modern Zionism: The Intellectual Origins of the Jewish State*, 2nd ed. (New York: Basic Books, 2017), 3–5.

41. Walter Laqueur, *A History of Zionism: From the French Revolution to the Establishment of the State of Israel* (New York: Shocken Books, 2003), chap. 2, Kindle; Avineri, *The Making of Modern Zionism*, 38.

42. Quoted in ibid., chap. 2.

43. Avineri, *The Making of Modern Zionism*, 37.

44. Laqueur, *A History of Zionism*, chap. 3.

45. Avineri, *The Making of Modern Zionism*, 8.

46. Quoted in Laqueur, *A History of Zionism*, chap. 3.

47. Hazony, *The Virtue of Nationalism*, 203.

48. Adrian Hastings, *The Construction of Nationhood: Ethnicity, Religion and Nationalism* (Cambridge, UK: Cambridge University Press, 1997), 4.

49. Ibid., 16.

50. Ibid., 24.

51. Smith, *Chosen Peoples*, 46, 80; Hastings, *The Construction of Nationhood*, 150.

Chapter 5: Our English Forerunner

1. Bede, *The Ecclesiastical History of the English People*, translated by Leo Shirley-Price (London: Penguin Classics, 1990), 1.

2. Adrian Hastings, *The Construction of Nationhood: Ethnicity, Religion, and Nationalism* (Cambridge, UK: Cambridge University Press, 1997), 46.

3. John Senior, Sarah Semple, Alex Turner, and Sam Turner, "Petrological Analysis of the Anglo-Saxon and Anglo-Norman Stonework of St Peter's, Wearmouth and St Paul's, Jarrow," Newcastle University and Durham University, 2014, https://www.ncl.ac.uk/media/wwwnclacuk/mccordcentre/files/report 2014 2.pdf, 12–15.

4. Ian Christopher Levy, *Introducing Medieval Biblical Interpretation: The Senses of Scripture in Biblical Exegesis* (Grand Rapids, MI: Baker Books, 2018), 41.

5. Quoted in Sherri Olson, *Daily Life in a Medieval Monastery* (Santa Barbara, CA: Greenwood Press, 2013), 63.

6. John Freely, *Before Galileo: The Birth of Modern Science in Medieval Europe* (New York: Peter Mayer, 2013), chap. 2.

7. Benedict Anderson, *Imagined Communities* (London: Verso Books, 2016), 6.

8. Hastings, *The Construction of Nationhood*, 36–37.

9. Ibid., 8.

10. Kevin Phillips, *The Cousins' Wars: Religion, Politics, and the Triumph of Anglo-America* (New York: Basic Books, 1999), 12.

11. Philip Corrigan and Derek Sayer, *The Great Arch: English State Formation as Cultural Revolution* (Oxford, UK: Basil Blackwell, 1985), 15.

12. Ibid., 18.

13. Hastings, *The Construction of Nationhood*, 39–41.

14. Corrigan and Sayer, *The Great Arch*, 19–21.

15. Hastings, *The Construction of Nationhood*, 43.

16. Ibid., 50–51.
17. Ibid., 49.
18. Hans Kohn, *The Idea of Nationalism* (New York: Macmillan, 1961), 157.
19. Ibid., 160.
20. Ibid., 157.
21. Liah Greenfeld, *Nationalism: Five Roads to Modernity* (Cambridge, MA: Harvard University Press, 1992), 51.
22. Corrigan and Sayer, *The Great Arch*, 51; Greenfeld, *Nationalism*, 51.
23. Quoted in Greenfeld, *Nationalism*, 33.
24. Anthony Marx, *Faith in Nation: Exclusionary Origins of Nationalism* (Oxford, UK: Oxford University Press, 2003), 59–60.
25. Greenfeld, *Nationalism*, 29–30.
26. Mark A. Noll, *In the Beginning Was the Word: The Bible in American Public Life, 1492–1783* (Oxford, UK: Oxford University Press, 2015), 57–62.
27. Ibid., 56–60, 62–63.
28. Ibid., 102, 90.
29. Greenfeld, *Nationalism*, 52, 54.
30. Marx, *Faith in Nation*, 61.
31. Noll, *In the Beginning Was the Word*, 65.
32. Greenfeld, *Nationalism*, 55.
33. Richard Helgerson, *Forms of Nationhood* (Chicago: University of Chicago Press, 1992), 249.
34. Greenfeld, *Nationalism*, 56.
35. Helgerson, *Forms of Nationhood*, 263–67.
36. Hastings, *The Construction of Nationhood*, 59.
37. Quoted in Greenfeld, *Nationalism*, 58.
38. Marx, *Faith in Nation*, 62–63.
39. Greenfeld, *Nationalism*, 62.
40. Marx, *Faith in Nation*, 62.
41. Corrigan and Sayer, *The Great Arch*, 61–62.
42. Quoted in Greenfeld, *Nationalism*, 63.
43. Hastings, *The Construction of Nationhood*, 56.
44. Krishan Kumar, *The Making of English National Identity* (Cambridge, UK: Cambridge University Press, 2003), 107.
45. Greenfeld, *Nationalism*, 60.
46. Ibid., 71.
47. Marx, *Faith in Nation*, 97.
48. Ibid., 100, 102.
49. Ibid., 101.
50. Ibid., 106–07.
51. Quoted in Greenfeld, *Nationalism*, 72–73.
52. Phillips, *The Cousins' Wars*, 44–47.
53. Kohn, *The Idea of Nationalism*, 166.
54. John Milton, *Aeropagitica* (Cambridge, MA: Harvard University Press, 1909), paras. 20–34.
55. Greenfeld, *Nationalism*, 76–77.
56. Quoted in Kohn, *The Idea of Nationalism*, 171–72.

57. Quoted in ibid., 170.
58. Phillips, *The Cousins' Wars*, 37–38.
59. Quoted in Kohn, *The Idea of Nationalism*, 175–76.
60. Quoted in Greenfeld, *Nationalism*, 70.
61. Quoted in Hastings, *The Construction of Nationhood*, 60.
62. Phillips, *The Cousins' Wars*, 12.
63. Kohn, *The Idea of Nationalism*, 183.
64. Greenfeld, *Nationalism*, 71; Phillips, *The Cousins' Wars*, 22.

Chapter 6: A Nation of Settlers

1. David A. Weir, *Early New England: A Covenanted Society* (Grand Rapids, MI: W. B. Eerdmans, 2005), 38.
2. Ibid., 36.
3. Richard S. Dunn, *Puritans and Yankees: The Winthrop Dynasty of New England, 1630–1717* (Princeton, NJ: Princeton University Press, 1962), 6.
4. Walter A. McDougall, *Freedom Just Around the Corner: A New American History, 1585–1828* (New York: HarperCollins, 2004), 58.
5. Quoted in Francis J. Bremer, *John Winthrop: America's Forgotten Founding Father* (New York: Oxford University Press, 2003), 156.
6. Ibid.; David Hackett Fischer, *Albion's Seed: Four British Folkways in America* (New York: Oxford University Press, 1989), 36.
7. McDougall, *Freedom Just Around the Corner*, 58; Fischer, *Albion's Seed*, 14.
8. Fischer, *Albion's Seed*, 16.
9. McDougall, *Freedom Just Around the Corner*, 57; Edward M. Lamont, *The Forty Years That Created America: The Story of the Explorers, Promoters, Investors, and Settlers Who Founded the First English Colonies* (Lanham, MD: Rowman & Littlefield, 2014), 223; Dunn, *Puritans and Yankees*, 4–5.
10. Dunn, *Puritans and Yankees*, 5; Bremer, *John Winthrop*, 138.
11. Quoted in Bremer, *John Winthrop*, 155.
12. Quoted in Lamont, *The Forty Years That Created America*, 226.
13. McDougall, *Freedom Just Around the Corner*, 58; Bremer, *John Winthrop*, 194.
14. Ibid., 194.
15. McDougall, *Freedom Just Around the Corner*, 59.
16. Bremer, *John Winthrop*, 163.
17. Dunn, *Puritans and Yankees*, 28; Bremer, *John Winthrop*, 232, 233.
18. Quoted in Bremer, *John Winthrop*, 232; Dunn, *Puritans and Yankees*, 28.
19. Carl Bridenbaugh, *Vexed and Troubled Englishmen, 1590–1642* (New York: Oxford University Press, 1968), 469; Bremer, *John Winthrop*, 234.
20. Quoted in Bridenbaugh, *Vexed and Troubled Englishmen*, 469.
21. Bremer, *John Winthrop*, 236.
22. Quoted in Dunn, *Puritans and Yankees*, 29.
23. Quoted in ibid., 28.
24. Bremer, *John Winthrop*, 236–39.
25. Dunn, *Puritans and Yankees*, 33–34; Bremer, *John Winthrop*, 236–39.
26. Quoted in Dunn, *Puritans and Yankees*, 33–34.

27. Ibid., 32–36.

28. Bremer, *John Winthrop*, 240.

29. Dunn, *Puritans and Yankees*, 35–36.

30. Greenfeld, *Nationalism*, 401.

31. Kevin Phillips, *The Cousins' Wars: Religion, Politics, and the Triumph of Anglo-America* (New York: Basic Books, 1999), 604. 2010 United States census data show that roughly 72 million Americans claimed British ancestry (defining British as English, Scottish, Welsh, and Irish), compared to the 71 million combined population of the United Kingdom and Ireland (not all of whom claim British ancestry).

32. Fischer, *Albion's Seed*, 6.

33. Quoted in Bridenbaugh, *Vexed and Troubled Englishmen*, 473.

34. Fischer, *Albion's Seed*, 25.

35. Quoted in Bridenbaugh, *Vexed and Troubled Englishmen*, 442.

36. Fischer, *Albion's Seed*, 25.

37. Bridenbaugh, *Vexed and Troubled Englishmen*, 463.

38. Ibid., 435.

39. Ibid., 464–65.

40. Fischer, *Albion's Seed*, 27–28; Bridenbaugh, *Vexed and Troubled Englishmen*, 458.

41. Quoted in Bridenbaugh, *Vexed and Troubled Englishmen*, 458.

42. Quoted in ibid., 446.

43. Fischer, *Albion's Seed*, 29–30.

44. Bridenbaugh, *Vexed and Troubled Englishmen*, 457.

45. Fischer, *Albion's Seed*, 31, 393–94.

46. Bridenbaugh, *Vexed and Troubled Englishmen*, 465.

47. Phillips, *The Cousins' Wars*, 25; Fischer, *Albion's Seed*, 37–38.

48. Phillips, *The Cousins' Wars*, 18.

49. Fischer, *Albion's Seed*, 46.

50. Phillips, *The Cousins' Wars*, 22.

51. Fischer, *Albion's Seed*, 44.

52. Ibid., 43.

53. Phillips, *The Cousins' Wars*, 27.

54. Ibid., 44–45.

55. Technically, East Prussia did not become a place until 1815, but you get the point.

56. Bridenbaugh, *Vexed and Troubled Englishmen*, 454.

57. Ibid., 445.

58. Mark A. Noll, *In the Beginning Was the Word: The Bible in American Public Life, 1492–1783* (Oxford, UK: Oxford University Press, 2015), 118.

59. Quoted in ibid., 118.

60. Quoted in Fischer, *Albion's Seed*, 47.

61. Sacvan Bercovitch, "'Nehemias Americanus': Cotton Mather and the Concept of the Representative American," *Early American Literature* 8, no. 3 (Winter 1974): 220–38.

62. Hans Kohn, *The Idea of Nationalism: A Study in Its Origins and Background* (New York: Macmillan, 1961), 269–70.

63. Cotton Mather, *Magnalia Christi Americana* (Hartford, CT: Silas Andrus & Son, 1855), 44.

64. Quoted in Kohn, *The Idea of Nationalism*, 270; Merle Curti, *The Roots of American Loyalty* (New York: Columbia University Press, 1946), 8.

65. Quoted in Noll, *In the Beginning Was the Word*, 117.

66. Fischer, *Albion's Seed*, 23.

67. Quoted in Daniel J. Elazar, *Covenant and Constitutionalism: The Great Frontier and the Matrix of Federal Democracy* (New York: Routledge, 2017).

68. Perry Miller, *The New England Mind: The Seventeenth Century* (Cambridge, MA: Harvard University Press, 1939), 409.

69. Quoted in Elazar, *Covenant and Constitutionalism*.

70. Miller, *The Unmaking of Americans*, 430–31.

71. Robert Kagan, *Dangerous Nation: America's Foreign Policy from Its Earliest Days to the Dawn of the Twentieth Century* (New York: Knopf, 2006), 9.

72. Quoted in Elazar, *Covenant and Constitutionalism*.

73. Quoted in Noll, *In the Beginning Was the Word*, 124–25.

74. Ibid., 107.

75. Quoted in Mark A. Noll, *A History of Christianity in the United States and Canada* (Grand Rapids, MI: Eerdmans, 1992), 401.

76. Quoted in Noll, *In the Beginning Was the Word*, 122–23.

77. Dunn, *Puritans and Yankees*, 11.

78. Bridenbaugh, *Vexed and Troubled Englishmen*, 472–73.

79. Fischer, *Albion's Seed*, 16.

80. Dunn, *Puritans and Yankees*, 36–37.

81. Virginia L. Ruland, "A Royalist Account of Hugh Peters' Arrest," *Huntington Library Quarterly* 18, no. 2 (February 1955): 178–82.

82. Michael Barone, *Our First Revolution* (New York: Crown, 2007), chap. 5, Kindle.

83. Noll, *In the Beginning Was the Word*, 166.

84. Barone, *Our First Revolution*, chap. 10, Kindle.

85. Quoted in Noll, *In the Beginning Was the Word*, 169–71.

Chapter 7: Our Nationalist Revolution

1. Pauline Maier, *American Scripture: Making the Declaration of Independence* (New York: Random House, 1997), 156–60.

2. Quoted in Walter A. McDougall, *Freedom Just Around the Corner: A New American History, 1585–1828* (New York: HarperCollins, 2004), 245.

3. Maier, *American Scripture*, 50–53.

4. Ibid., 109, 126.

5. "The Virginia Declaration of Rights, June 12, 1776," Library of Virginia, http://edu.lva.virginia.gov/online_classroom/shaping_the_constitution/doc/declaration_rights.

6. "From John Adams to Timothy Pickering, 6 August 1822," Founders Online, National Archives, https://founders.archives.gov/documents/Adams/99-02-02-7674.

7. Maier, *American Scripture*, 126.

8. Ibid., 160.

9. McDougall, *Freedom Just Around the Corner*, 222.

10.	Ibid.; Kevin Phillips, *The Cousins' Wars: Religion, Politics, and the Triumph of Anglo-America* (New York: Basic Books, 1999), 102.

11.	Liah Greenfeld, *Nationalism: Five Roads to Modernity* (Cambridge, MA: Harvard University Press, 1992), 402–03.

12.	Maier, *American Scripture*, 22–23; McDougall, *Freedom Just Around the Corner*, 219.

13.	Kohn, *The Idea of Nationalism*, 272. 1961.

14.	Greenfeld, *Nationalism*, 416.

15.	Quoted in Robert Kagan, *Dangerous Nation: America's Foreign Policy from Its Earliest Days to the Dawn of the Twentieth Century* (New York: Alfred A. Knopf, 2006), 30.

16.	Ibid., 34–35.

17.	John Adams, *Papers of John Adams*, vol. 1, *September 1755–October 1773*, edited by Robert J. Taylor (Cambridge, MA: Harvard University Press, 1977), 123–28.

18.	Joseph J. Ellis, *His Excellency George Washington* (New York: Random House, 2004), 55.

19.	Quoted in Alan Taylor, *American Revolutions: A Continental History, 1750–1804* (New York: Norton, 2016), 62, 510.

20.	Theodore Draper, *A Struggle for Power: The American Revolution* (New York: Random House, 1996), 200.

21.	Ellis, *His Excellency George Washington*, 56; Fred Anderson, *The War That Made America: A Short History of the French and Indian War* (New York: Penguin, 2005), 252–53; McDougall, *Freedom Just Around the Corner*, 197.

22.	Quoted in Ron Chernow, *Washington: A Life* (New York: Penguin, 2010), 176; Ellis, *His Excellency George Washington*, 56–58.

23.	Anderson, *The War That Made America*, 259–60.

24.	J.C.D. Clark, *The Language of Liberty, 1600–1832: Political Discourse and Social Dynamics in the Anglo-American World* (Cambridge, UK: Cambridge University Press, 1994), 13.

25.	Phillips, *The Cousins' Wars*, 170–77, 190–94.

26.	Ibid., 169; Clark, *The Language of Liberty*, 10.

27.	Quoted in Phillips, *The Cousins' Wars*, 105–06.

28.	Mark A. Noll, *In the Beginning Was the Word: The Bible in American Public Life, 1492–1783* (Oxford, UK: Oxford University Press, 2015), 106.

29.	Quoted in David Hackett Fischer, *Paul Revere's Ride* (New York: Oxford University Press, 1994), 163–64.

30.	Quoted in Kohn, *The Idea of Nationalism*, 278.

31.	Noll, *In the Beginning Was the Word*, 301.

32.	Quoted in ibid., 297; McDougall, *Freedom Just Around the Corner*, 232.

33.	McDougall, *Freedom Just Around the Corner*, 211; Noll, *In the Beginning Was the Word*, 313.

34.	Quoted in Phillips, *The Cousins' Wars*, 92, 97, 117.

35.	Ibid., 92; McDougall, *Freedom Just Around the Corner*, 228; Mark David Hall, *Roger Sherman and the Creation of the American Republic* (New York: Oxford University Press, 2013), 55.

36.	Maier, *American Scripture*, 31–33; McDougall, *Freedom Just Around the Corner*, 236.

37.	Noll, *In the Beginning Was the Word*, 331–35.

38.	Quoted in Maier, *American Scripture*, 33; Kohn, *The Idea of Nationalism*, 284.

39. Quoted in Taylor, *American Revolutions*, 308–09.

40. McDougall, *Freedom Just Around the Corner*, 290–95; Taylor, *American Revolutions*, 346–48.

41. Quoted in Taylor, *American Revolutions*, 350–51.

42. Quoted in McDougall, *Freedom Just Around the Corner*, 305.

43. Quoted in Taylor, *American Revolutions*, 388.

44. Kagan, *Dangerous Nation*, 113.

45. "From George Washington to Charles Carroll, 1 May 1796," Founders Online, National Archives, https://founders.archives.gov/documents/Washington /99–01–02–00480.

46. Matthew Spalding and Patrick J. Garrity, *A Sacred Union of Citizens: George Washington's Farewell Address and the American Character* (Lanham, MD: Rowman & Littlefield, 1996), 3.

47. Quoted in Ronald D. Rietveld, "Abraham Lincoln's Thomas Jefferson," in *White House Studies Compendium*, edited by Robert W. Watson (New York: Nova Science Publishers), 264.

48. Chernow, *Washington*, 754–55; Ellis, *His Excellency George Washington*, 234–36.

49. Michael Lind, *Hamilton's Republic: Readings in the American Democratic Nationalist Tradition* (New York: Free Press, 1997), 2–3.

50. Kagan, *Dangerous Nation*, 105.

51. Quoted in Craig L. Symonds, *Navalists and Antinavalists: The Naval Policy Debate in the United States* (Newark: University of Delaware Press, 1980), 23.

52. Kagan, *Dangerous Nation*, 105–06.

53. McDougall, *Freedom Just Around the Corner*, 350–51.

54. McDougall, *Freedom Just Around the Corner*, 288.

55. Kevin J. Hayes, *The Road to Monticello: The Life and Mind of Thomas Jefferson* (New York: Oxford University Press, 2008), chap. 31, Kindle.

56. Quoted in Peter S. Onuf, *Jefferson's Empire: The Language of American Nationhood* (Charlottesville: University of Virginia Press, 2000), 106.

Chapter 8: A Continental Nation

1. Hunt Janin and Ursula Carlson, *The California Campaigns of the U.S.-Mexican War, 1846–1848* (North Carolina: MacFarland and Company, 2015), chap. 4, Kindle; Kevin Starr, *California: A History* (New York: Modern Library, 2007), chap. 3, Kindle.

2. Hunt and Carlson, *The California Campaigns of the U.S.-Mexican War*, chap. 4.

3. Ibid., introduction.

4. Ibid., introduction, chap. 3.

5. Quoted in ibid., introduction, chap. 4.

6. Quoted in Robert Kagan, *Dangerous Nation: America's Foreign Policy from Its Earliest Days to the Dawn of the Twentieth Century* (New York: Knopf, 2006), 80.

7. Martin Sicker, *The Geopolitics of Security in the Americas: Hemispheric Denial from Monroe to Clinton* (Westport, CT: Praeger, 2002), 17.

8. Robert Morgan, *Lions of the West: Heroes and Villains of Westward Expansion* (Chapel Hill, NC. Algonquin Books of Chapel Hill, 2011), 216.

9. Alexander DeConde, *This Affair of Louisiana* (Baton Rouge: Louisiana State University Press, 1976), 57, 59.

10. Merle Curti, *The Roots of American Loyalty* (New York: Columbia University Press, 1946), 33, 36.

11. Ibid., 43.

12. Dennis Johnson, *The Laws That Shaped America: Fifteen Acts of Congress and Their Lasting Impact* (New York: Routledge, 2009), 6.

13. Ibid., 3, 6–8.

14. Ibid., 3.

15. Kagan, *Dangerous Nation*, 429; Johnson, *The Laws That Shaped America*, 11.

16. Johnson, *The Laws That Shaped America*, 11.

17. Ibid., 16, 29.

18. Kagan, *Dangerous Nation*, 132.

19. Johnson, *The Laws That Shaped America*, 5, 20–21.

20. Walter A. McDougall, *Freedom Just Around the Corner: A New American History, 1585–1828* (New York: HarperCollins, 2004), 391; Kagan, *Dangerous Nation*, 134.

21. Kagan, *Dangerous Nation*, 134.

22. Ibid., 77.

23. Ibid., 134.

24. McDougall, *Freedom Just Around the Corner*, 393.

25. Ibid., 393.

26. Anders Stephanson, *Manifest Destiny: American Expansion and the Empire of Right* (New York: Hill & Wang, 1995), 23.

27. McDougall, *Freedom Just Around the Corner*, 393.

28. DeConde, *This Affair of Louisiana*, 215–16.

29. Kagan, *Dangerous Nation*, 79.

30. Ibid., 136.

31. Stephanson, *Manifest Destiny*, 38, 42–43.

32. Quoted in Frederick Merk, *Manifest Destiny and Mission in American History: A Reinterpretation* (Cambridge, MA: Harvard University Press, 1963), 27.

33. Stephanson, *Manifest Destiny*, xi; Merk, *Manifest Destiny and Mission in American History*, 28.

34. Stephanson, *Manifest Destiny*, xi–xii. Merk, *Manifest Destiny and Mission in American History*, 28.

35. Stephanson, *Manifest Destiny*, 39.

36. Ibid.; Merk, *Manifest Destiny and Mission in American History*, 27.

37. Stephanson, *Manifest Destiny*, 42; Merk, *Manifest Destiny and Mission in American History*, 27.

38. Quoted in Stephanson, *Manifest Destiny*, 42; Steven Grosby, *Biblical Ideas of Nationality: Ancient and Modern* (Winona Lake, IN: Eisenbrauns, 2002), 224.

39. Quoted in Stephanson, *Manifest Destiny*, 40–44.

40. Walter A. McDougall, *Throes of Democracy: The American Civil War Era, 1829–1877* (New York: HarperCollins, 2007), 261.

41. Kagan, *Dangerous Nation*, 224.

42. McDougall, *Throes of Democracy*, 262.

43. Quoted in Stephanson, *Manifest Destiny*, 34.

44.   Robert W. Merry, *A Country of Vast Designs: James K. Polk, the Mexican War, and the Conquest of the American Continent* (New York: Simon & Schuster, 2009), 2.

45.   Kagan, *Dangerous Nation*, 224–25.

46.   Steven E. Woodworth, *Manifest Destinies: America's Westward Expansion and the Road to the Civil War* (New York: Alfred A. Knopf, 2010), 59.

47.   Stephanson, *Manifest Destiny*, 35.

48.   Quoted in Woodworth, *Manifest Destinies*, 72–73.

49.   Ibid., 73–74, 76–77.

50.   McDougall, *Throes of Democracy*, 277.

51.   Ibid., 282.

52.   Woodworth, *Manifest Destinies*, 148.

53.   McDougall, *Throes of Democracy*, 269.

54.   Stephanson, *Manifest Destiny*, 33.

55.   MacDougall, *Throes of Democracy*, 269–70, 280.

56.   Woodworth, *Manifest Destinies*, 109.

57.   Ibid., 110; Hunt Janin and Ursula Carlson, *The California Campaigns of the U.S.-Mexican War, 1846–1848* (North Carolina: MacFarland and Company, 2015), chap. 4, Kindle; Kevin Starr, *California: A History* (New York: Modern Library, 2007), 270.

58.   Woodworth, *Manifest Destinies*, 111, 112; Kagan, *Dangerous Nation*, 225.

59.   Woodworth, *Manifest Destinies*, 147–48.

60.   Kagan, *Dangerous Nation*, 225.

61.   Woodworth, *Manifest Destinies*, 148, 155.

62.   Janin and Carlson, *The California Campaigns of the U.S.-Mexican War*, 145, 186.

63.   Ibid., 145, 172, 214.

64.   Woodworth, *Manifest Destinies*, 249.

65.   Merry, *A Country of Vast Designs*, 474.

66.   Ibid., 475.

67.   Ibid.

68.   Peter Cozzens, *The Earth Is Weeping: The Epic Story of the Indian Wars for the American West* (New York: Alfred A. Knopf, 2016), 459.

69.   Fred Anderson, *The War That Made America: A Short History of the French and Indian War* (London: Penguin Books, 2005), 3–5.

70.   Ibid., 5–6.

71.   John Keegan, *Fields of Battle: The Wars for North America* (New York: Vintage Books, 1995), chap. 2.

72.   Ibid.

73.   Cozzens, *The Earth Is Weeping*, xxxiii.

74.   Quoted in Kagan, *Dangerous Nation*, 81–82.

75.   Ibid., 82.

76.   Ibid., 83.

77.   Thomas Jefferson, letter to Hendrick Aupaumut, 21 December 1808, founders .archives.gov/documents/jefferson/99-01-02-9358.

78.   Kagan, *Dangerous Nation*, 84.

79.   Quoted in ibid., 85.

80.   Ibid., 131.

81.   Keegan, *Fields of Battle*, chap. 5.
82.   Kagan, *Dangerous Nation*, 92.
83.   McDougall, *Throes of Democracy*, 413, 416.
84.   Ibid., 420–21.
85.   Kagan, *Dangerous Nation*, 142.
86.   Quoted in ibid., 152.
87.   Quoted in ibid., 150.
88.   Ibid., 150, 147, 203.
89.   "Document #38 Abraham Lincoln on the Mexican-American War (1846–48),"
      Brown University Library, https://library.brown.edu/create/modernlatinamerica
      /chapters/chapter-14-the-united-states-and-latin-america/primary-documents
      -w-accompanying-discussion-questions/abraham-lincoln-on-the-mexican
      -american-war-1846–48/.
90.   Mark E. Neely, Jr., *Lincoln and the Triumph of the Nation: Constitutional Conflict in
      the American Civil War* (Chapel Hill: University of North Carolina Press, 2011), 8.
91.   David Herbert Donald, *Lincoln* (New York: Simon & Schuster Paperbacks, 1995),
      283.
92.   "Image 4 of Abraham Lincoln Papers: Series 1. General Correspondence.
      1833–1916: Abraham Lincoln, [March 1861] (First Inaugural Address), Final
      Version," Library of Congress, https://www.loc.gov/resource/mal.0773800/?sp
      =4&st=text&r=0.031,0.372,0.938,0.744,0.
93.   Quoted in Donald, *Lincoln*, 134.
94.   Quoted in Dorothy Ross, "Lincoln and the Ethics of Emancipation: Universalism,
      Nationalism, Exceptionalism," *Journal of American History* 96, no. 2 (September
      2009): 379–99.
95.   Quoted in ibid.
96.   Abraham Lincoln, "Address to the New Jersey State Senate," February 21, 1861,
      Abraham Lincoln Online, http://www.abrahamlincolnonline.org/lincoln/speeches
      /trenton1.htm.
97.   "Image 4 of Abraham Lincoln Papers: Series 1. General Correspondence. 1833–
      1916: Abraham Lincoln, [March 1861] (First Inaugural Address), Final Version."
98.   Melvin B. Endy, Jr., "Abraham Lincoln and American Civil Religion," *American
      Society of Church History* 44, no. 2 (June 1975), 229–41.
99.   Quoted in Ross, "Lincoln and the Ethics of Emancipation."
100. Quoted in James Rawley, "The Nationalism of Abraham Lincoln," *Civil War
      History* 9, no. 3 (September 1963): 283–98.
101. Quoted in Eyal J. Naveh, *Crown of Thorns: Political Martyrdom in America from
      Abraham Lincoln to Martin Luther King, Jr.*, (New York: New York University Press,
      1990), 64.
102. Steven Grosby, *Biblical Ideas of Nationality: Ancient and Modern* (Winona Lake,
      IN: Eisenbrauns, 2002), 230.
103. Scot M. Guenter, *The American Flag, 1777–1924: Cultural Shifts from Creation to
      Codification* (Plainsboro, NJ: Associated University Presses, 1986), 68.
104. Quoted in ibid., 89, 69.
105. Ibid., 65, 75, 76.
106. Charles Sumner, *Complete Works*, vol. 16 (Boston: Lee & Shepard, 1900), 9.

107. Kevin Phillips, *The Cousins' Wars: Religion, Politics, and the Triumph of Anglo-America* (New York: Basic Books, 1999), 456.

108. Quoted in Susan-Mary Grant, *North over South: Northern Nationalism and American Identity in the Antebellum Era* (Lawrence: University Press of Kansas, 2000), 161.

109. Quoted in Wilfred M. McClay, *The Masterless: Self and Society in Modern America* (Chapel Hill: University of North Carolina Press, 1994), chap. 1.

110. Stuart McConnell, *Glorious Contentment: The Grand Army of the Republic, 1856–1900* (Chapel Hill: University of North Carolina Press, 1992), 2–3.

111. Quoted in ibid., 4.

112. Ibid., 14, 8.

Chapter 9: The Triumph of the Twentieth Century

1. Edmund Morris, *Theodore Rex* (New York: Random House, 2001), 502.

2. Michael J. Crawford and Donald C. Winter, *The World Cruise of the Great White Fleet: Honoring 100 Years of Global Partnerships and Security* (Washington, DC: Naval Historical Center, 2008), 38; Morris, *Theodore Rex*, 493, 503.

3. Quoted in Morris, *Theodore Rex*, 492–93.

4. Craig L. Symonds, *The U.S. Navy: A Concise History* (Oxford, UK: Oxford University Press, 2016), 64; Morris, *Theodore Rex*, 494.

5. Quoted in Morris, *Theodore Rex*, 494.

6. Crawford and Winter, *The World Cruise of the Great White Fleet*, 50.

7. Morris, *Theodore Rex*, 510.

8. Symonds, *The U.S. Navy*, 66; Crawford and Winter, *The World Cruise of the Great White Fleet*, 143.

9. Crawford and Winter, *The World Cruise of the Great White Fleet*, 348.

10. Quoted in Morris, *Theodore Rex*, 549.

11. Michael F. Blake, *The Cowboy President: The American West and the Making of Theodore Roosevelt* (Lanham, MD: TwoDot, 2018), 5.

12. Ibid., 5.

13. Leroy G. Dorsey, *We Are All Americans, Pure and Simple: Theodore Roosevelt and the Myth of Americanism* (Tuscaloosa: University of Alabama Press, 2007), 36.

14. Michael Lind, *Hamilton's Republic: Readings in the American Democratic Nationalist Tradition* (New York: Free Press, 1997), 56.

15. Quoted in ibid., 59.

16. Darrin Lunde, *The Naturalist: Theodore Roosevelt, A Lifetime of Exploration, and the Triumph of American Natural History* (New York: Penguin Random House, 2016), 141.

17. Morris, *Theodore Rex*, 512.

18. Blake, *The Cowboy President*, 220.

19. Lunde, *The Naturalist*, 141; Blake, *The Cowboy President*, 213–14.

20. Quoted in Blake, *The Cowboy President*, 212–14.

21. Lind, *Hamilton's Republic*, 154.

22. "Speech of President Roosevelt at Laying of the Cornerstones of Gateway to Yellowstone National Park, Gardiner, Montana, April 24, 1903," Theodore Roosevelt

Center at Dickinson State University, https://www.theodorerooseveltcenter.org/Research/Digital-Library/Record/ImageViewer?libID=o289720&imageNo=1.

23. "Address of President Roosevelt at Grand Canyon, Arizona, May 6, 1903," Theodore Roosevelt Center at Dickinson State University, https://www.theodorerooseveltcenter.org/Research/Digital-Library/Record/ImageViewer?libID=o289796&imageNo=1.

24. Quoted in Blake, *The Cowboy President*, 218.

25. Ibid., 5, 211–12, 221.

26. Quoted in Gary Gerstle, *American Crucible: Race and Nation in the Twentieth Century* (Princeton, NJ: Princeton University Press, 2017), 23.

27. Quoted in Dorsey, *We Are All Americans*, 32.

28. Quoted in Gerstle, *American Crucible*, 48–49.

29. Quoted in Dorsey, *We Are All Americans*, 31.

30. Lind, *Hamilton's Republic*, 57.

31. Quoted in ibid., 62.

32. Quoted in Dorsey, *We Are All Americans*, 37.

33. Quoted in Lind, *Hamilton's Republic*, 64.

34. Quoted in ibid., 63.

35. John Fonte and Althea Nagai, "America's Patriotic Assimilation System Is Broken," Hudson Institute, 2013, https://www.hudson.org/content/researchattachments/attachment/1101/final04–05.pdf.

36. Quoted in Gerstle, *American Crucible*, 26.

37. Edmund Morris, *The Rise of Theodore Roosevelt* (New York: Ballantine Books, 1980), 594.

38. Ibid., 594.

39. Sidney Milkis, "Theodore Roosevelt: Foreign Affairs," UVA Miller Center, https://millercenter.org/president/roosevelt/foreign-affairs.

40. Ibid.

41. Edmund Morris, *Colonel Roosevelt* (New York: Random House, 2011), 92.

42. Lind, *Hamilton's Republic*, 66.

43. Gerstle, *American Crucible*, 124.

44. Quoted in John B. Judis, *The Folly of Empire: What George W. Bush Could Learn from Theodore Roosevelt and Woodrow Wilson* (New York: Scribner, 2004), 105.

45. Quoted in ibid., 115.

46. Quoted in David M. Kennedy, *Over Here: The First World War and American Society* (New York: Oxford University Press, 2004), 383.

47. Quoted in ibid., 385.

48. Ibid., 356.

49. Margaret MacMillan, *Paris 1919: Six Months That Changed the World* (New York: Random House, 2002), 125.

50. Judis, *The Folly of Empire*, 105–09.

51. MacMillan, *Paris 1919*, 595.

52. Quoted in Judis, *The Folly of Empire*, 112–13.

53. Ibid., 113.

54. Kennedy, *Over Here*, 359.

55. Lind, *Hamilton's Republic*, 162–63.

56. Judis, *The Folly of Empire*, 117.

57.   Quoted in Ibid., 124.

58.   Jon Meacham, *Franklin and Winston: An Intimate Portrait of an Epic Friendship* (New York: Random House, 2003), 327.

59.   Judis, *The Folly of Empire*, 125; Lind, *Hamilton's Republic*, 162.

60.   Lewis A. Erenberg and Susan E. Hirsch, eds., *The War in American Culture: Society and Consciousness During World War II* (Chicago: University of Chicago Press, 1996), chap. 4, Kindle.

61.   Franklin D. Roosevelt, "Inaugural Address," reading copy, January 20, 1941, Franklin D. Roosevelt Presidential Library and Museum, https://www .fdrlibrary.org/documents/356632/390886/1941inauguraladdress.pdf /1ea00842-0ea7-4237-ab52-a96af4d6862f.

62.   Franklin D. Roosevelt, "FDR's D-Day Prayer," reading copy, June 6, 1944, Franklin D. Roosevelt Presidential Library and Museum, https://fdr.blogs .archives.gov/2019/06/05/fdrs-d-day-prayer/.

63.   Gerstle, *American Crucible*, 197, 461.

64.   Erenberg and Hirsch, *The War in American Culture*, chap. 4, Kindle.

65.   Ibid.

66.   David M. Kennedy, *Freedom from Fear: The American People in Depression and War, 1929–1945* (New York: Oxford University Press, 1999), 768.

67.   Ibid., 765–67.

68.   Gerstle, *American Crucible*, 230.

69.   Erenberg and Hirsch, *The War in American Culture*, chap. 3.

70.   Ibid., introduction.

71.   Cord A. Scott, *Comics and Conflict: Patriotism and Propaganda from WWII through Operation Iraqi Freedom* (Annapolis, MD: Naval Institute Press, 2014), chap. 2, Kindle.

72.   Erenberg and Hirsch, *The War in American Culture*, chap. 5.

73.   Ibid.

74.   Rod Pyle, "Apollo 11, 45 Years Later: What's the Mission," *Wired*, https://www .wired.com/insights/2014/07/apollo-11–45-years-whats-mission/.

75.   James R. Hansen, *First Man: The Life of Neil A. Armstrong* (New York: Simon & Schuster, 2005), 392–95.

76.   Ibid., 503–04.

77.   Ibid., 537.

78.   David J. Garrow, "Martin Luther King: The Making of an Orator," *Washington Post*, January 15, 1989, https://www.washingtonpost.com/archive/entertainment/ books/1989/01/15/martin-luther-king-the-making-of-an-orator/aede55b7–938a– 4d98–82b3–544177799d5f/?utm_term=.5b3fd8b3b288.

79.   Gary S. Selby, *Martin Luther King and the Rhetoric of Freedom: The Exodus Narrative in America's Struggle for Civil Rights* (Waco, TX: Baylor University Press, 2008), 7–9.

80.   Ibid., 51.

81.   Ibid., 9.

82.   Scott A. Sandage, "A Marble House Divided," in *Race and the Production of Modern American Nationalism*, edited by Reynolds J. Scott-Childress (New York: Routledge, 2013), 273–312.

83.   Martin Luther King, Jr., "'I Have a Dream,' Address Delivered at the March on

Washington for Jobs and Freedom," August 28, 1963, The Martin Luther King, Jr. Research and Education Institute, Stanford University, https://kinginstitute .stanford.edu/king-papers/documents/i-have-dream-address-delivered-march -washington-jobs-and-freedom.

84. Sandage, "A Marble House Divided," 274.

85. Gerstle, *American Crucible*, 296.

86. Quoted in ibid., 297.

87. Ibid., 300.

88. Quoted in Mary Beth Brown, *Hand of Providence: The Strong and Quiet Faith of Ronald Reagan* (Nashville: Thomas Nelson, 2004), 59.

89. "President Reagan's Remarks at the Franklin D. Roosevelt Library 50th Anniversary Luncheon," January 10, 1989, Ronald Reagan Presidential Library & Museum, https://www.reaganlibrary.gov/research/speeches/011089c.

90. Ronald Reagan, "Remarks to the Central American Peace Scholarship Program Participants, July 30, 1987," in *Public Papers of the Presidents of the United States: Ronald Reagan, 1987* (Washington, DC: White House, 1987), 899; Ronald Reagan, "Remarks at a White House Briefing for Private Sector Supporters of United States Defense Policies, September 23, 1986," in *Public Papers of the Presidents of the United States: Ronald Reagan, 1986* (Washington, DC: White House, 1986), 1235.

91. Quoted in Howell Raines, "President Is Firm on Welfare Cuts," *New York Times*, October 6, 1981, https://www.nytimes.com/1981/10/06/us/president-is-firm-on-welfare-cuts.html.

92. Ronald Reagan, "Republican National Convention Acceptance Speech," July 1, 1980, Ronald Reagan Presidential Library & Museum, https://www .reaganlibrary.gov/7-17-80.

93. Ronald Reagan, "Farewell Address to the Nation," January 11, 1989, Ronald Reagan Presidential Library & Museum, https://www.reaganlibrary.gov /research/speeches/011189i.

94. Quoted in John Fonte, "American Patriotism and Nationalism: One and Indivisible," *National Review*, May 1, 2017, https://www.nationalreview.com /2017/05/nationalism-patriotism-american-history-conservatives-progressives/.

95. Reagan, "Farewell Address to the Nation."

Chapter 10: The Treason of the Elites

1. Martin Duberman, *Howard Zinn: A Life on the Left* (New York: New Press, 2012), 214.

2. Ibid., 235–36.

3. Ibid., 1–22.

4. Ibid., 161–62.

5. Jonathan M. Wiener, "Radical Historians and the Crisis in American History, 1959–1980," *The Journal of American History* 76, no. 2 (September 1989): 399–434.

6. Howard Zinn, *A People's History of the United States* (New York: Harper & Row, 1980), 16.

7. Ibid., 59.

8.   Ibid., 215.

9.   He mentioned Gettysburg once, on page 231, but in the context of New York City draft riots, not the battle: "Union troops returning from the Battle of Gettysburg came into the city and stopped the rioting. Perhaps four hundred people were killed."

10. Oscar Handlin, "Arawaks," review of *A People's History of the United States* by Howard Zinn, *The American Scholar* 49, no. 4 (Autumn 1980): 546–50, https://d3aencwbm6zmht.cloudfront.net/asset/97521/A_Handlin_1980.pdf.

11. Quoted in Daniel J. Flynn, "Howard Zinn's Biased History," History News Network, June 9, 2003, https://historynewsnetwork.org/article/1493.

12. Victoria Brittain, "Howard Zinn's Lesson to Us All," *The Guardian*, January 28, 2010, https://www.theguardian.com/commentisfree/2010/jan/28/howard-zinn-america; "Howard Zinn—An American Mahatma," *Russia Today*, January 28, 2010, https://www.youtube.com/watch?v=xa76C4uEOss&feature=channel.

13. Dave Eggers, "Remembering Salinger," *The New Yorker*, January 29, 2010, https://www.newyorker.com/books/page-turner/remembering-salinger-dave-eggers.

14. Samuel P. Huntington, *Who Are We?: The Challenges to America's National Identity* (New York: Simon & Schuster, 2004), 143.

15. Kwame Anthony Appiah, *Cosmopolitanism: Ethics in a World of Strangers* (New York: Norton, 2006), introduction, Kindle.

16. William D. Desmond, *Cynics* (Berkeley: University of California Press, 2008), 21.

17. Quoted in Naomi Zack, *The Ethics of Mores and Race: Equality After the History of Philosophy* (Lanham, MD: Rowman & Littlefield, 2011), 41.

18. Quoted in Martha C. Nussbaum, "Patriotism and Cosmopolitanism," in *The Cosmopolitan Reader*, edited by Garrett W. Brown and David Held (Malden, MA: Polity Press, 2010), 157.

19. Quoted in Eric R. Schlereth, *An Age of Infidels* (Philadelphia: University of Pennsylvania Press, 2013), 80.

20. David Held, *Cosmopolitanism: Ideals and Realities* (Cambridge, MA: Polity Press, 2010), chap. 1, Kindle.

21. Immanuel Kant, *To Perpetual Peace*, translated by Ted Humphrey (Indianapolis: Hackett Publishing, 2003), 15.

22. William Doyle, *The Oxford History of the French Revolution* (Oxford, UK: Oxford University Press, 2002), chap. 7; Peter McPhee, *Liberty or Death: The French Revolution* (New Haven: Yale University Press, 2016), chap. 12.

23. Quoted in Bruce Robbins and Paulo Lemos Horta, *Cosmopolitanisms* (New York: New York University Press, 2017), 5.

24. Quoted in Appiah, *Cosmopolitanism*, introduction; Leo Tolstoy, *The Complete Works of Count Tolstoy: Miscellaneous Letters*, translated by Leo Wiener (Boston: Dana Estes & Co., 1905), 145.

25. Charles Dickens, *Bleak House* (London: Bradbury & Evans, 1853), 26.

26. Quoted in James D. Ingram, "Populism and Cosmopolitanism," in *The Oxford Handbook of Populism*, edited by Cristóbal Rovira Kaltwasser, Paul A. Taggart, Paulina Ochoa Espejo, and Pierre Ostiguy (Oxford, UK: Oxford University Press, 2017), 649.

27. Eric P. Kaufmann, *The Rise and Fall of Anglo-America* (Cambridge, MA: Harvard University Press, 2004), 159, 177, 306.

28. Horace M. Kallen, "Democracy Versus the Melting-Pot," part 2, *The Nation*, February 25, 1915, 217–18, http://www.expo98.msu.edu/people/kallen.htm.
29. Randolph S. Bourne, "Trans-national America," *The Atlantic*, July 1916, https://www.theatlantic.com/magazine/archive/1916/07/trans-national-america/304838/.
30. Quoted in Huntington, *Who Are We?*, 142.
31. Quoted in John Fonte, *Sovereignty or Submission: Will Americans Rule Themselves or Be Ruled by Others?* (New York: Encounter Books, 2011), 74.
32. Ibid., 74.
33. Quoted in Ibid., 76–78.
34. Richard Rorty, "The Unpatriotic Academy," *New York Times*, February 13, 1994, https://www.nytimes.com/1994/02/13/opinion/the-unpatriotic-academy.html.
35. Quoted in Huntington, *Who Are We?*, 145.
36. Quoted in ibid., 271.
37. Quoted in Fonte, *Sovereignty or Submission*, 94.
38. Quoted in Rorty, "The Unpatriotic Academy."
39. Quoted in Huntington, *Who Are We?*, 269.
40. Quoted in Fonte, *Sovereignty or Submission*, 96.
41. Huntington, *Who Are We?*, 264.
42. John Gray, "The World Is Round," review of *The World Is Flat: A Brief History of the Twenty-first Century* by Thomas L. Friedman, *The New York Review of Books*, August 11, 2005, https://www.nybooks.com/articles/2005/08/11/the-world-is-round/.
43. Ibid.
44. Somini Sengupta, "Mark Zuckerberg Announces Project to Connect Refugee Camps to the Internet," *New York Times*, September 26, 2015, https://www.nytimes.com/2015/09/27/world/americas/mark-zuckerberg-announces-project-to-connect-refugee-camps-to-the-internet.html.
45. Alex Shephard, "Facebook Has a Genocide Problem," *The New Republic*, March 15, 2018, https://newrepublic.com/article/147486/facebook-genocide-problem.
46. Huntington, *Who Are We?*, 265–67.
47. Thomas Bender, *Rethinking American History in a Global Age* (Berkeley: University of California Press, 2002), 224.
48. Ibid., 115.
49. John Adams, "From John Adams to Thomas McKean, 31 August 1813," Founders Online, National Archives, https://founders.archives.gov/documents/Adams/99–02–02–6140.
50. Alexis de Tocqueville, *Democracy in America*, translated by Henry Reeve, edited by Bruce Frohnen (London: Regnery Publishing, 2002 [1889]), 166.
51. *American Archives: Fourth Series; Containing a Documentary History of the English Colonies in North America, from the King's Message to Parliament, of March 7, 1774, to the Declaration of Independence of the United States*, vol. 1 (Washington, DC: M. St. Clair Clarke and Peter Force, 1837), preface.
52. George Athan Billias, "George Bancroft: Master Historian," The American Antiquarian Society, 2004, https://www.americanantiquarian.org/proceedings/44574433.pdf.
53. Kohn, *American Nationalism*, 40.

54. Quoted in ibid., 42.

55. Quoted in ibid., 43.

56. Jill Lepore, "Why a Nation Needs a New Story," *Foreign Affairs*, March–April 2019, https://www.foreignaffairs.com/articles/united-states/2019–02–05/new-americanism-nationalism-jill-lepore.

57. Quoted in George M. Fredrickson, *Diverse Nations: Explorations in the History of Racial and Ethnic Pluralism* (New York: Routledge, 2008), 61.

58. Quoted in Huntington, *Who Are We?*, 124–25.

59. Ibid., 174–75.

60. American Council of Trustees and Alumni, "A Crisis in Civic Education," January 2016, https://www.goacta.org/images/download/A_Crisis_in_Civic_Education.pdf.

61. American Council of Trustees and Alumni, "No U.S. History? How College History Departments Leave the United States Out of the Major," July 2016, https://www.goacta.org/images/download/no_u_s_history.pdf.

62. Jenna A. Robinson and Jay Schalin, "General Education: Our Response to Critics," The James G. Martin Center for Academic Renewal, December 4, 2013, https://www.jamesgmartin.center/2013/12/general-education-our-response-to-critics/.

63. Quoted in Mark Krikorian, *The New Case Against Immigration: Both Legal and Illegal* (New York: Penguin, 2008), 31.

64. Valerie Strauss, "Historians Blast Advanced Placement U.S. History Framework," *Washington Post*, June 11, 2015, https://www.washingtonpost.com/news/answer-sheet/wp/2015/06/11/historians-blast-advanced-placement-u-s-history-framework/?utm_term=.20330ac959ee.

65. Quoted in Elizabeth Kaufer Busch and Jonathan W. White, *Civic Education and the Future of American Citizenship* (Lanham, MD: Lexington Books, 2013), chap. 3, Kindle.

66. Quoted in Michael Lind, *The Next American Nation: The New Nationalism and the Fourth American Revolution* (New York: Simon & Schuster, 1995), 351–52.

67. Joseph Moreau, *Schoolbook Nation: Conflicts over American History Textbooks from the Civil War to the Present* (Ann Arbor: University of Michigan Press, 2004), 331.

68. Arthur Schlesinger, *The Disuniting of America: Reflections on a Multicultural Society* (New York: Norton, 1991), 51–52.

69. Find a Grave, https://images.findagrave.com/photos/2008/0/11014343_119922178084.jpg.

Chapter 11: One Nation, One People

1. Charles River Editors, *The Statue of Liberty: The History and Legacy of America's Most Famous Statue* (Charles River Editors, 2014), chap. 4, Kindle.

2. Ibid., chap. 3.

3. Ibid., chap. 4.

4. Ibid., chap. 5.

5. Ibid., chap. 6.

6. Ibid., chap. 7.

7.   Quoted in ibid., chap. 7.

8.   Ibid., chap. 8.

9.   Ibid., chap. 3.

10.   National Democratic Committee, *The Campaign Text Book of the Democratic Party of the United States for the Presidential Election of 1888* (New York: Brentanos, 1888), 81, https://babel.hathitrust.org/cgi/pt?id=mdp.39015030798378&view=1up &seq=93.

11.   Quoted in Charles River Editors, *The Statue of Liberty*, chap. 8.

12.   Elizabeth Mitchell, *Liberty's Torch: The Great Adventure to Build the Statue of Liberty* (New York: Grove Atlantic, 2014), 176–78.

13.   Eric P. Kaufmann, *The Rise and Fall of Anglo-America* (Cambridge, MA: Harvard University Press, 2004), 181.

14.   Eric P. Kaufmann, *Whiteshift: Populism, Immigration, and the Future of White Majorities* (London: Penguin Books, 2018), 56.

15.   Michael Lind, *The Next American Nation: The New Nationalism and the Fourth American Revolution* (New York: Free Press, 1995), 286.

16.   Benjamin Franklin, *The Select Works of Benjamin Franklin* (Boston: Phillips, Sampson & Co., 1855), 411.

17.   *The Papers of Alexander Hamilton*, vol. 25, *July 1800–April 1802*, edited by Harold C. Syrett (New York: Columbia University Press, 1977), 495–97.

18.   *The Papers of George Washington*, Presidential Series, vol. 17, *1 October 1794–31 March 1795*, edited by David R. Hoth and Carol S. Ebel (Charlottesville: University of Virginia Press, 2013), 161–62.

19.   *The Papers of James Madison*, vol. 13, *20 January 1790–31 March 1791*, edited by Charles F. Hobson and Robert A. Rutland (Charlottesville: University Press of Virginia, 1981), 17.

20.   Kaufmann, *Whiteshift*, 32.

21.   George J. Borjas, *We Wanted Workers: Unraveling the Immigration Narrative* (New York: W. W. Norton & Company, 2016), 51–52.

22.   Ibid., 52.

23.   Ibid., 55.

24.   Ibid.

25.   Ibid., 55–60.

26.   Ibid., 55.

27.   Ibid., 52.

28.   Ibid., 152.

29.   Ibid., 152–53.

30.   Ibid., 172, 194.

31.   Reihan Salam, *Melting Pot or Civil War?: A Son of Immigrants Makes the Case Against Open Borders* (New York: Sentinel, 2018), 41–42; Mark Krikorian, *The New Case Against Immigration: Both Legal and Illegal* (New York: Penguin, 2008), 22.

32.   Huntington, *Who Are We?*, 198–99.

33.   Ibid., 122–23.

34.   "Day-Long Pageant Pictures America United for War," *New York Times*, July 5, 1918, https://timesmachine.nytimes.com/timesmachine/1918/07/05/issue.html.

35.   John J. Miller, *The Unmaking of Americans: How Multiculturalism Has Undermined the Assimilation Ethic* (New York: Free Press, 1998), 64–65.

36. Ibid., 42–51.
37. "True Americanism," Address of Louis D. Brandeis at Faneuil Hall, Boston, July 5, 1915, Brandeis School of Law, https://louisville.edu/law/library/special-collections/the-louis-d.-brandeis-collection/business-a-profession-chapter-22.
38. Miller, *The Unmaking of Americans*, 68.
39. Quoted in ibid., 58–59.
40. Ibid., 55.
41. Ibid., 56.
42. Ibid., 52.
43. Huntington, *Who Are We?*, 201–02.
44. Ibid., 202.
45. Miller, *The Unmaking of Americans*, 49.
46. Ibid., 55.
47. Huntington, *Who Are We?*, 203–04.
48. Krikorian, *The New Case Against Immigration*, 25–26; Borjas, *We Wanted Workers*, 52.
49. Quoted in Krikorian, *The New Case Against Immigration*, 26–27.
50. Miller, *The Unmaking of Americans*, 56–58.
51. Huntington, *Who Are We?*, 202.
52. Borjas, *We Wanted Workers*, 53–54.
53. Ibid., 63.
54. Salam, *Melting Pot or Civil War?*, 16.
55. Quoted in Huntington, *Who Are We?*, 195–96.
56. Ibid., 195–96.
57. Salam, *Melting Pot or Civil War?*, 16.
58. Ibid., 85.
59. Borjas, *We Wanted Workers*, 102–03.
60. Ibid., 95–96.
61. Ibid., 100–01.
62. National Academies of Sciences, Engineering, and Medicine. *The Economic and Fiscal Consequences of Immigration* (Washington, DC: The National Academies Press, 2017), page 120, chapter 3, table 3–14.
63. National Academies of Sciences, Engineering, Medicine, and Committee on Population, *The Integration of Immigrants into American Society* (Washington, DC: National Academies Press, 2015), 314.
64. Borjas, *We Wanted Workers*, 97.
65. National Academies, *The Integration of Immigrants into American Society*, 314.
66. "A Growing Share of Latinos Get Their News in English," Pew Research Center, July 23, 2013, https://www.pewhispanic.org/2013/07/23/a-growing-share-of-latinos-get-their-news-in-english/.
67. Krikorian, *The New Case Against Immigration*, 30.
68. John J. Miller, "California's Bilingual-Ed Mistake," *National Review*, April 3, 2017, https://www.nationalreview.com/magazine/2017/04/03/californias-bilingual-education-program/.
69. Quoted in Lind, *The Next American Nation*, 291.
70. Quoted in ibid., 290.
71. Sheryll Cashin, *Loving: Interracial Intimacy in America and the Threat to White Supremacy* (Boston: Beacon Press, 2017), 128.

72. Ibid., 129, 134.

73. U.S. Census Bureau, "Overview of Race and Hispanic Origin: 2010," https://www.census.gov/prod/cen2010/briefs/c2010br-02.pdf.

74. Lind, *The Next American Nation*, 304.

75. "Multiracial in America," Pew Research Center, June 11, 2015, https://www.pewsocialtrends.org/2015/06/11/multiracial-in-america/.

76. Rich Lowry, "America Isn't a Melting Pot Anymore," *New York Post*, January 29, 2019, https://nypost.com/2019/01/29/america-isnt-a-melting-pot-anymore/.

Chapter 12: The Importance of Cultural Nationalism

1. Francis Davis, *The History of the Blues: The Roots, the Music, the People* (Cambridge, MA: Da Capo Press, 1995), chap. 1, Kindle.

2. Ibid.

3. Quoted in ibid.

4. Ibid.

5. Quoted in ibid.; Elijah Wald, *The Blues: A Very Short Introduction* (New York: Oxford University Press, 2010), chap. 1, Kindle; Paul Oliver, *The Story of the Blues* (Boston: Northeastern University Press, 1998), 17.

6. Dena J. Epstein, "The Folk Banjo: A Documentary History," *Ethnomusicology* 19, no. 3 (September 1975): 347–71.

7. Wald, *The Blues*, chap. 1.

8. Ibid., chap. 1.

9. Davis, *The History of the Blues*, chap. 1.

10. Michael Lind, *The Next American Nation: The New Nationalism and the Fourth American Revolution* (New York: Free Press, 1995), 267, 268, 269, 282.

11. Amy Kass, Leon Kass, and Diana Schaub, "Citizenship and Memory," *National Review*, May 30, 2011, https://www.nationalreview.com/2011/05/citizenship-and-memory-amy-kass-leon-kass-diana-schaub/.

12. John Fonte, *Sovereignty or Submission: Will Americans Rule Themselves or Be Ruled by Others?* (New York: Encounter Books, 2011), introduction.

13. *Reid v. Covert*, 354 U.S. 1 (1957).

14. Fonte, *Sovereignty or Submission*, 8.

15. Ibid., 254–55.

16. Ibid., 103.

17. Ibid., 108.

18. Quoted in Samuel P. Huntington, *Who Are We?: The Challenges to America's National Identity* (New York: Simon and Schuster, 2004), 338.

19. Quoted in Lind, *The Next American Nation*, 286.

20. Frederick Douglass, "The Myth of 'Yellow Peril'" in *Ripples of Hope: Great American Civil Rights Speeches*, edited by Josh Gottheimer (New York: Basic Books, 2003), 97.

21. Quoted in Lind, *The Next American Nation*, 270.

22. Ibid., 269.

23. "Race for United States, Regions, Divisions, and States: 1790," U.S. Census,

https://web.archive.org/web/20141008113215/http://www.census.gov
/population/www/documentation/twps0056/tabA-26.pdf.

24. Thomas Sowell, *Black Rednecks and White Liberals* (San Francisco: Encounter Books, 2005), 27.

25. Henry Louis Gates, Jr., and Donald Yacovone, *The African Americans: Many Rivers to Cross* (United States: SmileyBooks, 2013), 625.

26. Sowell, *Black Rednecks and White Liberals*, 27.

27. Ibid., 27.

28. Ralph Ellison, "What America Would Be Like Without Blacks," *Time*, April 6, 1970.

29. Albert Murray, *The Omni Americans: Some Alternatives to the Folklore of White Supremacy* (Cambridge, MA: Da Capo Books, 1990), 22.

30. Melanie Kirkpatrick, *Thanksgiving: The Holiday at the Heart of the American Experience* (New York: Encounter Books, 2016), 1, 148, 161.

31. Quoted in ibid., 162–63, 190–91.

32. Ibid., 8–9, 15.

33. Continental Congress, "A Proclamation," 1778, Pilgrim Hall Museum, http://www.pilgrimhallmuseum.org/pdf/TG_Continental_Congress_Proclamations_1778_1784.pdf.

34. George Washington, "A Proclamation," October 3, 1789, Pilgrim Hall Museum, http://www.pilgrimhallmuseum.org/pdf/TG_Presidential_Thanksgiving_Proclamations_1789_1815.pdf.

35. Kirkpatrick, *Thanksgiving*, 91.

36. Ibid., 98–99, 101–3.

37. Ibid., 77, 87.

38. Amy A. Kass, Leon R. Kass, and Diana Schaub, eds., *What So Proudly We Hail: The American Soul in Story, Speech, and Song* (Wilmington, DE: ISI Books, 2011), xvii.

39. Jimmy Stamp, "Who Designed the Seal of the President of the United States?," *Smithsonian Magazine*, January 23, 2013, https://www.smithsonianmag.com/arts-culture/who-designed-the-seal-of-the-president-of-the-united-states-5162560/.

40. Quoted in Wilbur Zelinsky, *Nation into State: The Shifting Symbolic Foundations of American Nationalism* (Chapel Hill: University of North Carolina Press, 1988), 199, 200, 200–01.

41. Quoted in Tim Marshall, *Worth Dying For: The Power and Politics of Flags* (London: Elliott and Thompson, 2016), 215, 42.

42. Ibid., 191.

43. Zelinsky, *Nation into State*, 76, 75–76.

44. Jeffrey B. Roth, "Star Spangled Banner Author May Have Been Tone Deaf," Reuters, July 3, 2014, https://www.reuters.com/article/us-usa-starspangledbanner/star-spangled-banner-author-may-have-been-tone-deaf-book-idUSKBN0F82GR20140703.

45. Quoted in Zelinsky, *Nation into State*, 70–72.

46. Athanasios Themos, Aphrodite Maltezou, Georgia Pantou, Giorgos Tsiangouris, and Christos Phlouris, "The Southwest Cemetery of Roman

Sparta: A Preliminary Account of the Results of Three Rescue Excavations,"
in *British School at Athens Studies*, vol. 16, *Sparta and Laconia: From Prehistory to
Pre-modern*, edited by William G. Cavanagh, Crysanthi Gallou, and Mercourios
Georgiadis (Athens, Greece: British School at Athens, 2009), 261–69; "Memorial
Day," The Center for Civil War Research, http://www.civilwarcenter.olemiss
.edu/memorial_day.shtml.

47.   Zelinsky, *Nation into State*, chap. 2.

48.   Victor Mather, "Yankees and Flyers Will Stop Playing Kate Smith After
Discovering Racist Songs," *New York Times*, April 19, 2019; John Timpane, "Kate
Smith Called for Racial Tolerance in This Forgotten 1945 Radio Address,"
Philadelphia Enquirer, April 25, 2019; Dean Balsamini, "Kate Smith's Niece
Demands 'Cowardly' Yankees Let Fans Decide on Ban," *New York Post*, May 4,
2019; Frank G. Prial, "Kate Smith, All-American Singer, Dies at 79," *New York
Times*, June 18, 1986.

49.   "God Bless America," Irving Berlin, http://www.irvingberlin.com/god-bless
-america.

50.   Ryan Gaydos, "Philadelphia Flyers Remove Kate Smith Statue, New York
Yankees Halt Her 'God Bless America' Amid Controversy," Fox News, April 22,
2019, https://www.foxnews.com/sports/philadelphia-flyers-kate-smith-statue
-removed.

51.   Jason Johnson, "Star Spangled Bigotry: The Hidden Racist History of the
National Anthem," The Root, July 4, 2016, https://www.theroot.com/star
-spangled-bigotry-the-hidden-racist-history-of-the-1790855893.

52.   "National Anthem Lyrics Prompt California NAACP to Call for Replacing
Song," November 8, 2017, CBS News, https://www.cbsnews.com/news/national
-anthem-lyrics-california-naacp-star-spangled-banner/; Colin Campbell and
Sean Welsh, "Baltimore to Keep, Clean Defaced Francis Scott Key Statue,"
Baltimore Sun, September 13, 2017, https://www.baltimoresun.com/maryland
/baltimore-city/bs-md-key-statue-painted-20170913-story.html.

53.   Tad Vezner, "Understanding Mayor Carter's Reference to National Anthem
as an 'Ode to Slavery,'" *Twin Cities Pioneer Press*, January 2, 2018, http://www
.twincities.com/2018/01/02/understanding-mayor-carters-reference-to-national
-anthem-as-an-ode-to-slavery/.

54.   Kirkpatrick, *Thanksgiving*, chap. 8.

55.   Belen Fernandez, "Thanksgiving: The Annual Genocide Whitewash," Al
Jazeera, November 23, 2017, https://www.aljazeera.com/indepth/opinion
/thanksgiving-annual-genocide-whitewash-171120073022544.html.

56.   Lori Aratani, "Historic Alexandria Church Decides to Remove Plaques
Honoring Washington, Lee," *Washington Post*, October 28, 2017, https://www
.washingtonpost.com/local/social-issues/historic-alexandria-church-decides
-to-remove-plaques-honoring-washington-lee/2017/10/28/97cb4cbc-bc1b-11e7
-a908-a3470754bbb9_story.html?utm_term=.298fd40e8a04.

57.   Alexander James, "George Washington University Students Vote to Remove
'Extremely Offensive' Nickname: Colonials," *Washington Examiner*, April 5, 2019,
https://www.washingtonexaminer.com/red-alert-politics/george-washington
-university-students-vote-to-remove-extremely-offensive-nickname-colonials.

Epilogue: The Anti-Nationalist Temptation

1. Ezra Klein, "Bernie Sanders: The Vox Conversation," Vox, July 28, 2015, https://
    www.vox.com/2015/7/28/9014491/bernie-sanders-vox-conversation.

2. Sheri Berman, *The Primacy of Politics: Social Democracy and the Making of Europe's
    Twentieth Century* (Cambridge, UK: Cambridge University Press, 2006), 162.

3. Michael Kazin, "A Patriotic Left," *Dissent*, Summer 2019, https://www
    .dissentmagazine.org/article/a-patriotic-left.

4. Dylan Matthews, "Bernie Sanders's Fear of Immigrant Labor Is Ugly—and
    Wrongheaded," Vox, July 29, 2015, https://www.vox.com/2015/7/29/9048401
    /bernie-sanders-open-borders.

INDEX